The Production and Use of
ECONOMIC FORECASTS

The Production and Use of ECONOMIC FORECASTS

Giles Keating

METHUEN

London and New York

First published in 1985 by
Methuen & Co. Ltd
11 New Fetter Lane, London EC4P 4EE

Published in the USA by Methuen & Co.
in association with Methuen, Inc.
29 West 35th Street, New York, NY 10001

Typeset by Colset Pte Ltd, Singapore
Printed in Great Britain at the
University Press, Cambridge

British Library Cataloguing in Publication Data

Keating, Giles
    The production and use of economic forecasts.
    1. Economic forecasting
    I. Title
    338.5'44   HB3730

    ISBN 0-416-35790-3
    ISBN 0-416-35800-4 Pbk

Library of Congress Cataloging in Publication Data

Keating, Giles.
    The production and use of economic forecasts.
    Bibliography: p.
    Includes index.
    1. Economic forecasting—Mathematical models.
    I. Title.
    HB3730.K37 1985   338.5'442   85-8992
    ISBN 0-416-35790-3
    ISBN 0-416-35800-4 (pbk.)

To my mother

Ο βίος βραχύς, ἡ δὲ τέχνη μακρή, ὁ δὲ καιρὸς ὀξύς, ἡ δὲ πεῖρα σφαλερή, ἡ δὲ κρίσις χαλεπή.

Life is short, the Science long, opportunity fleeting, experiment dangerous, judgement difficult.

Hippocrates, Aphorisms 1,1.

Contents

List of boxes

List of tables

List of figures

Acknowledgements

My experience in preparing economic forecasts and econometric models at the Confederation of British Industry and the London Business School has provided the basis for the work in this book, and my thanks are due to all my colleagues at those institutions for their advice and teaching. Much of the work on the book was done while I was at the LBS and I am particularly grateful for the use of the LBS model-building software. I should like to thank John Hey who devoted considerable time to reading the entire manuscript, and I am grateful to Alan Budd, Charles Burton, Bob Corker, Geoffrey Dicks, Badrul Haque, Sean Holly, Paul Levine, Andrew Longbottom and Peter Smith for comments on individual chapters and to Bunty King for typing. Sandy Noble provided a non-specialist's view of the whole manuscript, as did Henrietta Irving to whom is due special thanks for enduring all the traumas associated with this project.

Introduction

Economic forecasters attempt to predict the future by using economic theory to provide a systematic explanation of the past, which they assume will apply in future. Their work is central to government decision making in almost all major industrialized countries and to corporate planning in many large firms. This book describes the techniques used by forecasters and the problems they encounter, illustrating every major point with practical examples.

The forecasters' explanation of past behaviour is contained in a *macro-econometric model*, which is a series of equations that together purport to describe all important aspects of the economy. These equations are derived by assuming, on the basis of economic theory, that certain relationships hold, then using statistical analysis of historical data to test whether those relations existed and to quantify them. This process is one of the main parts of applied *econometrics*.

Forecasters use judgement as well as econometrics, particularly when analysing recent economic developments, which determine the whole course of the forecast and for which few government macro-economic data are available because of publication delays. Surveys, newspaper reports and other information must be used, and drawn together into an overall picture of the economy consistent with economic theory and econometric results. This process is known as *conjunctural analysis*.

A key feature of the book: a macro-econometric model estimated from actual historical data

An essential feature of the book is a specially developed macro-econometric model. The relatively small size of this, and its direct derivation from a theoretical model, make it particularly suitable for teaching purposes. Unlike other apparently similar models, the one in this book is estimated from actual macro-economic data for the post-war UK economy, using up-to-date econometric techniques. It is used to illustrate the process of model building (Chapter 4) with a step-by-step illustrated example of applied econometrics. It is also used to prepare a forecast for the UK economy up to 1988 (Chapter 5), and readers will be able to compare this projection with the events that actually occur. They will also be able to use the model to prepare their own forecasts using the latest data.

A further distinguishing feature of the macro-econometric model used here is that it is based on a relatively recent theoretical model, proposed by Buiter and Miller in 1981. Although this draws largely on relationships that will be familiar to many readers (an IS curve, an LM curve and a Phillips curve), it links these to an exchange rate equation, making it particularly appropriate for describing a small open economy such as the UK. This model explains events like those of 1979–81 as the result of anticipations about a future tightening of monetary policy, which cause the exchange rate to rise sharply, thus depressing competitiveness and so raising unemployment. Like any model, this focuses on some important aspects of the economy and abstracts from others, but it captures many of the relationships that have been most significant over the last fifteen years.

This model is intended for use with the assumption of *rational expectations*. This means that people are assumed not to make systematic mistakes when forming expectations. Since the model itself is in principle a description of how the economy has behaved in the past and will continue to behave, rational expectations are usually interpreted to mean that expectations are consistent with the projections of the model itself. A non-mathematical outline of analysis using the assumption of rational expectations is given in Chapter 8 and the discussion is illustrated with results from the macro-econometric model. This should be of considerable use to readers, given that other simulation results assuming rational expectations, and based on econometric models estimated from historical data, are derived from the models of the large forecasting groups, which are generally much more difficult to understand than the small model presented here.

Other major features of the book

In addition to deriving and making widespread use of its own small macro-econometric model, the book discusses the large models of the main UK forecasting groups. The history and objectives of the groups are described in Chapter 1, and after a review of their track record in Chapter 6, there is a discussion of the properties of the models in Chapter 7. Rather than attempt a full description of the models as they were in one particular year, which would inevitably be out-dated as the models are continuously changed, and which might obscure overall properties by concentrating on detail, this chapter examines the development of the models, explaining how small changes can affect the properties of the whole system. The small macro-econometric model used throughout the book is shown to have many features in common with recent versions of the much larger London Business School model. Chapter 7 also discusses likely areas for future research by the forecasting teams.

The emphasis on practical problems and the use of illustrations from real life extend throughout the book. The principles of conjunctural analysis, discussed in Chapter 2, are illustrated in Chapter 3 with a week-by-week account of developments in the UK during the final months of 1983, a period when the strength of economic recovery was highly uncertain. This discussion draws on the economic data, survey evidence, newspaper reports and other information as it was available at that time, and shows how this evidence is balanced against the results from the macro-econometric model used elsewhere in the book. The discussion of econometrics in Chapter 4 is based around a worked example, using a consumers' expenditure equation for the UK estimated from data from the mid-1950s up to the early 1980s. This shows the importance of starting from a general equation incorporating many items, and then gradually testing to see if some of them can be excluded, or combined, so that the end result is the more restricted equation suggested by theory. Each stage of this process is described in considerable detail to aid those unfamiliar with applied econometrics, but the procedure is followed right through to some less elementary tests not always found in econometrics textbooks.

The discussion of policy issues towards the end of the book involves some of the most exciting aspects of macro-economics and some of the most recent developments. Chapter 8 describes, with illustrations, how the effect of government action is greatly altered by the credibility of its policy announcements. After a description of applying *optimal control* to macro-econometric models, which involves a systematic search for the most effective policy (but is difficult to implement in practice), this chapter then explains that the government will in general be unable to implement the best policy unless the public believes that it will keep its promises. This is because the best policy is usually *time inconsistent*, i.e. there will be a temptation for the government to renege on it some time after having announced it.

The book has been written so that it can be understood by those with limited mathematical ability, but not at the cost of omitting any important relevant ideas that are usually expressed in mathematical notation. Such ideas are discussed mainly in words, with a mathematical explanation in the form of a 'box' for those who want to read it. Such notes are auxiliary to the main discussion and may be passed over if the reader so wishes.

There is no glossary; instead, where a technical term is first defined, it appears in italics. These definitions can be located rapidly using the index, in which such terms appear in italics with the page number of their definition also in italics.

1

The users and the forecasters

This chapter examines two of the main influences on the development of economic forecasting: the needs of those using forecasts and the structure of the groups producing forecasts. Events that indicate weaknesses in the forecasters' methods, and the evolution of economic theory, also have a very important influence and are discussed in Chapter 7.

1.1 The users

Policy making

Economic forecasting is central to government decision making in almost all major industrialized nations. It has retained this important position against a background, over the last fifteen years, of fierce controversy among economists about the ability of governments to influence the economy. When this controversy emerged in the early 1970s, the belief that fiscal and monetary policies can have large and sustained effects on unemployment was widespread among policy makers. Since then, an increasing number of governments around the world have changed to the view that such policies affect inflation but have little or no sustained effect on unemployment.

The continuing importance of forecasting for policy making against this background may appear surprising. Until the early 1970s, governments had a clear need for economic projections to help select and quantify the fiscal and monetary policies which they believed would have sustained effects on unemployment. For many present-day governments holding the contrary view, it might appear that economic forecasting has very limited use, because targets for monetary growth can be chosen with little or no reference to the economic relationships described by macro-econometric models.

However, the experience of the UK over the last ten years or so (under not only the Thatcher governments, but also the Callaghan–Healey administration which introduced monetary targeting to the UK) has shown that such governments also need economic forecasting. They need it to indicate the size of government borrowing that is consistent with their monetary growth targets, to suggest expenditure plans and tax rates which give that amount of borrowing, and to give some idea of the impact on interest rates and the exchange rate.

Whatever the viewpoint of the government, there are always groups anxious to influence its policies, and their use of economic forecasting and conjunctural analysis has become more widespread and more sophisticated over the last ten or fifteen years. Since 1975 the Confederation of British Industry (CBI) has published budget recommendations which include a full analysis of the prospects for the economy and for government finances, both on existing policies and under the organization's own proposals. The Trades Union Congress (TUC) policy recommendations have been based on a similar degree of analysis in recent years.

Pressure groups with fewer resources than the TUC or CBI also occasionally produce policy recommendations supported by projections on macro-econometric models. An example was the call for increased construction expenditure made by the Federation of Civil Engineering Contractors (FCEC) in 1981. See FCEC (1981). However, many pressure groups, even when campaigning for fairly large fiscal measures (for example, to help the old) give no indication of the macro-economic impact of their proposals.

In addition MPs on the important House of Commons Treasury and Civil Service Committee have used economic forecasts and macro-econometric models to examine critically the government's policies. This has been done partly through the House of Commons Library's membership of a commercial group that makes the Treasury model available to MPs, and partly by commissioning work directly from independent forecasting groups.

Companies and individuals

Almost all organizations and individuals in the economy make plans which involve assessment of the current and likely future state of the economy. The plans include large-scale investment by big companies, which may depend on prospects for the exchange rate, consumer spending and other macro-economic variables; the pay claims submitted by trade unions, which will be influenced by beliefs about the outlook for price inflation; and personal decisions to buy homes, which will be affected by the expected course of interest rates. In all these cases the decision will also be influenced by important factors which affect the organization or the individual, but not the whole of the economy. Depending on the relative importance for the decision being made, and on the total resources available for obtaining information, so the effort and expense used to find out about current and likely developments in the economy will vary.

At one extreme, most individuals and many companies, particularly small and medium-sized firms, make no use of economic forecasts apart from extracting projections of inflation, and also perhaps output, from the widely published press reports. Companies use these mainly for pay bargaining and possibly for planning costs and prices. The regular coverage given to the output of the main forecasting groups is particularly full in the *Financial Times*, which also publishes from time to time tables comparing all the main groups' forecasts for principal items. A problem with the publicity given by the media is that typically the limitations of forecasts are either ignored or over-emphasized. By contrast, the forecasting groups themselves generally try to indicate that although considerable uncertainty exists it can, in principle at least, be quantified. (See Chapter 6.)

For those who need more information than is available in the media, there are detailed publications produced by the groups that prepare the forecasts. In total, between five and ten thousand subscriptions to these publications are probably sold in the UK, at a cost from about £30 a year (for the quarterly *National Institute Economic Review*) up to around £600. These publications include analysis of recent developments, short-term projections reaching about two years into the future, and sometimes medium-term forecasts (about five years ahead). Assumptions are given for government policy and for main aspects of the world economy and the forecasts cover important items in the domestic economy, such as gross domestic product (GDP), inflation, unemployment, the current account and public borrowing (the PSBR). Other items such as output and investment by sector are sometimes included, to varying degrees of detail.

No service is offered by the forecasters to those who subscribe to their publications, although they will answer occasional enquiries. Large companies that want more information and assistance join one or more of the *forecasting clubs* run by several of the forecasting groups. In return for an annual subscription, typically several thousand pounds, such companies usually obtain briefings on the forecasts, access to the finalized forecasts perhaps several weeks ahead of publication, in greater detail than is generally available, and the facility to run the club's model on the companies' own assumptions often at an extra fee. The total number of firms belonging to such clubs in the UK is believed to be between seventy-five and a hundred.

A main attraction of this sort of access to a macro-econometric model is that it enables a company to tackle the problem of uncertainty about the future, by quantifying the effect on their business if the forecasts turn out differently from the view given by the forecasting groups. A large company selling consumer durables, for example, might use a macro-econometric model to investigate the impact of changes in interest rates on market size.

In addition to the forecasting clubs, an increasing number of consultancy services are now based partly on the use of macro-economic forecasts. In return for a substantial fee, companies are offered specialized projections for their industry, perhaps in conjunction with advice about their management methods. For example, Cambridge Econometrics (see Section 1.2) uses a disaggregated model to give forecasts of any sector of interest to a client.

Although very large companies often make use of the macro-econometric models of the forecasting groups in the ways described above, none of them has a comparable model of their own, although some have small or specialized models. The reason is that setting up a macro-econometric model, modifying it when new data or new theories indicate inadequacies, and obtaining the latest historical data require very considerable, specialized resources.

Despite the growth in the use of macro-economic forecasts by companies over the last fifteen years, many features in the models remain more appropriate to their original purpose of advising government than to the newer role of aiding business planning. A major reason for the large size of the Treasury model, for example, is the inclusion of many different types of tax instruments and detailed modelling of the public sector. Without this detail the model would be significantly cheaper and quicker to use, but just as useful to companies.

Another problem for companies is that modelling expediency can take priority over their needs. An example of this is given by the aggregation of all private non-residential fixed investment into a single item in the 1984 version of the LBS model, an expedient adopted to avoid problems that were resulting from re-classification of investment among different parts of the private sector as leasing grew. This was a severe drawback for commercial users, anxious to distinguish, for example, between manufacturing investment in plant and machinery (machine tools, robots, etc.) and distributive trades investment in construction (new supermarkets, warehouses, etc.).

The use of macro-econometric models for research

Economists from outside the forecasting groups rarely make use of macro-econometric models when evaluating theories. Typically, they write down an equation, the theory indicating which items to include; the equation is estimated from historical data, and the results are tested to see if they are consistent with the theory.

It would be possible to make an additional test by inserting this new equation into a macro-econometric model, probably replacing an existing part of the model. If this altered the properties of the whole system from sensible to implausible, it might be possible to conclude that the new equation was unsatisfactory; but this is often not possible, for there may have been offsetting errors before the change. This is one of the main reasons why economists from outside the forecasting groups rarely use macro-econometric models in this way. Another reason is that access to the macro-econometric models for such economists is difficult, although the new macro-econometric modelling bureau makes these models more accessible. This bureau is described in the next section.

The forecasting groups themselves carry out a considerable amount of research work, most of which is incorporated into their macro-econometric models. These groups share many objectives with other researchers, but when new data or developments in economic theory indicate inadequacies in an existing macro-econometric model, they can face a conflict between the normal objectives of researchers and their special obligations. They are obliged to be ready to publish projections on the dates expected by their subscribers, and if they run a forecasting club they must always offer access to a macro-econometric model. Given the limited time available, the forecasters may have to apply statistical techniques without the desirable degree of rigour, or use judgement. (See Chapter 5.) Despite such short-term expediency, most forecasting groups have the long-term objective of including only research work of the highest standard in their macro-econometric models, moving towards this target whenever time permits.

1.2 The forecasters

There are now over a dozen main groups publishing regular forecasts of the UK economy based on macro-econometric models, and several other groups (mainly stockbrokers) who produce forecasts using judgement. See Table 1.1. About half of the major groups rely heavily on government funding, much of it channelled through the Economic and Social Research Council (ESRC, formerly the Social Science Research Council or SSRC). In this section, we describe the major groups, emphasizing the influence of financial pressures and discussing their institutional arrangements. In Chapter 7, we explain how the macro-econometric models used by the groups have developed.

The earliest forecasts

Economic forecasting in the UK began in the Treasury shortly after the Second World War. There had been experiments with forecasting models in the US just before the war and formal models describing the US economy were developed during the 1950s (see for example, Klein and Goldberger, 1955), but the UK Treasury relied instead on judgement. The Treasury forecasts were published annually as background to the budget, usually in the form of qualitative statements, although occasionally figures were given. From 1959, a second group started publishing regular forecasts for the UK economy. This was the National Institute for Economic and Social Research (NIESR), which began by giving qualitative forecasts only, producing quantitative projections from 1961. The NIESR is an independent research body, which began forecasting and related research with the help of funds from the Treasury and the Ford foundation. A further group, the Henley Centre, also started producing regular forecasts, based on judgement, at the start of the 1960s. In contrast to the NIESR and the Treasury, this received no public funding, nor did it formalize its forecasting methods until the early 1980s.

In 1965 the government set up the Social Science Research Council to distribute some of the public funds available for research and training in the social sciences. The SSRC gave grants to several teams that had started developing macro-econometric models or were about to begin, typically

Table 1.1 Main UK organizations publishing forecasts of the UK economy

	Date Started (2)	Club?	Name of main forecasting publications with no. of issues/year and approx. price in 1984
Government HM Treasury	late 1940s	no	*Financial Statement and Budget Report*, published annually with the Budget, £5 *Autumn Statement*, published annually in the autumn, £5
Bank of England	1973	no	*Bank of England Quarterly Bulletin*, 4 issues, £25 p.a.
Academic research institutes National Institute for Economic and Social Research	1959	no	*National Institute Economic Review*, 4 issues, £25 p.a.
London Business School	1966	yes	*LBS Economic Outlook*, 12 issues, £90 p.a. *LBS Financial Outlook*, 4 issues, £350 p.a.
Cambridge Economic Policy Group	1971	no	*Cambridge Economic Policy Review* (1), 1 or 2 issues, £20 p.a.
Liverpool University	1981	no	*Liverpool University Quarterly Economic Bulletin*, 4 issues, £50 (personal £20) p.a.
Cambridge Growth Project/Cambridge Econometrics	late 1970s (2)	yes	see note (3)
City University Business School	1983	no	*City University Economic Review*, 4 issues, £40 p.a.
Commercial Treasury Model St. James's Group	1977/78	yes	see note (3)
Item Club	1977/78	yes	see note (3)
Others – outside the City Oxford Economic Forecasts	late 1970s	yes	*Oxford Review of Economic Policy*, 4 issues, £45 (personal £25) p.a.
Henley Centre	1960s	no	*Henley Centre Framework Forecasts*, 12 issues, £600 p.a.
City Phillips and Drew	1970s	no	*Phillips and Drew Economic Forecasts*, 12 issues, see note (4), £350 p.a.
Simon and Coates (Many other stockbrokers prepare less detailed forecasts)	1981	no	*Simon and Coates The Economic Analyst*, 12 issues, see note (4)

Notes: (1) No issues published in recent years.

(2) First publication. CGP started model building some fifteen years before Cambridge Econometrics was formed.

(3) Publications available only to club members, although main points of forecast appear in the press.

(4) These stockbrokers give their economic forecasts free to their clients.

In addition to the UK-based organizations shown, the OECD based in Paris publishes forecasts of the UK economy in *OECD Economic Outlook*.

on renewable terms of three to five years. Grants were given to the London Business School (LBS), the Cambridge Economic Policy Group (CEPG), Southampton University, the NIESR, and Professor Richard Stone's Cambridge Growth Project (CGP). The last two of these groups also received funds directly from the Treasury.

Of these groups, the LBS started publishing regular forecasts in 1966 (just before it received its first SSRC grant), the CGP research programme had begun in 1960 but regular projections were not published until the late 1970s, the CEPG started an annual report in 1971 containing medium-term policy projections, the Southampton project was to close without ever publishing regular forecasts, and the NIESR had already begun publishing forecasts as noted above.

Institutional changes in the 1970s

In the mid-1970s, important changes occurred in the financing and structure of the forecasting groups. The SSRC announced that it would not renew the grant for the Southampton model, and this project was wound up in 1976. The Southampton approach differed significantly from the others in that individuals were responsible for estimating equations, or groups of equations, independently. The intention was that the separately estimated equations could be combined to form a complete macro-econometric model. (See Heathfield (1984) for a description of the work done.) By contrast the other groups were usually controlled by one or two team leaders who exercised fairly tight control over the research work used in the macro-econometric models. This type of control is a feature of all the forecasting teams in existence today, including the new groups.

At the same time that the Southampton project was closing down, the government (via the Treasury and the SSRC) indicated that it wished to reduce the emphasis on public funding and increase private sector finance for forecasting. Two groups, the CGP and LBS, were most affected by this, with the CEPG and NIESR continuing to receive a high proportion of their funds from the public sector.

The CGP set up a new, independent organization called Cambridge Econometrics, launched in 1978. This is a commercial company, but is covenanted to transfer some of its profits to Cambridge University in order to support research at the CGP. In return, the new organization has access to the CGP macro-econometric model. Cambridge Econometrics has its own independent staff, although two of its directors are also part of CGP. The commercial services offered include consultancy and there is also a forecasting club of the type described in the previous section. Because the CGP model is disaggregated into many sectors, detailed reports can be offered on individual industries. See Barker (1976) for a description of the CGP model. Unlike most of the other forecasting groups, Cambridge Econometrics releases only very limited parts of its forecasts to the general public via the media.

The LBS also reacted to the government's requirements by setting up a

Box 1.1   The size of the forecasting industry

How large is the economic forecasting industry in the UK? The 1981 SSRC report cited in the text suggests a total turnover of some £3 million in 1980 (at 1980 prices) for the main publicly funded groups plus three of the biggest private groups (this covers only forecasting and directly connected research work). Adding in an estimate for the groups excluded from this figure, the total for the UK as a whole in 1980 was probably around £4 million. This almost certainly represents a significant real increase on the size of the industry three years earlier (some figures for which are given in Ball, 1978).

Of the £3 million quoted by the SSRC, over two-thirds was provided by the public sector and the rest came from a variety of private sources. Of this finance, almost half was spent on the activities of the Treasury, the Bank of England and other government agencies. Another £1 million was used by the LBS, the CEPG, the CGP and the NIESR, and the table gives details of their budgets. The remaining half a million pounds represented the work of the three private forecasters (the ITEM club, the St James' Group, and Phillips and Drew) included in the SSRC's total.

Table 1.2   Budgets of main publicly financed independent forecasters, 1980

	LBS	NIESR	CGP	CEPG
Total budget (£ thousand)	212	555	98	211
Breakdown				
Public sector funds	126	440	74	
Publication sales	15	–	–	211
Subscriptions	71(1)	–	–	
Other private sector	–	115	23(2)	
Number of employees	11	20	8	12

Source: SSRC (1981).
Notes: (1) Includes surplus carried forward.
       (2) Income from Cambridge Econometrics.
       Figures may not sum precisely to totals due to rounding error.

club of subscribing companies (LBS calls this its 'consortium'). In contrast to the arrangements adopted by CGP, the LBS consortium is not run by a separate commercial company, but by the forecasters themselves. The LBS continued to receive finance from the SSRC for research activities and in 1977 started producing a forecasting publication called *Economic Outlook*, and a further publication called *Financial Outlook* was produced from 1983. Profits from these provided an additional source of finance.

The Bray Amendment

Since 1973, the Treasury, like most of the other forecasting groups, had published a manual listing and explaining the equations in its forecasting model. This was of interest to researchers wishing to examine Treasury work on an individual equation but was of little practical use to others. This was partly because the manual (published annually) was about twelve to eighteen months out of date when it first appeared, and partly because even experienced forecasters obtained little idea of the overall properties of the model merely by studying the equations. Setting up the model on a computer using the information from the manual would have been a very large task and there is no record of any attempts to do this.

There was a strong case for making Treasury modelling work more easily available and this was achieved in 1975 when Jeremy Bray (Labour MP and mathematician) successfully proposed an amendment to the Industry Act of that year. The Bray Amendment formalizes the practice, established in the 1950s, of publishing Treasury forecasts. It stipulates that the Treasury must publish projections for GDP, inflation and other important items twice a year. Current practice is for these to appear with the budget and also at the same time as the Chancellor of the Exchequer's autumn statement.

The Bray Amendment also requires the government to make the Treasury model available for public use in computer readable form, together with all necessary historical data. Commercial users are charged a royalty, of the order of £100 per forecast in 1980, which is waived for academic users. In practice, there is no direct access to the Treasury model. Academic users have access via the ESRC bureau at Warwick, which was not operative until 1984 and is described later in this section, while others users have access via one of the commercial forecasting clubs set up late in the 1970s.

One of these clubs is the Independent Treasury Modelling Group (ITEM), run by a computer software subsidiary of British Petroleum. The other is the St James's Group, run by the Economist Intelligence Unit (the consultancy arm of the *Economist* newspaper); this was taken over by Chase Econometrics early in the 1980s. These clubs have obtained almost all of their revenue from subscriptions paid by member companies, and from computer and consultancy charges, plus a small amount from publications. They have received no government grant.

The version of the Treasury model that is available to the public through the commercial clubs and the Warwick bureau is generally between one and two years out of date. The Treasury provides only a summary of the assumptions on which its own forecasts are based, and no indication at all is given of how the results from the model have been adjusted using judgement. This makes it impossible to reproduce the Treasury forecasts, and so the projections of the ITEM club are no more likely to reflect official forecasts than those of, for example, the LBS.

The discrepancy between the Treasury's own version of its model and the published version is unsatisfactory for users, particularly when the two versions have significantly different properties. This problem is worsened when, as in 1981, major revisions to the model (described in Chapter 7) coincide with a period of great uncertainty in the economy.

The early 1980s: the Warwick bureau and other institutional change

By mid-1979, when the Conservative government came to office, the UK forecasting industry had seen five years of rapid expansion. The number of groups producing projections, and the availability of publications, had increased greatly. In addition to the groups already mentioned, the CBI started publishing short-term economic forecasts in 1975, drawing on its surveys (see Chapter 2) and its other sources of information from companies. Several stockbrokers also began publishing forecasts at this time, intending them mainly as a service to clients, and as a means of obtaining press publicity. Among these stockbrokers, Phillips and Drew are one of the best known. The CBI has not published the models that it uses, nor have any of the stockbrokers, most of whom rely on judgement rather than a formal model.

Reflecting its doubts about the effectiveness of economic forecasting (expressed in a speech by the incoming Chancellor), the new government asked the SSRC to review the level of public sector financial support, with a view to obtaining more funds from the private sector. The SSRC's report, published in June 1981, rejected the view that privatization might allow substantial reductions in the public funding of forecasting. Instead the SSRC suggested only a small cut in grants from the government, although it indicated that a significant redistribution might occur among the forecasting groups. See SSRC (1981).

The following year the specific allocations of funds, effective from 1983, were announced. The principal changes were that CEPG lost much of its public funding, and NIESR lost a much smaller proportion. The relatively new group at Liverpool University, which published its first projections in 1980, received improved funding. The recently formed team at the City University Business School (CUBS) received a new grant.

Some commentators saw this distribution as politically motivated, penalizing those whose views differed from the government's and favouring those who agreed. This view arose partly because the Liverpool group emphasized the effect of expectations, while CUBS concentrated on supply factors, both of which were areas that the government felt were treated inadequately by the other groups and through which it hoped its policies would operate. (For a discussion of the macro-econometric models of these groups, see Chapter 7.)

The 1981 SSRC report also considered whether there would be benefits from merging the forecasting teams into several larger units or even one very large unit. This idea was rejected, but the report called for closer co-operation. This was to take two forms. Regular joint research meetings were to be held, to ensure that the teams had much greater knowledge of one another's work than was possible before, when the only formal contact had been through occasional joint conferences. In addition, a small forecasting centre was to be set up. Tenders were invited for this and in 1983 it was announced that it would be at the University of Warwick under the directorship of Professor Wallis. With the SSRC now renamed the Economic and Social Research Council (ESRC), this centre is known as the ESRC Macro-econometric Modelling Bureau.

The Bureau makes available to a wide academic audience all the macro-econometric models developed by groups who receive government funding. The Bureau itself does not develop models or prepare forecasts, although it analyses and comments on the models of the various forecasting teams. Every year, each of the forecasting groups deposits at the Bureau a computer-readable copy of its model and associated data, and the Bureau arranges for all of these models to be accessible through a single piece of computer software. (An exception is the CGP model which has to be treated separately because of its size.) This in principle allows universities nationwide to have access to all of the models. The versions of the models available via this system are generally out of date by between about six and eighteen months, in most cases because of the technical difficulties in transferring models between computers.

2

Conjunctural analysis

Government macro-economic data are generally published with a delay, many important series not appearing until nearly two months or more after the period to which they relate. To give forecasters and others a more up-to-date view of economic developments, conjunctural analysts draw together survey data, 'anecdotal' information and a limited amount of government macro-economic data into an overall picture of the economy that is consistent with economic theory and econometric results. Without conjunctural analysis, economic forecasts would be subject to increased errors, because much of the recent past would have to be 'forecast' (see Chapter 5). Forecasters and econometricians also use information from conjunctural analysis to indicate whether assumptions used in estimating their macro-econometric models have been violated.

In this chapter we explain why government macro-economic data are inadequate, discuss other sources of information about the economy, and indicate how all the information is used by the conjunctural analyst. Chapter 3 gives a practical example of this process.

2.1 Problems in using government macro-economic data

Official macro-economic data are derived from a variety of sources. The unemployment figures (in the UK) are derived from a simple count of the numbers registering. The index of industrial production is based partly on returns which companies are obliged to complete, while the aggregate personal income figures are constructed partly from income tax returns (for full details of data sources, see Maurice, 1968). Whatever the source of official macro-economic data, it is not adequate for monitoring the current economic situation. This is because of two practical problems: the delay in publication and measurement error. There is also a third problem inherent in the data, which is examined at the end of this section.

Publication delay

Government economic statistics are published at given times on dates announced usually about two months or more in advance. In some cases the dates follow the same pattern for year after year. For example, since the 1960s the retail prices index has been published at 11.30 a.m. on the second Friday of the month after that to which it relates (unless bank holidays intervene or the first Friday is very early in the month). Once announced, timetables are strictly adhered to, only strikes or other exceptional difficulties causing an alteration.

A pre-arranged timetable is useful to, for example, economists and journalists. However, a more important effect is to prevent political interference with the publication dates. This contributes to the independence of the government statistical service. Pre-determined publication dates were introduced in the 1960s when Sir Claus Moser was head of the government statistical service. Until then, governments could freely adjust the release dates of statistics. This would allow, for example, publication of bad trade figures at the same time as some major non-economic news in order to reduce adverse foreign exchange market reaction.

Despite strict adherence to official publication dates, figures are generally made available in confidence to government ministers, Civil Servants and journalists just before their official release. Members of the public usually learn of the most newsworthy statistics very rapidly (say within half an hour of publication) through the media, and many of the more important data series can be obtained through the post the day after publication by subscribing to the appropriate news release. However, detailed or specialized data may be difficult to obtain until it appears in *Economic Trends*, *Financial Statistics* or one of the other government publications a week or more after official release.

The delay between the period to which a figure relates, and the date on which it is published, depends both on when information is collected and on the time taken in processing it. This means that the delay varies considerably. Rather than wait until all information is available, which in some cases takes years, preliminary estimates are published for most figures making use of partly estimated data. Such preliminary estimates are subject to considerable revision after publication.

Table 2.1 gives, for various important UK economic data series, some idea of the delay before initial publication. For comparison, exchange rates, interest rates and survey data are included in this table; they will be considered in Section 2.2. The monthly unemployment figures are one of the most rapidly available government statistics, being published within about twelve days of the date to which they relate. This very short delay reflects the relative ease with which these figures are compiled. Several other monthly statistics are available after about one and a half to three weeks delay. Among the more important of these are the producer price indices (input and output), retail sales and provisional money stock estimates. The remaining monthly data are published somewhat later.

Preliminary quarterly estimates of consumers' expenditure, with a fairly large estimated element, appear after a delay of about three weeks. Further preliminary quarterly data, including the output estimate of GDP, appear about one and a half months after the end of the quarter to which they relate. However, the bulk of the quarterly data, including the expenditure estimate of GDP and its components, are not available until

The production and use of economic forecasts

Table 2.1 Delay in publication of economic data

Statistic	Source	Monthly or quarterly	Typical delay before publication
Exchange and interest rates			none
Capital issues	Bank of England	M	about 2 days
Official reserves	HM Treasury	M	about 2 days
Vehicle production	Dept Trade	M	about 1 week
Unemployment	Dept Employment	M	about 12 days
CBI surveys	CBI	M	up to 12 days
Wholesale price indices	Dept Trade	M	about 1½ weeks
Central government transactions	HM Treasury	M	about 1½ weeks
Building society figures	BSA	M	1½ to 2 weeks
Usable steel output	BSC/BISPA	M	about 2 weeks
Retail sales	Dept Trade	M	2 to 3 weeks
Money stock (various measures) and banking figures	Bank of England	M (Banking)	about 3 weeks
Consumers' expenditure (preliminary estimate)	CSO	Q	about 3 weeks
PSBR	CSO	M	about 3 to 5 weeks
Trade figures	Dept Trade	M	about 3 to 4 weeks
New vehicle registrations	Dept Transport	M	about 4 weeks
Bank lending and other counterparts to money stock	Bank of England	M (Banking)	about 1 month
Retail prices index	Dept Employment	M	1 month or just over
Housing starts and completions	Dept Environment	M	5 to 6 weeks
Index of industrial production	CSO	M	about 1½ months
Analysis of bank lending	Bank of England	Q (Banking)	about 1½ months
Index of average earnings	Dept Employment	M	about 1½ months
GDP (output estimate)	CSO	Q	just over 1½ months
Manufacturers' and distributors' stocks	Dept Industry	Q	just over 1½ months
Capital expenditure of manufacturing, distributive and service industries	Dept Industry	Q	just over 1½ months
Employment in production industries	Dept Employment	M	about 2 months
Full balance of payments	CSO	Q	about 2¼ months
GDP (expenditure estimate) and components	CSO	Q	about 2¾ months
Personal income and expenditure and company appropriation account	CSO	Q	about 3 months
Institutional investment	CSO	Q	nearly 4 months
Complete transactions in financial assets	CSO	Q	about 4 months

Note: For an explanation of 'Banking' months and quarters, see page 32.

Table 2.2   Data revisions

Statistic	Average revision after 5 years
Retail prices index	nil
GDP	0.8
Consumers' expenditure	0.4
General government consumption	1.0
Fixed investment	2.3
Exports of goods and services	1.7
Imports of goods and services	0.6
Current account balance	0.1
PSBR	0.2

Sources: GDP and its components are estimated from charts in Hibbert (1981). Current account balance and PSBR revisions are taken from a five year sample of third quarter data.

Notes: For GDP and its components, this is the average absolute revision in percentage points after 5 years, to the year on year percentage change. For the current account balance and the PSBR, this is the average absolute revision in £billion after 5 years (4 for the PSBR), at a quarterly rate. The RPI is not subject to revision.

after a delay of nearly three months. The remaining quarterly data, including most of the ambitious flow of funds data showing income and expenditure for broad sectors of the economy and the corresponding financial transactions, appear after about four months.

Annual data for items not covered by monthly or quarterly series, such as capital stock, are published by the government in *National Income and Expenditure* (known as the *Blue Book*) about nine months after the end of the year to which they relate. In addition some extra material appears after an even longer delay; for example information about income distribution given in *Inland Revenue Statistics*.

These publication delays mean that a conjunctural analyst relying solely on government macro-economic data would have no information at all about current economic events and only a fairly incomplete picture of events occurring several months before. Moreover, as Table 2.2 shows, most government data are subject to considerable revision after initial publication. For example, the average revision (see table for precise definition) in figures for GDP is 0.8 per cent, which is substantial given that the growth between years is typically of the order of 2 per cent. Also, the revisions are sometimes very much larger than the averages shown in the table. For example, publication of figures showing a substantial current account deficit at the end of 1976 caused a crisis of confidence which appears to have been mainly responsible for a large fall in the sterling exchange rate. Yet this deficit has been virtually halved by revisions made since its initial publication.

Measurement error

Even after all revisions, the data are subject to measurement error. This is partly because of the black economy (see Section 2.3) but also reflects a large number of other factors. Much of the data is based on surveys rather than a complete count, so there is sampling error. Timing differences cause considerable problems, notably in the trade statistics, which are compiled mainly from the customs declarations submitted by traders. The timing of these does not bear a constant relationship to the moment at which ownership changes, which is itself difficult to define precisely. Errors also arise from foreign exchange revaluations, which affect both financial statistics and trade figures. Another source of error is the lack of a clear distinction between changes in prices and changes in volumes. This problem is particularly significant for stocks because there is no simple, fixed relation between the prices at which companies value their stocks and the prices they charge for current output.

The combination of publication delay and unreliability of early estimates makes it essential that the conjunctural analyst has other types of information, from surveys and the other sources described below, and also that all information is viewed as a whole. This sometimes makes it possible to identify an erroneous data item which does not fit into the overall pattern. This is the core of the conjunctural analyst's job and is discussed more fully in Section 2.4 below.

A problem inherent in macro-economic data

There is a further problem, inherent in macro-economic data, which makes it essential for the conjunctural analyst to complement official data with material from other sources. Full information about the economic activities of all individuals and organizations in the economy would include among other things details of contracts, negotiations and expectations. Such information even for only a week would require vast amounts of storage; its collection and processing would use sufficient resources to affect substantially the economy and would probably be regarded as an unacceptable incursion into personal freedom, even if people were able to answer the necessary questions. Instead of trying to assemble all this information, governments collect macro-economic data, which are summary statistics for the population of all information about economic activities.

The conjunctural analyst, by using sources other than official data, can look behind these summary statistics. As illustration, consider the index of manufacturing output, which provides an estimate of total production in one broad sector of industry. This is useful, but may hide a wide diversity between sub-sectors, between firms of varying size, between regions, between firms with capital stock of varying ages, and so on. There is only very limited official data for some of these, and no official information at all for others. Such diversity could violate the assumptions used to derive the equations in macro-econometric models and perhaps change the policy conclusions drawn from those models. Survey data and other sources of information (described below) will often indicate which types of companies are performing in a different way from the rest, thus warning the conjunctural analyst when the official data are misleading.

2.2 Other sources of information

This section describes three main types of information used by conjunctural analysts and economic forecasters to complement the official macroeconomic data.

The first main source is from surveys, conducted by various private and public organizations. These cover recent or projected actions and also business or consumer confidence. The most important UK surveys are shown in Table 2.3. The Confederation of British Industry (CBI) industrial trends survey began in 1958 and now has a large weighted sample of about fifteen hundred to two thousand manufacturing firms. It is conducted quarterly and includes questions on recent and expected trends (i.e., changes over the past four months and over the coming four) in a wide range of items including output, orders and prices. There are also questions about confidence, and about investment plans over the next twelve months. The major quarterly survey is complemented by a brief monthly survey, containing only five questions, which is sent to the same participants. The results are available broken down by detailed subsectors, by size of firm, and, to some extent, by region.

Other important UK surveys shown in Table 2.3 include the new CBI/*Financial Times* survey of the distributive trades started in 1983, which covers retailing, wholesaling and dealerships. Very little official data are available on the last two of these sectors, so this survey, which has many similarities to the CBI's established survey of manufacturing, is an important development for conjunctural analysts. The table also includes

Table 2.3 Main UK economic surveys

Survey	Frequency	Sector covered
CBI industrial trends survey	quarterly	manufacturing industry
CBI monthly trends enquiry	monthly	manufacturing industry
Department of Trade investment intentions survey	twice-yearly	fixed investment by manufacturing, distributive and services industries
National Federation of Building Trades Employers survey	quarterly	construction industry
CBI/*Financial Times* distributive trades survey	quarterly with short surveys in intervening months	retailing, wholesaling and dealerships
Incomes Data Services pay report	twice monthly	pay settlements for all the economy
CBI pay databank	monthly	sample of pay settlements across the economy
Gallup consumer survey	quarterly	trends in consumer sentiment

Note: A description of the CBI surveys is given in Klein and Moore (1981).

the National Federation of Building Trades Employers' (NFBTE) survey of the construction industry, which together with the CBI industrial trends survey forms the UK part of the European Community's harmonized business survey. Not shown in the table are the detailed and very expensive surveys covering demand for individual products and carried out by market research firms.

There are several advantages of survey data compared to official macro-economic data. The surveys are generally published much more rapidly. For example, the CBI survey data appear within two weeks of the end of the two to three week survey period, which is a shorter publication delay than for any important official macro-economic data except the unemployment figures (see Table 2.1). Another advantage of survey data is that they include responses to questions about confidence, a topic not covered by the official figures. Also, survey data are not subject to revision.

However, there is a drawback. Much of the data from the surveys shown in Table 2.3 is not explicitly quantitative. Most questions in the CBI and NFBTE surveys are of the form, 'What has been the trend with regard to new orders (or employment, or output, etc.) over the last four months: up, unchanged, or down?' The resulting data are the percentages replying to these three categories, and the information is often summarized as a *balance*, which is the percentage replying 'up' minus the percentage replying 'down'. See Theil (1966) for justification of the use of the balance, and Keating (1983) for discussion. Because the data are in this form, there is a tendency to use survey data to detect turning points rather than to quantify trends. However, there has been considerable success in obtaining quantified information from the survey data by relating past survey figures to official outturns; see for example Savage (1975).

The second main source of alternative information available to conjunctural analysts and forecasters is from directly observable prices. These include exchange rates (which are the price of one currency in terms of another), interest rates, oil and commodity prices. Such data are available almost instantaneously via on-line computer information services and almost as rapidly through other media.

The third type of alternative information is *anecdotal*. This comes from a wide variety of sources and includes information about current trading conditions which the conjunctural analyst obtains simply by speaking to those in business. It includes information about pay negotiations, industrial action and settlements; about company investment plans, plant closures, negotiations or agreements for new orders, liquidations, new issues on the stock market, announced price changes, take-over bids and so on. It includes the weather which affects the energy and agricultural sectors directly and can affect other sectors. It also includes political developments and government policy announcements, both major (such as entire budgets) and relatively minor (such as the setting of council house rents).

Some of this information will appear through formal sources, for example in company reports, in Hansard or in press notices, but the conjunctural analyst's main means of obtaining most of it will be through the media. The *Financial Times* is currently the best source for this type of information in the UK, although it has no monopoly.

Some anecdotal information is about events which have a significant effect on the whole economy, for example, major company investment plans, pay settlements affecting many people, and government policy announcements. Such events give the conjunctural analyst hard data about what is going on in the economy. By contrast, much anecdotal information is about events which, by themselves, are insignificant for the economy as a whole. The conjunctural analyst must study this to see whether there seems to be any widespread tendency in actions or in sentiments (for example, among pay negotiators). When a new piece of information conflicts with the picture already becoming established, the conjunctural analyst will increase the search for information in that area, to try to resolve the conflict.

2.3 Review of national accounts practice

The system of national accounts is fundamental to conjunctural analysis and to economic forecasting, and is reviewed in this section, with emphasis on its ability to explain how transactions are financed. Readers with a full knowledge of the national accounts can omit this section without loss of continuity. Values taken by many of the items mentioned are shown in Table 3.1 of the next chapter and the latest figures are available in the government's *Economic Trends* or *Financial Statistics* in most cases.

In the national accounts, total output of the whole economy is called *gross domestic product*, often abbreviated to *GDP*. 'Gross' indicates that this measure of output is calculated without making any deduction for depreciation, while 'domestic' distinguishes GDP from *gross national product*, which is obtained by adding net income from abroad to GDP. It is possible to define GDP in terms of the prices which buyers pay for goods and services. This is known as GDP at *market prices*. Alternatively, GDP can be defined as that part of the price which is paid to the factors of production, which is known as GDP at *factor cost* and equals GDP at market prices minus taxes on expenditure net of subsidies. Both these definitions of GDP can be computed using the prices and incomes at which transactions actually take place, or alternatively both can be adjusted to allow for inflation by revaluing them to the price and income levels of some base year (1980 is used in this book). The unadjusted figures are said to be at *current prices* (the phrases *current market prices* or *current factor cost*, as appropriate, are also used), while the figures adjusted for inflation are said to be at *constant prices*.

As an elementary accounting identity, total output of the economy equals total expenditure equals total income. In practice, independent

measurement yields three different estimates known respectively as the
'output measure of GDP', the 'expenditure measure of GDP' and the
'income measure of GDP'. The difference between these three measures
varies substantially between one quarter and another, so that it is possible
for one measure to suggest an increase in the volume of GDP while
another implies a fall.

It is often thought that the difference between the income and expenditure measures of GDP provides some measure of the black economy. As
explained in Box 2.1, this is not correct, partly because the government
statisticians try to correct for any such effect, and partly because the
difference reflects a variety of errors and omissions not connected with the
black economy.

In the national accounts, the expenditure measure of GDP is divided
into components:

> GDP (expenditure measure, at factor cost)
> = consumers' expenditure
>   + general government final consumption
>   + investment in fixed assets and stocks
>   + exports
>   − imports
>   − government receipts of expenditure taxes, net of subsidies

The government statisticians provide quarterly data for all these components, at constant and at current prices, and a more detailed breakdown
is available; for example investment can be split between houses and other
capital goods. Some macro-econometric models have less detail than is
shown here but the larger models have more.

The output and income measures of GDP can also be disaggregated into
broad categories as shown below. Data for the output measure are
available only in constant prices, while data for the income measure are
available only at current prices; both are calculated at factor cost:

> GDP (output estimate)
> = industrial production (includes manufacturing output, North
>   Sea oil and other industries)
>   + distributive and services output including government
>   + agricultural output

> GDP (income estimate)
> = income from employment
>   + gross trading profits
>   + rent
>   + other domestic income
>   − stock appreciation

As well as giving the three measures of GDP, the national accounts
explain how economic activity is financed. For this purpose the economy

Box 2.1   The black economy

This box explains the relationship between the black economy and the national accounts, and shows that the difference between the income and expenditure measures of GDP gives no information about the black economy.

The income measure of GDP is based largely on information from the Inland Revenue and so it tends to under-record true incomes, because of earnings not declared on people's income tax returns – the 'black economy'. The government statisticians make an upward adjustment to allow, at least partly, for this. The expenditure measure is believed to under-record true spending by a smaller amount, because it relies to a large extent on surveys of household and company spending, which are thought to be less subject to inaccurate replies than returns to the Inland Revenue. No adjustment for the black economy is made to the expenditure estimate.

If the statisticians made no adjustment, the difference between the income and expenditure measures of GDP would provide some information about the black economy, although it would also reflect other errors and omissions, and would exclude black economy transactions recorded in neither measure of GDP. Since the published figures include the adjustment to the income measure, the discrepancy between the measures cannot be regarded as giving any indication about the black economy, reflecting instead other types of measurement error. See Figure 2.1.

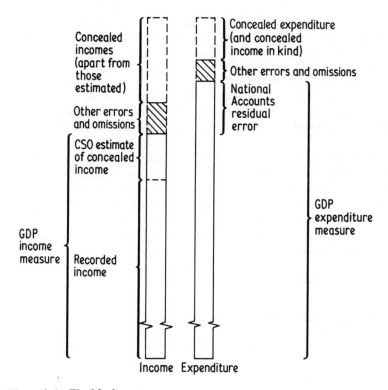

Figure 2.1   The black economy
   Source: Adapted from chart in *Economic Trends* (see CSO, 1983). Not to scale.

is divided into several sectors (see Maurice, 1968, for full definitions): industrial and commercial companies; the personal sector; the public sector; the monetary sector (i.e. banks); other financial institutions (e.g. building societies); and the overseas sector (which includes all economic agents outside the domestic economy). One of the reasons for choosing this particular division of the economy was the hope that the economic agents within each sector would be sufficiently homogeneous for their behaviour to be treated as if they all acted in the same way. In practice the agents within each sector often act in diverse ways and violate the assumptions made when deriving macro-econometric models, causing forecasters to impose judgemental adjustments (see Chapter 5).

Each domestic sector receives income from providing the services of a factor of production (e.g. people receive wages in return for their labour), plus net receipts of interest and dividends from other sectors (this net figure is typically positive for the personal sector and negative for companies), plus current grants from other sectors (e.g. people receive unemployment benefits from the public sector), minus payments of income taxes. For each sector, its *saving* is defined as all these receipts, minus consumption, plus, for the public sector only, receipts of income and expenditure taxes. Each sector's *financial balance*, or *net acquisition of financial assets* (NAFA), is defined as saving, plus capital transfers (typically very small), minus investment in fixed assets and stocks. Exceptionally, the overseas sector NAFA is defined as its receipts of income from sales of imports to UK residents, plus its net receipts of interest, etc., minus its payments for purchases of goods and services exported by the UK (this is the current account of the balance of payments with the sign reversed).

Typically the personal sector's financial balance is large and positive, because savings comfortably exceed the sector's investment expenditure (much of which is on new houses). For industrial and commercial companies, the balance is sometimes significantly negative and sometimes positive, depending in part on profitability. For the public sector, the balance is usually a large negative figure, reflecting a shortfall of tax and other receipts below expenditure and the government's consequent need to borrow.

Given the definition of financial balances, we can write:

Sum of all sectors' financial balances
= sum of post-tax incomes
  + government receipts of income taxes
  + government receipts of expenditure taxes, net of subsidies
  + sum of interest, dividends and grants
  + imports minus exports
  − sum of consumption
  − sum of investment
  + sum of capital transfers

A transfer payment made by one sector (which may be a grant or a payment of interest or dividends) must be reflected in a receipt by another sector, so the sum of interest, dividends and grants is zero, as is the sum of capital transfers. Noting also that GDP (expenditure measure, at current factor cost) equals consumption (by persons and government), plus investment, plus exports, minus imports, minus government receipts of expenditure taxes net of subsidies, the above expression becomes:

> Sum of all sectors' financial balances
> = sum of post-tax incomes
>   + government receipts of income taxes
>   + zero
>   – GDP (expenditure measure, at current factor cost)
>   + zero

Adding income taxes to the sum of post-tax incomes, we obtain the sum of all incomes before tax, which is the income measure of GDP:

> Sum of all sectors' financial balances
> = GDP (income measure)
>   – GDP (expenditure measure at current factor cost)

In principle, these two measures of GDP are equal, so the sum of the financial balances should be zero. In practice they differ by a residual error, as noted above, and so the sum of the financial balances equals this error.

The financial balances provide a measure of the total receipts of funds by each sector, minus total outgoings. A positive balance means that the sector has excess funds, not being used for spending, which are available for net purchases of financial assets, i.e. the sector is a net lender. A negative balance means that the sector is a net borrower. The importance of the financial balance is illustrated by the rapid deterioration in the industrial and commercial companies deficit in 1974, which indicated dangerous liquidity problems for many companies, causing the Labour government to act speedily to reduce company taxes.

Within any sector, individuals are often in diverse circumstances, some needing to borrow and others needing to lend, whatever the sector's overall financial balance. In addition, individuals often act as borrowers and lenders at the same time (e.g. many people have both a mortgage and some savings at the building society at the same time). Hence any sector is usually carrying out a large amount of lending and a large amount of borrowing at any time, but the difference must equal the financial balance (apart from measurement error).

This lending and borrowing is in the form of a wide range of financial liabilities and assets, both short term and long term. For people, short-term liabilities include bank overdrafts, while long-term assets include holdings of company equities. These equities are one of the long-term liabilities of companies. This illustrates a general point: items which are financial assets for one sector must always be the liabilities of another.

The various measures of growth in money stock can all be obtained by adding together transactions in certain types of assets. For example, changes in sterling M3, used for targeting monetary growth by the Conservative government after 1979, are defined as increases in the holdings of notes and coins and sterling bank deposits by the personal, industrial and commercial companies, and other financial institution sectors.

2.4 The conjunctural analyst's methods

This section explains how a conjunctural analyst builds up a picture of the economy in the current quarter and Chapter 3 gives a practical example of this procedure. In practice, as indicated by Table 2.1, only very limited data are available for a recently ended quarter, so conjunctural analysts are in the process of refining their estimates for the previous quarter at the same time as they are studying the current quarter. This complication is ignored here.

There is considerable variation among conjunctural analysts in the emphasis they give to different aspects of the economy, reflecting their interests. For example, government borrowing figures are of more concern to analysts in the gilts departments of stockbroking firms than to analysts in the motor industry. Despite this difference in emphasis, the method followed by all conjunctural analysts follows broadly the pattern set out below.

The conjunctural analyst's procedure is to use information, as it becomes available, to estimate components of the expenditure and income measures of GDP at current prices, and of the expenditure and output measures at constant prices, and also to estimate financial transactions. Typically an estimate for any one of these items may draw on information from all the various different sources discussed earlier in this chapter. For example, consider stock building. An estimate for this would rely partly on disaggregated import figures, because the analyst knows from econometric work and from experience that imports (particularly of raw materials) respond rapidly to stock movements; CBI survey data on past and expected movements in manufacturers' and distributors' stocks would also be used, and so would official coal and oil stock figures; also anecdotal and survey information about retailers' sales expectations at the start of the quarter could be combined with indicators of the sales actually achieved to give some warning of unplanned stock building or destocking.

Towards the end of the quarter, estimates will have been made for a reasonably large proportion of the components of GDP and of the financial transactions. At this stage, a complete estimated set of national accounts can be prepared, with missing items filled in by results from a macro-econometric model or by guesswork. This provides a series of consistency checks: the two current price estimates of GDP should be equal (apart from effects due to measurement error), as should the two constant price estimates; the financial balances for all the sectors should sum to zero (again, apart from any measurement error in the GDP estimates); and the estimated financial balances obtained from information about income and expenditure should equal the estimate of net financial transactions for each sector. Sufficient information is usually available earlier in the quarter to give estimates of parts of the national accounts, thus allowing use of some of these consistency checks.

Very often, the initial estimates prepared by the conjunctural analyst will not satisfy these consistency checks. An example would be if the expenditure measure of GDP (at constant prices) fell and the estimate for the output measure rose. Inconsistencies do not necessarily imply that the analyst's estimates are wrong because (as mentioned in Section 2.3), the official data sometimes contain measurement errors giving this type of effect. Nevertheless if such an inconsistency is implied by the analyst's initial estimates, the normal procedure is to eliminate it by altering the estimates. This is because at this stage, the available information is so limited that inconsistencies are more likely to reflect errors in the analyst's estimates than measurement error in the statistics.

It is not always clear which item or items should be adjusted to remove an inconsistency, in which case it is usual to alter the least certain items, or those that are furthest from the values suggested by the macro-econometric model used by the analyst. However, it is sometimes possible to remove two or more inconsistencies by altering a single item, suggesting fairly strongly that the estimate of that item is wrong. For example, suppose that the estimated GDP expenditure measure (at constant prices) is considerably below the estimated GDP output measure, while at the same time a positive estimate for the industrial and commercial companies sector financial balance (indicating net lending) appears to conflict with money supply statistics that show a large amount of borrowing from the banks. The obvious way to remove both inconsistencies at once is to increase the estimate for the volume of company investment on fixed assets, or stocks, or both. This implies a higher expenditure estimate of GDP and a lower company financial balance (i.e. an increased demand for borrowing by companies). In this situation, the conjunctural analyst checks to see how the estimates for company stock building and fixed investment were obtained, noting whether a higher estimate is consistent with such limited information as is available.

When a macro-econometric model is available, it is usually convenient to carry out this process by preparing a forecast for the current quarter on the model and then replacing the forecasts by estimates based on conjunctural analysis as information becomes available. In the example of conjunctural analysis in practice presented in the next chapter, we start with forecasts obtained from the small macro-econometric model of Chapter 4, explain how information is obtained over the course of a quarter and used to derive estimates, and show how the estimates are adjusted to ensure consistency.

3

Conjunctural analysis in practice

This chapter shows how a conjunctural analyst builds up a picture of the UK economy for the fourth quarter of 1983. The description begins at the end of October, when the first anecdotal and official figures start to appear, and continues on a week-by-week basis up to the end of December, when a reasonable amount of information is available. At the end of every fortnight from mid-November onward, there is a review of the conjunctural analyst's current assessment for the fourth quarter values of key economic variables. The final section of the chapter sets out in detail the analyst's views as they stand at the end of December, and these figures for the fourth quarter are then used as one of the inputs to the forecast discussed in Chapter 5.

At the end of October 1983, there are full national accounts data up to the second quarter of 1983 and the conjunctural analyst has already made estimates for the third quarter (in practice, these estimates would be refined at the same time as the analyst is building up a picture of the fourth quarter, but for clarity only occasional references will be made to this). These data and estimates for the first three quarters of 1983 are shown in Table 3.1, together with the forecasts for the fourth quarter produced by the model of Chapter 4 without as yet using any conjunctural analysis information. This table therefore summarizes the information about major national accounts data series available at the end of October.

3.1 Monday, 29 October to Sunday, 6 November 1983

Output

The October CBI industrial trends survey of manufacturing industry is published on Tuesday. For each question respondents reply by ticking one of three boxes to indicate whether the trend is upwards, downwards or unchanged. The survey results are given as the percentage of respondents replying to each category and are sometimes summarized as a 'balance'. This is the percentage replying up minus the percentage replying down. The October trends survey shows 31 per cent of respondents reporting increased total orders during the recent past, 45 per cent no change and 21 per cent a fall. (The last 3 per cent ticked 'not applicable'.) This gives a balance of + 10 per cent, compared to a balance of + 13 per cent in the previous quarterly survey carried out in July. See Table 3.2.

Table 3.1 Recent data and model forecasts for 1983 fourth quarter

	GDP output (1)	GDP expenditure measure	Consumer spending	Gov't expenditure	Fixed investment	Stock-building	Non-oil exports	Non-oil imports	Net oil trade	Factor cost adjustment	Consumer prices 1980 = 100	Personal disposable income £bn. current prices	Bank base rates % p.a.	Effective exchange rate 1980 = 100
Code used in model of Ch. 4	–	GDPE	C	G	Working variable IFP	Change in KII	X	M	O	Working variable F	PC	YD	RLB	EER
1982 1	48.3	49.0	34.1	14.8	6.8	+ 0.0	13.8	13.2	0.5	7.7	117.0	45.9	13.8	95
2	48.6	49.2	34.3	14.6	6.7	+ 0.2	13.9	13.5	0.7	7.7	120.0	46.5	12.9	94
3	48.9	49.4	34.9	14.8	7.0	– 0.6	13.0	13.0	1.0	7.8	121.3	47.1	11.3	95
4	49.0	50.7	35.5	15.0	6.9	– 0.7	13.6	13.2	1.3	7.8	122.7	48.2	9.7	93
1983 1	49.3	51.8	35.4	15.4	7.0	+ 0.6	13.5	13.9	1.2	7.6	124.7	49.0	10.8	84
2	49.3	50.7	35.9	14.9	6.8	+ 0.1	13.3	14.0	1.0	7.6	125.8	49.6	10.0	88
(estimate) 3	49.9	50.8	36.1	15.3	6.9	– 0.2	13.3	14.0	1.2	7.8	127.4	50.6	9.5	88
Model Q4 forecast	n.a.	51.7	36.7	15.4	7.1	0.0(2)	13.9	14.4	1.0	7.9	129.3	51.8	9.0	87
% change Q4 on Q3	n.a.	+ 1.5	+ 0.8	+ 0.4	+ 3.1	n.a.	+ 4.6	+ 3.0	n.a.	n.a.	+ 1.5	+ 2.3	n.a.	n.a.

All figures are in £ billion at 1980 prices, seasonally adjusted, unless indicated.
Notes: (1) The output estimate of GDP is published as an index 1980 = 100. For ease of comparison with the expenditure estimate, it is conventionally assumed equal in 1980 to the 1980 level of the expenditure measure.
(2) Includes adjustment – see Chapter 5.

Table 3.2   CBI industrial trends survey, a summary

		Oct. 82	Jan. 83	Apr. 83	Jul. 83	Oct. 83
Numbers employed	past 4 months	−44	−50	−44	−35	−27
	next 4 months	−43	−45	−29	−25	−24
Volume of new orders	past 4 months	−30	−13	+16	+13	+10
	next 4 months	− 4	+ 5	+23	+16	+12
Volume of output	past 4 months	−19	−11	+13	+15	+15
	next 4 months	− 4	− 5	+22	+17	+16

Source: CBI.
Note: All figures are percentage balances.

The survey also asks about expected developments over the immediate future. There is a balance of + 12 per cent for the question on total orders in the near future and + 16 per cent for future output.

Since the replies are weighted by size and by industry group, a positive balance ought to imply an increase for the manufacturing industry as a whole (unless there is an odd distribution of experiences among firms, with a few companies facing large falls and a lot facing very small increases). See Keating (1983). On this interpretation the reduction in the balance on the expected output series, from + 17 in July to + 16 in October shown in the table, implies a marginal decline in the rate of increase of output – not a fall in the level of output. However, there is an alternative viewpoint which asserts that the respondents ignore the wording of the question and tick 'up' when their output is at a high or acceptable level in relation to some normal figure, and 'down' when output is perceived to be low. On this interpretation the balance measures the level, not the rate of change, of output and the change between July and October is indicative of a marginal fall in output. The evidence is not conclusive but tends to reject this alternative view. Questionnaires sent to survey respondents, asking them how they fill in the form, suggest that the vast majority interpret the question correctly and tick 'up' only when they perceive an increase.

Assuming that the first interpretation is correct, the survey evidence indicates that manufacturing orders and output have grown in recent months and will continue to rise, at a slightly slower rate, in the near future. See Ballance and Burton (1983).

On Thursday the September figures for housing starts and completions are published by the Department of the Environment. These seasonally adjusted data show a decline in private sector housing starts, which peaked at about 16,000 houses in January and are now only 12,000. See Table 3.3. Despite the decline, this figure is well above the levels reached during the worst of the recession in 1980 and 1981. It is possible that the recent fall is misleading; there was a tendency among builders to build more, smaller houses during the recession and construction patterns may recently have been returning to normal. This view is supported by the figures for value

Table 3.3　Housing starts (private sector, in thousands, at a monthly rate)

Year	Month	Monthly rate
1980		8.2
1981		9.6
1982		11.7
1982	Sept.	11.1
	Oct.	11.5
	Nov.	11.6
	Dec.	12.3
1983	Jan.	16.1
	Feb.	15.0
	Mar.	14.9
	Apr.	12.7
	May	13.5
	June	14.6
	July	13.5
	Aug.	13.4
	Sept.	12.0

Source: *Economic Trends.*
Note: Data are seasonally adjusted.

of new orders placed with contractors, deflated to constant prices. These ought to be unaffected by alterations in the types of houses built. The September figures show a sharp pick-up from the summer months, back towards the high level recorded at the start of the year.

Labour market

The October unemployment figures published on Thursday show a decline both in the headline total (unadjusted, including school leavers) and in the adult figure (seasonally adjusted, excluding school leavers). See Table 3.4. The latter measure generally provides a better month-by-month guide to underlying movements in unemployment because the number of school leavers fluctuates sharply according to time of year. However, it is not insulated from all irregular effects. For example school leavers who take a job and then return to the register are included in the adult total. The average of the adult figure for the last three months is sometimes used to try to smooth out irregularities. This measure fell in October for the first time in four years. Further evidence of growth in labour market activity comes from the vacancies figures, also published on Tuesday, which show an increase for the fifth successive month. These figures only measure vacancies reported to Jobcentres, estimated at roughly a third of the whole economy figure.

The adult unemployment figure fell by 10,000 in October and by an average of 2000 in the last three months compared to the previous three. These declines are tiny compared to the rates of increase of 100,000 a month recorded during the worst of the recession. It seems safest to interpret them as evidence that unemployment has stabilized rather than

Table 3.4 Unemployed excluding school leavers

Year	Month	Unemployed excluding school leavers		Vacancies notified to employment offices
		000s	Percentage of employees	000s
1980		1560.8	6.4	143.0
1981		2413.1	10.0	97.0
1982		2793.2	11.7	111.3
1982	Oct.	2885.4	12.1	113.9
	Nov.	2905.5	12.2	114.4
	Dec.	2948.8	12.4	117.6
1983	Jan.	2982.7	12.5	122.0
	Feb.	3000.6	12.6	124.0
	Mar.	3025.7	12.7	126.1
	Apr.	3021.1	12.7	134.5
	May	2969.9	12.4	131.1
	June	2967.7	12.4	139.3
	July	2957.3	12.4	153.4
	Aug.	2940.9	12.3	162.0
	Sept.	2951.3	12.4	163.6
	Oct.	2941.2	12.3	167.0

Source: Employment Gazette.
Note: Unemployment data are seasonally adjusted.

implying that it has started to fall, particularly given the CBI trends survey which suggested further job losses in manufacturing over coming months.

The new Youth Training Scheme (YTS) – replacing the former Youth Opportunities Scheme – has just begun and is almost certainly reducing the number counted as unemployed. The total impact on the register of such schemes is currently estimated at 400,000 (slightly above the level of a year ago). This estimate is subject to a very wide margin of error because it requires arbitrary assumptions about the jobs lost as a side-effect of the existence of the YTS.

Demand

Further important information on demand and output appears from the Society of Motor Manufacturers and Traders (SMMT) on Friday. Car sales in October are some 3.4 per cent up on a year earlier, while sales in the first ten months of 1983 are 16.3 per cent above the same months of 1982. The pattern of sales is always greatly distorted by the wish to obtain the new registration letter in August, and this pattern was particularly marked this year. The October figure seems to indicate that sales are continuing at a high level and have not fallen back from the August figure by more than the normal seasonal amount. The SMMT figures show that imports took 60 per cent of the market in October, compared to an average of about 55 per cent last year. This is in spite of a commitment by Ford to produce domestically more of the cars sold in the UK.

Financial markets

Movements in the foreign exchange and short-term money markets were relatively small. However the UK equity market saw significant increases, the FT industrial ordinary index rising by almost 4 per cent over the week. This was partly in reaction to the information described above. The equity market was also boosted by the announcement of plans for the UK's biggest ever takeover bid, for £0.8 billion, with the diversified tobacco company BAT taking over insurers Eagle Star. The impact of this on the market as a whole depends on a wide range of factors but there is almost certain to be a large net increase in demand for all equities, pushing up prices for a wide range of companies. The CBI trends survey questions on corporate liquidity show that manufacturers improved their net liquidity (liquid assets less borrowing) over the last year at the fastest rate recorded since the survey began in 1974. This is consistent both with reduced demand by companies for bank borrowing and with increased takeover activity.

3.2 Monday, 7 November to Sunday, 13 November 1983

Demand

The retail sales volume figures for September, published three weeks ago, show a sharp rise to 116 (index 1978 = 100). This is above the August value and well up on figures from earlier in the year. On Monday, the revised estimate for this number is published. It shows an unusually large revision, upwards to 117.3, the highest figure ever recorded. See Table 3.5.

Table 3.5   Volume of retail sales

Year	Month	Weekly average
1980		104.3
1981		105.5
1982		108.2
1982	Sept.	109.3
	Oct.	109.3
	Nov.	110.0
	Dec.	112.2
1983	Jan.	110.1
	Feb.	111.1
	Mar.	111.9
	Apr.	112.9
	May	113.7
	June	114.0
	July	113.9
	Aug.	112.8
	Sept.	117.3

Source: Economic Trends.
Note: Figures are weekly averages, units are index 1978 = 100.
Data are seasonally adjusted.

This figure surprises many commentators, particularly those in the City, who have for some time been arguing that the boom in consumer spending was unsustainable. The reason for this view is that the savings ratio fell earlier in the year further and faster than anyone expected. A decline to an even lower level in the second half of the year seems highly unlikely and real personal disposable income is thought to be rising only marginally. The retail sales figure covers only about half of total consumer spending. The rest includes cars and their running costs, rent, rates, heating and lighting, other transport and entertainment. Car sales are known to be doing very well (see week ended 6 November) and there is no information to suggest declines in any of the other items. Thus total consumer spending in September must have been very buoyant, so either the savings ratio has against all expectations fallen even further from its low second quarter level, or real incomes have been stronger than estimated.

Prices

The October producer price indices are also published on Monday. There is an output price index covering the prices received by manufacturers for goods sold in the home market and an input price series covering their raw materials and fuel. The output prices index rose 5.5 per cent over the twelve months to October. This gives some indication about likely developments in retail prices in the new year, by when it will have worked through to the shops. However, retail prices can move in a different way for a while because of items not covered by the producer price index such as services, housing and petrol. The input price index tends to move erratically; recently it appears to have been rising significantly faster than the output price series. This suggests either a squeeze on manufacturers' margins, which is inconsistent with the information about profits, or cuts in labour costs through rapid productivity growth.

Monetary aggregates

On Tuesday the provisional figures for monetary growth in banking October are issued by the Bank of England. The monthly monetary data are all measured in banking months, which cover a four or five week period ending in the middle of the calendar month. Today's data relate to the four weeks ending on 19 October. The purpose of this period of measurement, which causes difficulties when considering monetary data in conjunction with other economic series, is to avoid the substantial variations in bank balances that occur towards the end of calendar months depending on the precise timing of wage and salary payments.

During banking October, sterling M3 rose by 1.5 per cent, the broader PSL2 by 1.0 per cent and the narrower M1, 1.5 per cent. Although sterling M3 grew most rapidly this month, the annualized rates of growth of these aggregates since the beginning of the current target period in mid-February are 10.8 per cent, 13.1 per cent, and 12.7 per cent respectively, so

PSL2 has been growing most rapidly. The reason for this is discussed below.

The Bank of England does not officially give counterparts to Tuesday's figure for another ten days but meanwhile there is enough other information to explain why sterling M3 rose substantially in October, after falling in September. The London clearing banks' figures (which cover some, but not all, of the organizations whose deposits contribute to sterling M3) suggest that private sector borrowing was much larger in October than in September. Stockbrokers who report on daily transactions in the markets (plus some limited preliminary figures for government borrowing) suggest that lower gilts sales may be another important reason.

The index PSL2 is a broad measure of liquidity, which includes not only bank deposits and notes and coin, but also other items such as building society deposits. The latter are not included in sterling M3, and since the building societies raised their interest rates at end June (while the banks reduced theirs in August), they have been enjoying an increased inflow at the expense of bank deposits. This suggests that sterling M3 has been understating liquidity growth while PSL2 is undistorted because funds have been switched from one part of PSL2 (bank deposits) to another (building society deposits).

With the most optimistic of the monetary aggregates only just within the upper end of the 7 to 11 per cent target range and a more accurate measure probably slightly above, the monetary indicators appear to suggest that inflation will accelerate over the next year or two. Even with 3 per cent output growth – which is much higher than any forecaster is currently suggesting – a constant velocity would imply inflation of around 8 per cent. There is a chance, though, that velocity might fall as it has done over the last year. This would imply a rather lower inflation rate. The reason for falling velocity is that an increasing proportion of the assets included in the monetary aggregates are in practice held for savings, not for transactions motives.

Output

On Thursday the vehicle production figures for October appear. Car output, seasonally adjusted, was 1.5 per cent up on its September level but substantially below the third quarter average. Commercial vehicle production remains at a low level. The car output figure was affected by strikes at three manufacturers. These figures are important to the conjunctural analyst, for they account directly for approaching 5 per cent of total manufacturing output and are an indicator of activity in other parts of manufacturing. This aids preliminary estimation of the total industrial production index, which is not published for another month. The car output figures also give clues about stock building when compared with the SMMT data on car sales (week ended 6 November). While precise comparison is difficult, the movements in the output figures and in the data for sales of domestically built cars are close enough to suggest no major change in car stock levels during October. (This does not tell us about stocks of imported cars.)

Further preliminary evidence about industrial production appears on Friday when the October usable steel output figures are published. These are also rather lower than the third quarter average, although well above the very depressed levels of a year ago. The car and steel production figures taken together suggest that October manufacturing output is likely to have been similar to September, implying that it was below the third quarter average.

Incomes

All the forecasters have predicted substantial rises in company profits in 1983 as output expands and employment remains static or falling. Two sets of company results this week provide strong support for this view. Sainsbury's profits show a 28 per cent rise for the six month period ending in October on the same period a year earlier. Shell also report a very large rise, much of it due to its UK operations.

Prices

The October retail prices index appears on Friday. The twelve-monthly rate of increase reached a trough of 3.7 per cent in May and June (the election period) and has since been rising, reaching 5.1 per cent in September. See Table 3.6. This rise had been widely predicted, for the low May and June figures reflected special factors including the pattern of changes in mortgage rates and exceptionally low seasonal food prices. These special factors ceased to affect the index or were reversed by

Table 3.6   Retail prices index

Year	Month	Percentage change
1980		18.0
1981		11.9
1982		8.6
1982	Oct.	6.8
	Nov.	6.3
	Dec.	5.4
1983	Jan.	4.9
	Feb.	5.3
	Mar.	4.6
	Apr.	4.0
	May	3.7
	June	3.7
	July	4.2
	Aug.	4.6
	Sept.	5.1
	Oct.	5.0

Source: Economic Trends.
Note: Percentage change on a year earlier. Not seasonally adjusted.

September. Most forecasters have argued that inflation will continue on a rising trend even now that the impact of the special factors has ended. This is because of rising labour costs and widening profit margins as economic activity gradually recovers.

Friday's figure suggests that this view may be wrong. The index in October rose by less than 0.3 per cent, bringing the twelve-monthly increase marginally down to 5.0 per cent. The reasons for this lower than expected figure are uncertain. One possibility is that output has been growing more rapidly than predicted, allowing companies to expand productivity more speedily than allowed for in the forecasts.

Financial developments

The building societies' monthly figures for October are published on Friday. These indicate that inflows to deposits are continuing at record levels, unsurprising given the competitiveness of the societies' interest rates and last week's PSL2 figures. The building societies also show further heavy commitments to mortgage lending. Loans have been running at a high level for over a year and the total value of loans for house purchase is even higher when added to bank mortgages. (Banks started offering mortgages on a large scale only in 1981 and although they have this year reduced the number of loans, their activities remain significant.) This very high rate of mortgage borrowing has been partly reflected in the construction of new dwellings, which is well above last year's depressed level (see week ended 6 November) and has partly been used to finance the purchase of council houses from the government by tenants. Together these two factors have been insufficient to account for more than about half of the mortgage loans. The rest has 'leaked out' of the housing market to be used for general consumer spending.

Despite the rapid inflows to the societies, a meeting on Friday decides not to lower the interest rates paid on deposits and charged on mortgages. This is because, even with current inflows, the demand for mortgages is only just being met. Nor are there large movements in other short-term interest rates. Exchange rates remain reasonably stable and the UK equity market, despite the profits announcements noted above, moves up only marginally.

3.3 13 November – Preliminary assessment of the fourth quarter

We are now halfway through the fourth quarter yet the amount of information is limited. The more optimistic interpretation of the CBI trends survey suggests that manufacturing output will rise this quarter at about the same rate as in the last quarter, some 1 to 1.5 per cent. Against this, the October figures for car and steel production suggest a flatter picture. The vehicle figures were affected by strikes now ended and so the impression from the trends survey is probably more accurate.

The forecast made by the model suggests that the more rapidly growing components of demand in the fourth quarter will be investment and exports, with consumption growing more slowly. See Table 3.1. Such a mixture of demand components has in the past been associated with manufacturing output growing faster than services and other sectors. Yet the survey evidence suggests a rise in manufacturing output between 1 and 1½ per cent, implying that other sectors must grow more rapidly than manufacturing in order to give the increase of 1½ per cent predicted for GDP as a whole. This seems inconsistent with the mixture of demand components and implies that GDP growth may be less than the model is forecasting.

Supporting this view are the unemployment figures. These now appear to be more or less stationary. With the trend rise in the labour force running at about ½ per cent per annum, or just over 0.1 per cent a quarter, a 1½ per cent rise in GDP would very roughly imply output per person employed growing at about 1.4 per cent in the fourth quarter. This would be exceptionally rapid and seems unlikely.

If we want to adjust down the model's prediction of GDP growth, we need to find evidence that the model has overestimated one or more of the GDP demand components (or underestimated imports). The biggest component is consumers' expenditure. For this the model is predicting a rise of about 0.8 per cent between the third and fourth quarters. The only direct information so far available about consumer activity in the fourth quarter is the SMMT October car sales figure. This suggests that demand is flat or rising very slowly. Apart from this, we know that retail sales in September were 3.5 per cent above the average for July and August. This means that even with a fairly large fall from the high September figure, fourth quarter retail sales could still be somewhat above the third quarter. Further evidence comes from the continuing high level of mortgage loans, many of which are leaking into general consumer spending. The money stock figures, which suggest rapid growth in other types of private sector bank borrowing, also imply continued increases in personal sector loans, because the buoyancy of company liquidity means that people and not firms are borrowing these funds. Overall, this evidence all seems broadly consistent with the model's prediction for consumption.

On government spending, the high rate of public borrowing in banking October suggests continued high expenditure, although the Chancellor's spending cuts announced in July must start to have an effect soon. Our first guess is for a marginal increase in government spending between the third and fourth quarters but we may revise this in the light of later public borrowing data. The only other demand component on which we have information at this stage is exports, where the CBI trends survey suggests a flat picture for manufactured exports compared to the sharp increase predicted by the model for total non-oil exports. However, this part of the CBI trends survey is less reliable than others.

This suggests that we can make a weak case for adjusting down exports and hence GDP, bringing our forecast down more into line with the *picture suggested by the CBI survey and the unemployment figures. This would be in line with current received opinion as expressed in a **Financial Times** leader of 5 November, which describes the pace of recovery as 'imperceptibly slow'.*

However, it is possible to make out a different case. The unexpectedly low retail prices figures and the evidence of buoyant profits and company liquidity are both consistent with firms' success in reducing costs through productivity increases. Perhaps productivity is growing rapidly, thus explaining both the static unemployment figures and the 1½ per cent fourth quarter GDP increase predicted by the model. This is contrary to the view expressed earlier, but would be possible if manufacturing output grew by significantly more than the 1 to 1½ per cent implied by the CBI survey. More evidence is needed to help us judge which story is correct.

3.4 Monday, 14 November to Sunday, 20 November 1983

The Chancellor's autumn statement on Thursday contains no significant policy changes. Its accompanying forecast is dramatically different from current received opinion. GDP is estimated to have risen 3 per cent in 1983 and the same growth is expected to be sustained throughout 1984. Moreover retail price inflation is forecast to fall back to 4.5 per cent by the end of 1984, with perhaps some small rise before them. This contrasts with projections of 1¾ – 2¼ per cent growth in 1984, plus rising inflation, produced by most independent forecasters.

Demand

The provisional October retail sales figures are published on Monday. These show a decline of about 2 per cent from the record September level but are still higher than any other figure recorded this year and are about ½ per cent above the third quarter average. The official view is that the September number was erratic and that the trend may still be upward. Even with the fall in October, retail sales remain considerably higher than predicted earlier in the year by most forecasters.

Further information about demand appears with Wednesday's data on government finances. These show that public expenditure in cash terms has been running well ahead of target in the first seven months of the financial year, to October. Because this is a cash figure it may reflect either a higher than anticipated price or a greater volume than planned. It seems that both have been above target, although there is no clear evidence. This suggests that spending by government as well as by consumers has contributed to the growth in domestic demand. It indicates that Nigel Lawson's spending cuts, announced in July (to have impact from late 1983) just after the election and after he had only recently become Chancellor, were not as premature as many commentators had thought. For a Chancellor determined to keep government spending and borrowing reasonably close to target, they now appear a timely and, if anything, modest measure.

Income/costs

Average earnings in the whole economy rose 8.5 per cent over the year to September, or 7.75 per cent when allowance is made for distortions due to irregular back pay, etc. For manufacturing only, the corresponding figures were 9.5 per cent and 8.75 per cent. The latter figures are well in excess of the 5.5 per cent or so reported to the CBI pay databank as the typical figure for settlements in manufacturing. The difference, or 'wage drift', is unusually large. In part it is because overtime has increased fairly rapidly over the year, while short time working has fallen. This means increased hours per employee – with the extra hours generally paid at a higher rate – so boosting the average earnings index, by an estimated 1 to 1.5 per cent. Payments under productivity schemes are estimated to have added a similar amount to the index, as employees gain some of the benefit from rapidly rising output per head. This leaves some of the drift unexplained – one possible cause is the recent failure to recruit young, low-paid employees.

Financial markets

On foreign exchange markets, the dollar advanced strongly against the DM and also rose against sterling. The effective rate for sterling fell by about 0.5 per cent. Short-term interest rates were more or less unchanged while equities rose about 1 per cent and then fell back almost to the week's starting point.

3.5 Monday, 21 November to Sunday, 27 November 1983

The National Institute publish a forecast that disagrees greatly with the Treasury's. The NIESR expect GDP to rise only 1 per cent during 1984, or 2 per cent between the whole of 1983 and 1984. They also expect the inflation rate to reach almost 7 per cent next year. This projection was prepared before publication of the Treasury forecast.

Balance of payments current account

The major data this week are about exports, imports and the current balance, all for October. The current balance continued the irregular movements of recent months, the large surplus of £400m. recorded in September giving way to a deficit of approximately £200m. in October. Over the last six months, the current balance has on average been almost exactly nil. This compares with a surplus in 1982 that averaged £450m. per month. The main reason for the disappearance of the surplus has been a sharp rise in imports, in response to the increase in domestic demand, at a time when exports have been flat or grown only slowly in reflection of weak European demand. United Kingdom unit labour cost competitiveness has also been below its long-term average over the last year, although much better than the very poor figures recorded in 1980–81.

The export and import figures for October continue the erratic pattern of recent months. These irregular movements are smoothed by taking the average for the last three months compared to the three preceding. These measures show a 3 per cent volume rise both for exports of non-oil goods and for non-oil goods imports. The continued growth in imports is unsurprising given the strength of domestic demand. The rise in exports, although possibly just an erratic movement, gives some hope that UK firms are starting to benefit from the current buoyancy of the US economy even though the European markets (which take a larger share of UK trade) remain stagnant.

Employment

Thursday also sees publication of several series on employment and hours. Unlike most official data, these never appear in a press release. Instead their first appearance is in an official publication, *Department of Employment Gazette*. Figures for manufacturing employment in August, seasonally adjusted, have been revised to show a marginal increase, the first since 1979. However, the provisional figure for September, appearing for the first time, shows a small fall. Given this and the CBI survey data (week ended 6 November) it looks as though the underlying trend is still downward, although at a much slower rate than over the last year. Other figures in the *Department of Employment Gazette* confirm that average hours worked by manufacturing employees rose rapidly in September. (In addition, data on days lost through strikes show very little increase despite the pick-up in economic activity. This is of considerable interest if it represents a change in the pattern of labour relations.)

Demand

The CBI industrial trends survey covers only manufacturing industry. A similar, separate survey, organized jointly by the CBI and the *Financial Times,* covers the distributive trades. Like the manufacturing survey, this gives information about the immediate past and near future, in advance of the publication of official statistics. In addition, some of the distributive trades survey questions, about sales by wholesalers, cover an important item that is ignored by the official statistics. The survey released this week, covering late October/early November, is the fourth survey conducted and is the first to be published. It provides strong evidence that retail spending in addition to normal seasonal patterns will continue to grow from its currently high level over the whole of the Christmas period. (The survey provides little information for periods further ahead.) Motor trades, however, are reported to be less buoyant reflecting the remarkably high level of sales in August, which is unlikely to be sustained. Significantly, wholesalers who sell to industry also report good business in the recent past, which they expect to continue.

Financial markets

The dollar continues to rise against other currencies, with a further signif-icant increase against sterling. There is no sign of any upward move in UK short-term interest rates to help defend the current parity, as sterling's effective rate declines slightly again. The FT index of UK industrial ordinary shares gains more than 2 per cent over the week. Among other items this reflects very good profit figures from Metal Box (doubled in the six months ended 30 September) and an optimistic projection of equity prices from the London Business School.

3.6 27 November – assessment of the fourth quarter

There has been no new information during the last fortnight about GDP as a whole, but there is important new evidence on some of the components. October retail sales, although below the high September figure, were 0.5 per cent above the third quarter average. This means that only fairly small increases in November and December are needed to give a rise in retail sales in line with the 0.8 per cent predicted by the model for total consumer spending in the fourth quarter. Information from the CBI/FT distributive trades survey is also consistent with this forecast.

Another important piece of evidence about consumption comes from the average earnings figures. These indicate that the incomes of those in work were rising about 2 to 3 per cent per annum faster than retail prices at the end of September and there is no evidence to suggest a slowdown since. With unemployment more or less stable, this means that total personal sector real incomes have also started to grow at about this rate. This contrasts with what many forecasters had been expecting. It implies that increases in consumer spending, which over the last year have been possible only because of a falling savings ratio, are now being financed partly out of higher real incomes. This makes it more likely that there can be a further increase in consumer spending in the fourth quarter as predicted by the model.

We now have average earnings running significantly ahead of prices. In addition evidence from company reports and from the buoyancy of equity prices suggest rapid profits growth. These two can only be reconciled by productivity growth being exceptionally fast, paying for both the increase in real earnings and the growth in profits. This suggests that the second of the two explanations put forward in the 13 November assessment is correct, i.e. output per person is rising by about 1½ per cent this quarter in the economy as a whole, GDP is growing 1½ per cent as predicted by the model, and manufacturing output is rising more rapidly than the 1 to 1½ per cent estimate based on the CBI survey.

On this view non-oil exports in the fourth quarter will rise rapidly, in line with the model projection (see Table 3.1), rather than changing little as suggested in the 13 November assessment. The October trade figures suggest rapid growth in both non-oil exports and non-oil imports, thus supporting the model's forecast. The latest evidence on government spending seems in line with the estimate included in Table 3.1.

The evidence to date is now in line with the rapid growth, high productivity picture presented by the model rather than with the view based on lower increases in output and productivity.

3.7 Monday, 28 November to Sunday, 4 December 1983

Output/exports

The November CBI monthly trends enquiry for manufacturing industry appears on Monday. This contains only the five questions asked in months when the major quarterly survey is not prepared. It shows a sharp increase in the balance for the question about output in the near future. This suggests, on either interpretation of the survey, that manufacturing output will rise in the next month or so. Also the balance for the question on export order books shows a distinct improvement. This provides support for the view that the export figures noted last week may mark the start of an upward trend. See Table 3.7.

Table 3.7 CBI monthly trends enquiry

Month	*1982* *1983*											
	Dec	*Jan*	*Feb*	*Mar*	*Apr*	*May*	*Jun*	*Jul*	*Aug*	*Sep*	*Oct*	*Nov*
Total order book	−55	−55	−46	−33	−41	−26	−24	−34	−24	−25	−33	−21
Export order book	−53	−55	−43	−31	−38	−25	−24	−35	−34	−28	−31	−25
Volume of output	−11	− 5	+ 8	+16	+22	+18	+19	+17	+19	+20	+16	+24

Source: CBI.
Note: All figures are percentage balances.

Unemployment

Thursday's unemployment figures, for November, show another decline, both for the headline total and for the seasonally adjusted adult figure. The latter is down 4000, a smaller fall than recorded in October (see week ended 6 November).

The number of reported vacancies actually declined slightly in November, after increases over the whole of the previous year. Taken together with evidence that manufacturing employment is still falling (week ended 27 November), these figures suggest that the trend in unemployment has stopped growing but not yet started to fall.

Wages

The threatened strike at Ford is called off on Thursday when negotiators agree on a 7½ per cent pay deal. The Ford deal is one of the most important private sector agreements. This figure is well above the figure of about 5 per cent which is the average for agreements reported to the CBI pay databank over the four months since the current 'pay round' began in August. However, the buoyancy of the car market has put Ford unions in a particularly powerful position. This particular deal may turn out to be above average.

Demand

Private sector housing start figures for October, published on Friday, show a substantial rise on the particularly low September figure. The October figure is now back almost to the peak levels reached at the start of 1983. (See week ended 6 November for September figures.)

Separate figures for total new orders (industrial and residential) placed with contractors show a buoyant third quarter. Orders in the first three quarters of 1983 are 15½ per cent above the level in the same period of 1982. Despite this, the Federation of Civil Engineering Contractors' October workload survey was the gloomiest for six years. One possible reconciliation is that the beneficial effect of orders already received has yet to work its way through.

Financial markets

The Department of Trade's company liquidity survey for the third quarter, published on Friday, shows a substantial improvement in company liquidity. This is in line with the heavy destocking in that quarter (week ended 20 November), with reports of improved profits and with results from the CBI survey data. It suggests that the recent rapid rise in private sector bank borrowing has been largely by the personal sector, not by companies. This view is supported by anecdotal evidence from bankers and also by the large funds being raised directly by companies through new issues in the buoyant equity market.

The FT index rose again, by about 2.3 per cent on the week, with BAT industries and the German firm Allianz raising their bids for insurers Eagle Star to £0.9 billion or more. Sterling's rate against the dollar was little changed although its effective rate fell marginally. United Kingdom short-term interest rates were unchanged.

3.8 Monday, 5 December to Sunday, 11 December 1983

Prices

The producer prices index, measuring output prices for manufacturing, rose by 5.7 per cent over the year to November. This compares to 5.5 per cent over the year to October (see week ended 13 November). This slight increase implies some small upward pressure on retail prices in coming months but confirms that manufacturers are having considerable success in paying for rising raw material prices, wage increases, and wider profit margins out of increased productivity rather than rapidly rising output

Table 3.8   Producer price indices

Year	Month	Input prices	Output prices
1980		8.5	14.0
1981		9.2	9.5
1982		7.3	7.8
1982	Oct.	3.6	6.8
	Nov.	3.6	6.4
	Dec.	4.9	6.3
1983	Jan.	5.2	5.6
	Feb.	5.7	5.2
	Mar.	5.8	5.1
	Apr.	5.9	5.4
	May	6.8	5.6
	June	7.3	6.0
	July	6.4	5.4
	Aug.	8.3	5.3
	Sept.	9.6	5.4
	Oct.	8.2	5.5
	Nov.	7.2	5.7

Source: Economic Trends.
Note: The output price index measures the price received by UK manufacturers for domestic sales. The input price index measures their raw material and fuel costs. Both indices are base 1980 = 100, and are not seasonally adjusted. Figures shown here are percentage change on a year earlier.

prices. The erratic input price index rose just over 7 per cent in the year to November. See Table 3.8.

Expenditure/output

The SMMT figures for car sales suggest, after allowing for seasonal factors, a marginal increase in car registrations between October and November. This means that business is being sustained at recent high levels (apart from seasonal effects) although it is no longer growing rapidly. Significantly the share of imports in total sales has fallen from the high figure of 60 per cent recorded in October to 57 per cent in November. This may partly reflect implementation by Ford of its earlier pledge to produce more cars in the UK. This is consistent with the official figures for November vehicle production, published on Thursday, which show a significant rise from the October figures.

Money stock

M1, sterling M3 and PSL2 all rose by between ½ and ¾ per cent in banking November, about half the rate recorded last month. The annualized growth rates since the start of the target period in February are 12 per cent, 10½ per cent and 12¼ per cent respectively. Reasons for these diverse movements were discussed under week ended 13 November. Official comment emphasized that growth over the last six months had been within target for all three aggregates and that there are no plans to raise short-term interest rates. Figures from the London clearing banks suggest that lending to the private sector in November has returned to around the average rate recorded for the rest of the year, following the exceptionally rapid increase in October. This provides a partial explanation for the slowdown in monetary growth between the months.

Financial markets

A week of some drama in financial markets, with the dollar strong against all currencies. Sterling falls about ½ per cent against the dollar to an all-time low and the FT industrial ordinary share index climbs steeply to an all-time high before falling somewhat, though still more than 2 per cent up on the week. United Kingdom short-term money market interest rates edge up marginally. The reason for the strength of the dollar appears to be concern that no action to limit US Federal deficits will be taken until after the 1984 elections, leading meanwhile to increased US interest rates.

3.9 11 December – assessment of the fourth quarter

One source of very important information during the last two weeks and little else. This is the November CBI survey of manufacturing industry which, in contrast to the October survey, shows a marked improvement in the short-term outlook for both output and exports. The new survey suggests that manufacturing output in the fourth quarter will grow significantly faster than in the third quarter. This is strong evidence in support of the 1½ per cent GDP and production growth predicted by the model. The latest unemployment figures, which are again unchanged, also seem to support this view, as do the improved construction industry figures.

3.10 Monday, 12 December to Sunday, 18 December 1983

Expenditure

Retail sales volume in November is provisionally estimated to have risen 1.1 per cent from the October figure, which was down on the exceptionally high September number. Sales in the last four months compared to the previous four are up 2 per cent, suggesting a strong underlying rate of increase.

Output

Industrial production in October fell ½ per cent on September, disappointing many commentators. Preliminary evidence from vehicle and steel production data (week ended Sunday 13 November) had suggested that an increase was unlikely, but a fall had not been expected particularly after three months of stagnation.

It is possible either that the official figures understate output, or that October was erratically low. CBI survey evidence (week ended 4 December) suggests that since November the trend in manufacturing output is definitely upwards. This is supported by last week's vehicle production figures and by this week's steel output data, which show a significant increase in November.

Earnings and prices

The underlying rise in whole-economy average earnings over the year to October was 7¾ per cent, the same as in September. See Table 3.9. Production industry earnings rose more rapidly, reflecting a further rise in hours worked. Retail price inflation in October was 5 per cent and the tax and prices index (which allows for the effect of direct taxes) rose only 4 per cent, indicating that those with jobs have seen real take-home pay rise about 3¾ per cent over the year. With unemployment now static, this implies rises in total personal sector spending power in recent months, accounting for the buoyancy of spending.

On Friday figures appear for retail price inflation in November. These show a fall to 4.8 per cent. It is already possible to predict that the December figure will show an increase, because the index in December 1982 was reduced by a cut in mortgage rates that will not be repeated this year.

Table 3.9 Average earnings

Year	Month	Percentage increase in earnings
1981		13.0
1982		9.6
1982	Oct.	8.75
	Nov.	8.5
	Dec.	8.0
1983	Jan.	8.0
	Feb.	8.0
	Mar.	7.75
	Apr.	7.5
	May	7.5
	June	7.5
	July	7.5
	Aug.	7.75
	Sept.	7.75
	Oct.	7.75

Source: Employment Gazette.
Note: This table shows the underlying percentage increase compared to a year before in the index of average earnings for the whole economy. This underlying series is adjusted to exclude distortions, caused for example by large lump sums paid in respect of back-dated pay settlements.

Financial markets

Full money stock figures for banking November confirm that private bank borrowing fell back from the high October figure to around £1 billion, close to the monthly average for the rest of the year. (Public borrowing remained stable while gilts sales rose from the lower level of November.

Figures for building societies showed a continued high level for both inflows and new mortgage commitments.)

On foreign exchange markets, the dollar advanced further. Sterling was down about ½ per cent against the dollar, to another all-time low. Despite this, short-term UK interest rates remained stable, the authorities seeming to acquiese in the fall in sterling. At the same time GEC reported sharply reduced profits. This reflected factors special to that company: cuts in interest rates over the last year reduced GEC's earnings on its 'cash pile'. Profits measured on a national accounts basis do not include such earnings, so this does not provide evidence inconsistent with projections of increased profits. The FT index rose marginally on the week.

3.11 Monday, 19 December to Thursday, 22 December 1983

Trade

The November current account figures are published on Thursday 22 November. A high figure for exports (goods excluding oil) gives a 4 per cent rise in the last three months compared to the previous three. The corresponding non-oil goods import figure is a 3½ per cent increase. The price indices for both exports and imports rose only 1 per cent over this period. The high export volume figure is sufficient to push the current balance back into surplus, with a figure of about £300m.

Financial markets

On the foreign exchange markets, sterling rose about ½ per cent against the dollar from the very low level of last week and UK short term rates fell marginally. The Chancellor, describing government exchange rate policy, said, 'We do not have a target, but we are not indifferent.' The FT industrial ordinary share index reached a new all-time peak, falling back slightly to end more than 2 per cent up on the week.

3.12 23 December – the end-quarter assessment

Having argued in the 11 December assessment that the November CBI trends survey confirmed the model-based view of rapidly rising GDP and productivity, we now have a disappointing official figure for October industrial production which appears to cast doubt on that view. This gives the conjunctural analyst a clear conflict among different information sources. On one hand the model, the CBI survey (with the very latest, end-December figures backing up the November survey) and the information about components of demand all seem consistent with rapid GDP growth of around 1½ per cent in the fourth quarter or even slightly more. On the other hand one month of official industrial production data suggest a more depressed picture.

The weight of evidence in support of the more rapid growth seems overwhelming and this is the view we will follow. There has in recent quarters emerged a particularly large discrepancy between the output-based measure of GDP and the expenditure-based figure (the latter is used in the model of Chapter 5), with the output measure being well below the expenditure. It seems very likely that the depressed picture given by the industrial production index (which is the major component of the output measure of GDP) reflects a further increase in this discrepancy. In principle the two measures of GDP should move in the same way. In practice they do not because they rely on different data sources. Some commentators have argued that the output measure is understating the true level of output because rapid structural change means there are many new firms failing to fill in the government's production returns. These new firms are likely to be the fastest growing. In due course they may submit returns and the output measure may then be revised upwards.

We now have the retail prices index for October and November and a good estimate of the December figure. These suggest that on average the index in the current quarter will be about 5 per cent above its level a year ago. This implies a similar movement in the consumer price index (the variable used in the model of Chapter 5). This is because the mortgage rate, which is the main factor affecting the RPI but not the consumer price index, is almost the same now as a year ago. This means that the model's projection of a 5½ per cent rise in consumer prices compared to a year ago is about ½ per cent too high and needs to be adjusted down. Together with the new earnings figures, for October, this suggests that real personal disposable incomes are higher than predicted.

Other new information during the last two weeks included the November retail sales figures, which showed a sharp increase on October, plus anecdotal evidence of unusually buoyant Christmas shopping. Taken together with the rapid rise in real personal incomes this information suggests that consumers' expenditure in the fourth quarter has probably been slightly higher than forecast.

The November trade figures are consistent with the non-oil export and import projections made by the model. However, the upward adjustment that will be made to consumer spending will also have the effect of pushing imports up, to above the level suggested by the trade figures. To offset this, a downward adjustment needs to be made to imports.

Information about other components of demand remains limited. The data on government finances are available only in current prices and so are consistent with a range of figures for the volume of public spending, including the estimate shown in Table 3.1. Nor is there much information about private fixed capital spending and stock building, apart from some indications given by the CBI surveys. The best we can say at this stage is that none of the available information on these items implies that the model should be adjusted in these areas, but nor does it really confirm the model forecasts.

Table 3.10 Conjunctural analysis estimates for 1983 fourth quarter

GDP expenditure measure	Consumer spending	Gov't expenditure	Fixed investment Working variable	Stock-building Change in KII	Non-oil exports	Non-oil imports	Net oil trade	Factor cost adjustment Working variable	Consumer prices 1980 = 100	Personal disposable income £bn. current prices	Bank base rates % p.a.	Effective exchange rate 1980 = 100
GDPE	C	G	IFP		X	M	O	F	PC	YD	RLB	EER

Code used in model of Ch. 4

	GDPE	C	G	IFP	Change in KII	X	M	O	F	PC	YD	RLB	EER
1983 1	51.8	35.4	15.4	7.0	+ 0.6	13.5	13.9	1.2	7.6	124.7	49.0	10.8	84
2	50.7	35.9	14.9	6.8	+ 0.1	13.3	14.0	1.0	7.6	125.8	49.6	10.0	88
3	50.8	36.1	15.3	6.9	− 0.2	13.3	14.0	1.2	7.8	127.4	50.6	9.5	88
4	51.9	36.8	15.4	7.1	0.0	13.9	14.3	1.0	7.9	128.8	51.8	9.0	87

Note: All figures are in £ billion at 1980 prices, seasonally adjusted, unless indicated.

Putting this information together, we conclude:

(i)   The broad picture presented by the model of rapidly rising output and productivity in the fourth quarter is correct, even though it conflicts with the evidence from official series for output.

(ii)   The consumer price forecast from the model should be adjusted down ½ per cent.

(iii)   The fourth quarter consumers' expenditure projection should be adjusted up slightly, by about ¼ per cent.

(iv)   The import figure was more or less consistent with the trade figures but will tend to be increased by the upward adjustment to consumption, so it will have to be adjusted down. There is no information to suggest alterations to other demand components at this stage.

(v)   Overall the effect of the last two changes is to raise the fourth quarter GDP figure marginally from the level originally predicted.

Table 3.10 shows the estimates for the fourth quarter based on these conclusions.

4

Economic models

All economic forecasts are made by using models of the economy. This chapter explains what an economic model is and how it is derived.

4.1 What is an economic model?

An economic model is a description of the whole or part of the economy, omitting those aspects of the economy that the model-builder believes to be relatively unimportant. The description may take the form of words or diagrams or mathematical expressions (or occasionally other forms). *Theoretical* models are derived entirely from assertions about how people act or about how institutions operate. Such models can indicate that one variable (e.g. world oil prices) influences another (e.g. UK retail prices) and can often show the direction of such effects, but do not give their size. *Econometric* models are derived by using statistical techniques to estimate how large these effects have been over the historical periods for which data are available. Thus econometric models include quantitative estimates for the influence of one variable on another and can be used for forecasting. This chapter deals with *macro-econometric models*, which provide a quantitative description of the whole economy and are used by almost all of the groups producing forecasts of the UK economy. These models vary greatly, both in complexity and in the theory on which they are based (see Chapter 7), but all consist of a series of equations each of which relates one macro-economic variable (e.g. consumers' expenditure) to others (e.g. consumer incomes). These equations are usually written into a computer program which uses them for repetitive calculations during forecasting, but a small macro-econometric model such as that presented later in this chapter can be used for forecasting by hand.

The construction of a macro-econometric model involves both specification and estimation. Specification is the extension and modification of equations from a theoretical model to make allowance for the complexities of the real world and to permit testing of alternative theoretical models. Estimation is the application of statistical techniques to historical data to quantify and test the effects specified in the equations. In this chapter, Section 4.2 sets out a theoretical model of the UK economy and introduces the notation and definitions needed to understand macro-econometric models. Section 4.3 discusses specification, showing how the theoretical model is extended and modified. Sections 4.4, 4.5 and 4.6 describe and illustrate estimation, and the final section suggests further reading.

4.2 A theoretical model of a small open economy

The four equations in Box 4.1 together form a theoretical model of a small open economy such as the UK. They will be used in this section to illustrate

Box 4.1 A simple linear-in-logs model of an open economy

LM curve	$\log(MO_t/PC_t) = \alpha_1 \log(GDPE_t) - \alpha_2 RLB_t + \alpha_3 + \epsilon_{M_t}$
IS curve	$\log(GDPE_t) = -\beta_1 \left[\dfrac{RLB_t}{400} - \log \dfrac{PC_t}{PC_{t-1}} \right]$
	$\quad - \beta_2 [\log(PC_t) - (\log WWPI_t - \log EER_t)]$
	$\quad + \beta_3 + \epsilon_{3_t}$
UK prices: adjust towards world prices measured in sterling	$\log(PC_t) = \gamma_1 \log(PC_{t-1}) + \gamma_2 [\log(WWPI_t) - \log(EER_t)] + \epsilon_{P_t}$
Exchange rate (uncovered interest parity)	$\log(EER_t) = \log(XEER_t) + (RLB_t - RSW_t)/400$

Symbols used	*Meanings* (variables are endogenous unless otherwise stated)
MO_t	Money supply MO, exogenous policy variable
$GDPE_t$	Gross domestic product, expenditure measure (i.e. total output in the whole economy)
RLB_t	UK short term interest rates
PC_t	Domestic price index
$WWPI_t$	World price index (exogenous)
EER_t	UK exchange rate (foreign currency per unit of sterling)
RSW_t	World short term interest rates (exogenous)
$XEER_t$	Expectations of value to be taken by the exchange rate one period ahead (temporarily treated as exogenous – see text)

In the model as a whole, the government's exogenous choice of monetary policy affects interest rates, which in turn affect the nominal exchange rate, which in turn affects domestic prices and wages. Competitiveness is determined by the nominal exchange rate and by UK wages. Exports and imports, and hence output and employment, respond to the changes in competitiveness. Because the nominal exchange rate responds rapidly in response to exogenous changes and UK wages adjust slowly, competitiveness can be away from its equilibrium level for a long time. Eventually, after a long time without exogenous changes, it moves back towards its equilibrium level and at that level exports and imports are brought more or less into balance. The simulations of Chapter 8 show examples of this process and a description is also given in Buiter and Miller (1981).

There is one apparent difference of substance between the model shown in this box and the Buiter–Miller system. In the latter, domestic prices are related to monetary growth while in the model here there is an explicit move back towards foreign prices. Once the four equations are solved as a system, this difference is unimportant.

many of the terms used by model-builders, and the notation will be explained in detail. Later sections of this chapter illustrate how a macro-econometric model can be built, based on a development of this simple four-equation system. This macro-econometric model will then be used in Chapter 5 to produce a forecast for the UK economy to 1988.

The first two equations in the box, and possibly the others, will be familiar to many readers. The model begins with an equation representing an LM curve, and the second equation is an IS curve (IS and LM curves are defined later in this section). The third equation suggests that UK prices react, gradually, to competitive pressure from abroad and the fourth equation states that the exchange rate is determined by expectations and by relative interest rates. These equations are based on the model used by Buiter and Miller (1981) to analyse the Thatcher administration's monetary policy and its impact on the 1980–81 recession in the UK. The analysis of Buiter and Miller relies on material that is not introduced until later and so discussion of the properties of the model as a whole is postponed to Chapter 8, although there is some discussion of individual equations in this section.

The variables of the model

In the equations, items in capital letters such as PC (the consumer prices index) and GDPE (real gross domestic product) are the *variables* of the model. They measure prices, volumes or some other economic factor and they vary over time. A key to their definitions is given in the box. Historical data are available for all the variables. For MO, these data are monthly but for GDPE and other important variables data are available for periods no shorter than quarters. (See Chapter 2.) Because of this, the macro-econometric model derived later in this chapter is based on quarterly data, as are many of the macro-econometric models used by the forecasting institutes.

The equations shown in Box 4.1 describe the events in a quarterly time period but they also capture, in a very over-simplified way, the dependence of that quarter's events on the past and on expectations of the future. The influence of the past comes through the item PC_{t-1}.

This item can be understood by noting that the model is usable as a description of economic events in any quarter. The subscript t indicates the value taken by a variable in the quarter currently being described, while $t-1$ indicates the value taken by a variable in the previous quarter. For example, suppose that the fourth quarter of 1983 is being analysed using the model; then PC_t refers to the value of the consumer price index in 1983 fourth quarter and PC_{t-1} refers to the value of the index in 1983 third quarter. Similarly, PC_{t-4} refers to the level of the index in the quarter a year earlier than the one being analysed. Any such reference is called a *lagged variable*.

The theoretical model captures the influence of expectations about the future through the variable XEER, which represents expectations of the value that the exchange rate will take on one period ahead. More details about this are given in Section 5.7 and in Chapter 8.

Variables in economic models can be divided into two types: those that are *endogenous* and those that are *exogenous*. The distinction is fundamental. Endogenous variables are explained by the model while exogenous variables are determined outside the model. Exogenous variables influence the endogenous variables but there is no effect in the opposite direction.

For some purposes it is possible to treat variables as if they were exogenous, even though they fail to satisfy the above criteria. For example, lagged endogenous variables and exogenous variables can often be treated in the same way during estimation; these two categories of variable are referred to by the generic term *predetermined*.

In the model shown in Box 4.1, four variables are treated as endogenous: GDPE, PC, EER and RLB. There is an equation to explain each of these. Three variables are treated as exogenous: WWPI, RSW and MO. (In addition there is the expectations variable, XEER, treatment of which is discussed in Section 5.7 and Chapter 8; for the moment it will be treated as exogenous.) The first two exogenous variables describe events in the world economy. Assuming that the UK is small enough to have only a negligible impact on the world economy, these two variables satisfy the criteria given above for exogenous variables. By contrast the variable MO is a UK government policy variable. To treat it as exogenous is to ignore the influence on government policy of developments in the UK economy. In principle it is possible to allow for this influence by extending the model to include equations describing the formation of government policy. This is extremely difficult in practice and is rarely done, although Chapter 5 explains that during forecasting judgement can be used to allow for such influence. Chapter 8 describes how this judgement can be formalized using optimal control methods.

The parameters of the model

The greek letters with numbered subscripts, such as α_1, are called the *parameters* or *coefficients* of the model. In contrast to the variables, the parameters are assumed not to change over time, nor can they be observed directly, although economic theory usually suggests whether they are positive or negative. For analysis using theoretical models, they are left as unknown quantities. For forecasting and other work using macro-econometric models, quantified estimates of their values are necessary, and are obtained by statistical analysis of historical data on the variables.

The parameters reflect partly the preferences of individuals (and other economic agents such as companies) and partly the institutional structure of the economy. For example, consider α_1, which measures the relationship between real cash holdings and GDPE. This coefficient reflects partly people's dislike of having to go to the bank (the less they like going, the more cash they will hold to finance their spending and the higher α_1 will be). It also reflects the institutional structure, because easy payment by cheque or credit card implies low holdings of cash.

For macro-econometric models, it is vital that the parameters remain constant both over the period covered by the historical data used for estimation, and on into the period for which forecasts are made. When a parameter is believed to change, the appropriate procedure is usually to introduce an extra variable into the equation, multiplied by an extra parameter, to capture the effect. For example, growth over time in the use of credit cards and cheques can be dealt with by adding to the equation an extra variable measuring the number of bank accounts and credit cards. Without this extra variable, the assumption that α_1 is constant over time would be invalid. Reliance on this invalid assumption would cause bias both in the estimated parameter values and in forecasts. (See Section 4.4 for explanation of bias.)

Changes in parameters over time due to altered perceptions of government policy should in principle be dealt with by introducing an extra variable into the equation to capture the effect of such perceptions (it may even be necessary to multiply one of the existing variables by a new variable representing policy). In practice this is very difficult and is done rarely. Models in which parameters are liable to change for this reason are said to be subject to the *Lucas critique*. This important issue is discussed further in Chapter 8.

The error terms

At the end of each of the first three equations is the greek symbol epsilon. This has two subscripts; a capital letter indicating which equation it is part of (M for money supply, etc.) and also a t indicating that, like the variables, this item changes over time. These epsilons are *error terms*, containing all the effects not captured by other parts of the equation. This covers a wide range of factors, such as atypical timing of holidays and also sheer perversity which occasionally causes people to act in an unusual way. These effects are almost certain to vary over time, which is why the error terms have a t subscript, but in contrast to GDPE and interest rates they are unobservable. This problem is dealt with by treating the error terms as random variables, which are assumed to have an average value of zero and a probability distribution which indicates how far they are likely to be from zero. This probability distribution is itself unknown but during estimation of the model parameters, an estimate of its variance can be derived. (The variance is a measure of how far from its average a random variable is likely to be.) Section 4.4 gives more details.

The use of logarithms

Throughout all four equations, logarithms of variables (except for the two interest rates RLB and RSW) are used. Use of this particular functional form is convenient, both because it facilitates algebraic analysis of the equations and because it means that the coefficient on each equation is also an elasticity. For example, α_1 is the elasticity of real money demand with respect to GDPE. Despite its convenience, this choice of functional form is arbitrary and it imposes the property of constant elasticity. This restriction should if possible be tested during estimation.

Interpretation of equations

This completes the description of the relevant notation and definitions. The remainder of this section explains briefly the economic interpretation of each equation.

The first equation represents the demand for money, in real terms, showing that it tends to rise when GDPE increases (because people need more cash to finance the higher level of transactions) and that it tends to fall when interest rates are high because then more interest is lost from holding funds in the form of money. (The type of money used in this equation is MO, which consists only of notes and coin and of the very small bankers' operational deposits held at the Bank of England; none of these is interest-bearing.) Assuming that the government fixes the amount of money that it is willing to supply, and also assuming that supply equals demand, then this is an *LM curve*, i.e. it indicates combinations of output and interest rates at which money demand equals money supply.

The second equation shows that output (variable GDPE) tends to fall when real interest rates are high (real interest rates are given by nominal interest rates RLB minus the rate of inflation, which is the change in the consumer price index PC). In addition, output tends to fall when domestic prices PC are high relative to overseas prices converted to sterling (this conversion is done by dividing world prices WWPI by the exchange rate EER), because competitiveness is poor so imports tend to rise and exports tend to fall. This equation is an *IS curve*, i.e. it gives combinations of GDPE and interest rates at which savings equal investment. It can (in principle) be derived from separate equations for consumption and investment, by setting investment equal to the difference between income and consumption (less government consumption and net exports). This equation explains movements in output entirely in terms of changes in demand; some allowance for changes in supply (e.g. growth over time in productive potential) is discussed in Section 4.3.

Both the LM curve and the IS curve must be satisfied, i.e. GDPE and interest rates must take on values at which both money supply equals money demand, and savings equal investment. These values could be found by re-arrangement of the first two equations of the model. For any given set of values for the exogenous variables (WWPI, MO, RSW), assuming for the moment that the other two endogenous variables EER and PC are also given, there is only one combination of GDPE and interest rates that satisfies both the first two equations. This is known as the solution to the model. For the theoretical model presented in the box, this solution can only be worked out in terms of the symbols used, but in a macro-econometric model, with quantified values for the coefficients and also for the exogenous variables, it is possible to compute a quantitative solution for GDPE and interest rates. The point of intersection of the IS and LM curves on a diagram is also a way of finding a solution to this model. However, the position and slope of those curves, and hence the solution values of GDPE and interest rates, are affected by the two remaining endogenous variables in the model, the exchange rate (EER) and domestic prices (PC). To find solution values for these it is necessary to consider the remaining two equations of the model as well as the IS and LM curves.

Interpretation of the prices and exchange rate equations

The third equation shows UK consumer prices depending partly on their own level one quarter ago and partly on world prices converted to sterling. In the 'long run', i.e. after many quarters without exogenous shocks, this equation always brings UK prices back into line with foreign prices (measured in sterling), whatever the starting point. In the short run, i.e. over a few quarters or perhaps a few years, the one-quarter-ago level of UK prices slows down the adjustment towards this long-run position. This equation is based on the theory that competitive pressure will eventually force UK prices into line with those abroad but in the short run the slowness of the wage bargaining process to react to external pressures will prevent this happening. If the coefficient γ_1 is zero, then there will be no slow adjustment; instead UK prices will always move exactly in line with world prices measured in sterling (apart from the error term), and if γ_1 is small then there will be a period of adjustment but it will not be very marked. Thus the size of γ_1 provides a measure of how rapidly UK prices and wages adjust to external events.

The final equation describes the foreign exchange market. It suggests that any expected appreciation of sterling against other currencies (i.e. the expected exchange rate XEER being above the current period exchange rate EER) must be matched by UK interest rates RLB being below world interest rates RSW by exactly the amount of the expected appreciation. The opposite interest rate differential is necessary when a depreciation is expected. See Box 4.2. This is the theory of uncovered interest parity.

If the expected exchange rate XEER is known, then the four equations taken together form a simultaneous equation system in the four endogenous variables GDPE, RLB, PC and EER. The solution to this system is known as the solution to the model.

The model was designed to be used on the assumption that exchange rate expectations are consistent with the forecasts for the exchange rate generated by the model itself. Discussion of the properties of this model under this assumption is postponed to Section 8.3.

It is unlikely that the results of estimating the four equations set out in Box 4.1 would be satisfactory, because they are based on a simple, highly abstract model of the economy. The next section discusses how an abstract model such as this can be developed to make it suitable for estimation.

Box 4.2   Exchange rate forecasts

The exchange rate equation in the model is based on uncovered interest parity. This means that any expected appreciation in the exchange rate must be matched by UK interest rates being lower than foreign interest rates by exactly the size of the expected rise. (When a depreciation is expected, UK interest rates must exceed those abroad.) This can be written as an equation. Write today's exchange rate as EER and write XEER for market expectations of the level to be taken by the exchange rate at the next time when trading will take place. In real foreign exchange markets, trading takes place more or less continuously while in the forecasting model presented here, trading takes place at discrete three month intervals. The expected percentage capital gain from buying sterling now and holding it until trading next takes place is:

$$\text{Expected percentage capital gain} = \frac{\text{XEER}_t - \text{EER}_t}{\text{EER}_t} \times 100$$

(Transactions costs are ignored.) Someone planning to hold sterling expects to get both this capital gain and an interest payment. Writing the UK interest rate as RLB (in per cent at annual rate), the total expected return on sterling is given by the sum of expected income plus capital gain:

$$\text{Total expected return on holding sterling for three months} = \text{RLB}_t/4 + \frac{\text{XEER}_t - \text{EER}_t}{\text{EER}_t} \times 100$$

(The factor of 4 converts the interest rate from annual to quarterly, ignoring compounding. Alternative models can be constructed in which both interest rate and expectation refer to longer or shorter periods and continuous trading can also be modelled.) Write the foreign currency interest rate (in per cent per annum) as RSW. Then the return on holding foreign currency is:

$$\text{Return on holding foreign currency for three months} = \text{RSW}_t/4$$

We assume that foreign exchange markets are dominated by speculators who shift funds into the country offering the highest total returns (capital gain plus income). Such arbitrage causes exchange rates to change until total returns are the same for all currencies. This is the uncovered interest parity condition. It means that the above expression for the total return on sterling must equal the total return on holding foreign currency:

$$\text{RLB}_t/4 + \frac{\text{XEER}_t - \text{EER}_t}{\text{EER}_t} \times 100 = \text{RSW}_t/4$$

This can be re-arranged to give the expression used in the forecasting model, noting the relationship $\{1 - (\text{RLB}_t - \text{RSW}_t)/400\}^{-1} \simeq 1 + (\text{RLB}_t - \text{RSW}_t)/400$:

$$\text{EER}_t = \text{XEER}_t \times \{1 + (\text{RLB}_t - \text{RSW}_t)/400\}$$

which is almost exactly equivalent to:

$$\log \text{EER}_t = \log \text{XEER}_t + (\text{RLB}_t - \text{RSW}_t)/400$$

In practice, there are industrial companies and others operating in foreign exchange markets who are not trying to obtain the highest total return. They have funds to invest now and know that eventually they have to make a payment in one particular currency. They are anxious to hold that currency in order to avoid the risk of an adverse movement in exchange rates and so they will if necessary take a slightly lower expected return than is offered in a different currency. This type of behaviour means that the above formula is only an approximation to the way that foreign exchange markets work.

This explanation of exchange rate determination appears to ignore trade flows and competitiveness, but this need not be so when the exchange rate equation is combined with other equations, as in the previous box.

4.3 Specification

This section describes the process of specification, which consists of modifying and expanding a theoretical model (such as that set out above) to give equations that are realistic enough to be suitable for estimation. We consider three types of modification and expansion: allowing for alternative theories; allowing for the relationships among variables over time; and the introduction of other types of extra detail.

Allowing for alternative theories

The derivation of macro-econometric models offers the opportunity to resolve some of the disputes among economists, by confronting theories with evidence from historical data. Where there is argument over the size of the influence of one variable on another, estimated parameters should help resolve the dispute. Where there is argument over theory, it should be possible to specify a set of equations that is general enough to encompass both (or all) of the theories and again the estimated parameters will provide evidence to suggest which theory is supported by the data. This approach can be illustrated using the model described above.

The first equation shown in Box 4.1 includes short-term interest rates (RLB) as one of the items explaining the real demand for money (MO/PC). Extreme monetarist theories suggest that the demand for money is unaffected by interest rates implying that the coefficient α_2 is zero. This extreme theory can easily be tested against the model shown in the box, which asserts that interest rates are one of the factors affecting money demand, by carrying out a simple statistical test during estimation to see if the data reject the hypothesis that α_2 is zero. Similarly, the extreme theory of instantaneous purchasing power parity, which asserts that UK prices adjust instantly in line with movements in world prices converted to sterling, can be evaluated by testing the hypothesis that γ_1 in the third equation is zero. In both cases, the extreme theory is said to be *nested* within the more general form of equation that is being estimated.

There are some alternative theories that are not already nested within the equations shown in Box 4.1. For example, another extreme theory states that all markets, including those for capital and for labour, clear instantly. This implies that the only factors affecting output will be those that alter the position of supply and demand curves (proponents of this type of theory usually stress movements in supply curves). According to this view, the variables that influence GDPE include changes in the population of working age, due for example to an earlier 'baby boom' (this would affect the supply of labour and might also affect the pattern of demand for consumer goods and housing); another factor would be changes in productive capacity due to technological development. On this view, the variables included in the GDPE equation of Box 4.1 are prices that result from market clearing processes and contain only a transformation of the information from the variables, such as those mentioned above, that fix the position of the supply and demand curves. This extreme theory implies that the variables in the GDPE equation in Box 4.1 will have no ability to explain GDPE once the extra supply and demand variables are added into the equation.

To test this alternative, extreme, theory against that shown in the box, all the extra supply and demand variables would have to be included in the GDPE equation and this new expanded specification would then be estimated. According to the theory of the model in Box 4.1, the coefficients on all the new variables would be zero; on the alternative extreme view, β_1 and β_2 would be zero. A third possibility exists; all the coefficients, on both existing and additional variables, may have non-zero coefficients. This would reflect a third type of theory in which markets do not clear but, in contrast to the model of Box 4.1, GDPE is none the less influenced by factors that move supply and demand curves as well as by prices.

This expanded specification is more general than that given in Box 4.1 and is described as encompassing all three theories. It is a flexible specification that allows the data to indicate which of the competing theories is most likely to be correct. Where there is uncertainty about which theory to use, this general type of specification should be used.

There are drawbacks to using this more general specification. The extra variables complicate the system and, assuming that not all their coefficients are shown to be zero, the resulting macro-econometric model will not have the known properties of a reasonably simple theoretical model, instead having the probably unknown and almost certainly more complex properties of a more general theoretical model. Also, unless all the extra variables are treated as exogenous, extra equations will have to be specified, increasing the size of the system and generating their own problems of specification. A further drawback to the introduction of extra variables is that when the number of years for which historical data are available is short, estimation accuracy may become very low.

These apparent drawbacks are arguments for simple macro-econometric models, based on fully understood theory. They are not arguments against the use of a general model specification. There is no point in specifying a very simple model if there are extra variables that ought to be included but have been omitted, or if there are restrictions imposed on the included variables (e.g. two variables may be constrained to have equal coefficients) that ought not to be imposed. When the simplifying assumptions are wrong, the resulting model will also be wrong.

Dynamic specification

Dynamic specification is the choice of equations that allow for an appropriate response of one variable to another over time. Its importance can be illustrated by considering the first equation in Box 4.1. This shows real demand for money rising as soon as gross domestic product (variable GDPE) increases or interest rates (variable RLB) fall, with no delayed reaction. A brief examination of past events suggests that this instant response is probably unrealistic, implying that attempts to estimate such an equation might produce unsatisfactory results. This suggests that it is desirable to specify a more general equation that allows for the possibility of both an immediate response and a further, delayed reaction. During estimation the data will indicate which is correct, or there may be a combination of instant and delayed response.

One simple way to specify an equation that allows for both an immediate and a delayed reaction is to add lagged values of the variables that already appear on the right hand side. In the money demand equation of Box 4.1, this means adding the lagged variables log $GDPE_{t-1}$ and RLB_{t-1}, each multiplied by an extra coefficient that has to be estimated. This approach has the drawback of allowing for only a limited range of possibilities, because it includes variables lagged one period but not variables lagged by, say, two periods or four periods. A more general specification is obtained by adding real money demand lagged one quarter, $\log (MO_{t-1}/PC_{t-1})$, to the right hand side of the equation. This is called a *lagged dependent variable*. Via this item, those lagged values of gross domestic product and interest rates that are excluded from the equation do still have an indirect effect. For example, interest rates lagged two quarters do not appear in the equation, but they affect real money stock lagged one quarter (because the equation is valid for that quarter's real money stock) which in turn affects this period's real money stock.

An equation which includes lagged variables and so allows for delayed responses is known as a *dynamic specification*. It is more likely to give satisfactory estimation results than a simple equation with no lagged variables such as the money demand equation in Box 4.1. Despite having extra variables, the dynamic specification remains closely related to the simple form. To explain this relationship, it is necessary to define the *steady state* of an equation.

A steady state is reached when all the variables in an equation are unchanging, or growing at a constant rate (this state can alternatively be called the *long run*). The steady state of an entire model containing many equations is defined in the same way. A brief examination of historical data suggests no obvious period in which the economy settled down to a steady state. Despite this, the idea is of considerable importance. This is because it allows reconciliation of ideas used in simple theoretical models, for example market clearing, with the more complex phenomena often observed in the real world. This reconciliation is achieved by specifying macro-econometric models that allow for fairly complex adjustment over time, but with variables gradually tending towards a steady state in which some simple theory is valid. Such models are not inconsistent with the observation that steady states never seem to have occurred in the past. This is because the economy may take a long time to return even approximately to its steady state and in the meanwhile irregular movements in exogenous variables (e.g. world prices) may retard its progress. Also, describing the economy by a model that has a steady state in which markets clear (giving full employment automatically) does not rule out the possibility of using government policy to raise employment. This is because policy changes may be able to speed up the return to equilibrium in such a model.

The equation for real money demand given in Box 4.1 is the steady state of the more complex dynamic specification suggested above. Assuming that there was a very long period over which gross domestic product and interest rates were unchanged, then the more complex equation would predict demand for money settling down to a constant, and could be re-arranged into the form of the simpler equation in Box 4.1. There is a complication: the coefficient on the lagged dependent variable, which is to be obtained during estimation, must have a magnitude less than one. If it equalled one or more, then money demand would go on growing indefinitely. The requirement that this coefficient be less than one to prevent this occurring is called a *stability condition*. Checking estimation results to ensure that stability conditions are satisfied is very important. In models consisting of several equations it involves checking not merely the size of individual coefficients but also the relationship among coefficients on different equations.

The reasons given above for adding lagged variables to the equation specification was empirical, i.e. a brief examination of history suggested that the extra variables were needed for the equation to fit the data. There are alternative justifications, based on the argument that costs of adjustment or market imperfections prevent an immediate move to the steady state, even though that state is desirable or is a position in which markets clear. *Error correction mechanisms* are justifications of this type. They typically show the change in the dependent variable depending partly on any change in its steady state level and partly on the discrepancy between last period's steady state level and last period's actual dependent variable. The correction for last period's discrepancy gives these mechanisms their name. The dynamic specification suggested above, which had the current period and one lag for each of the independent variables and one lag for the dependent variable, is a re-arranged error correction mechanism.

Error correction mechanisms are derived from arbitrary assumptions about the costs of adjustment and about the costs of being away from the steady state. For some applications, it may be possible to argue that a different assumption about costs is more appropriate. Despite this, error correction mechanisms are useful as a simple type of dynamic specification and have been widely used in empirical work.

To move from the theoretical model of Box 4.1 to equation specifications that are ready for estimation, it is necessary to provide a dynamic specification for all the equations. This involves the introduction of extra, lagged variables to all the equations. A fully worked example of the estimation process is given in Section 4.5.

Adding extra detail

Various modifications have now been proposed to the four-equation theoretical model presented in the previous section, but even with these, the specification would be too abstract to explain most historical data. Extra detail must be added, both by expanding equations already in the model and by adding extra equations.

There are a number of variables that were excluded from the theoretical model for simplicity but which must be included in the equations that are to be estimated. Some of the most important examples are: a measure of the tendancy for people to use fewer notes and coin as cheques and credit cards are used more (this has already been mentioned and must be included in the equation for real money demand); some allowance for the production of North Sea oil and gas must be made in the equation for GDPE; and a variable measuring indirect tax rates (such as VAT rates) must be included in the consumer prices equation. Another important feature of the real economy that is completely missing from the theoretical model is an allowance for the growth in productive potential. A crude way to deal with this is to assume that in the absence of cyclical fluctuations GDPE would tend to rise at some trend growth rate. Between the mid-1950s and the early 1980s GDPE grew by well over 50 per cent, in spite of falls in its level in some recession years. This represents an average annual growth rate of 2.3 per cent and this is the trend growth figure assumed in the model used in this book.

The choice of the number of equations used to describe each part of the economy is a matter of judgement and depends partly on the resources available. At one extreme it would be possible to estimate a model with only the four equations shown in Box 4.1, modified in the ways outlined so far in this section. At the opposite extreme are macro-econometric models such as those at the Treasury and London Business School which contain well over 500 variables. The first approach fails to use much of the information provided by data and by theory, while the second approach requires very substantial resources. Also, it is difficult to ensure that very large models have properties that are in line with economic theory.

The approach adopted for the macro-econometric model presented in this book is to balance the advantages and drawbacks of the two extremes. In the judgement of the model-builder, this is best done by expanding somewhat the theoretical model of Box 4.1, to include some nineteen endogenous and thirteen exogenous variables. The remainder of this section describes briefly the extra equations and explains why they were chosen.

Extra equations: components of expenditure

In the expanded model, the equation for GDPE given in Box 4.1 is replaced by five separate equations for different components of expenditure, and by the gross domestic product (expenditure measure) identity (see Chapter 2 for definition of this identity). The advantages and costs of doing this are discussed below. The full, expanded model, including all the new equations, is shown in Appendix 1, and for ease of reference the long-run versions of all the model equations are shown in Box 4.10 at the end of this chapter.

In the first of these new equations, exports (non-oil, at constant market prices, denoted X in the equations) depend on competitiveness and world trade. In the second equation, private sector gross fixed investment (again at constant market prices) is set at the level needed to adjust the total private sector fixed capital stock (at constant market prices, denoted KI) back towards its long-run level, which is defined as a constant proportion of GDPE. The adjustment is delayed when real wages are abnormally high because profits, and so the returns on capital, are then lower. The third new equation is similar to the second, with stock building (at constant market prices) adjusting to bring the total stock of inventories (at constant market prices, denoted KII) back towards its long-run level, which is again defined as a constant proportion of GDPE. This adjustment process is delayed when real interest rates are high. In the fourth equation, imports (non-oil, at constant market prices, denoted M) depend partly on the level of UK domestic demand (particularly UK expenditure on stock building, which tends to have a high import content) and partly on competitiveness. In the fifth equation consumers' expenditure (at constant market prices, denoted C) adjusts towards the level at which it is a given proportion of consumer post-tax real incomes; this proportion is high when inflation is low, and vice versa, reflecting people's need to save more at times of high inflation in order to top up their stock of financial assets so as to maintain that stock at a constant level in real terms.

This description of the five extra equations is brief but the corresponding equations in the large UK macro-econometric models are reasonably similar and are fully described elsewhere. See Brittan (1983) for the National Institute model and Budd *et al.* (1984) for the London Business School model.

The gross domestic product identity states that GDPE (which is the expenditure measure, at constant factor cost) equals the sum of all the expenditure components (each of which must be at constant market prices): consumers' expenditure, private sector gross fixed investment, stock building, non-oil exports, net trade in oil, and government spending on goods and services; all minus non-oil imports and minus the adjustment to factor cost at constant prices. (This adjustment equals taxes on expenditure net of subsidies and there is no separate variable for it in this model; instead an allowance is made for it in the equation for GDPE.) No equation has been mentioned for net trade in oil or for government spending, because these two variables are treated as exogenous.

By substituting the five equations for expenditure components into the identity and re-arranging, it is possible to derive an equation for GDPE with real interest rates and competitiveness on the right hand side. This would be an IS curve, similar to the one given in Box 4.1, but more complex; unlike that IS curve, the one derived from this substitution would include some extra variables such as government spending. It is not necessary to carry out this algebra to use the more detailed system for forecasting or policy analysis. The fact that it can be done suggests that the properties of the more detailed model will probably be similar to those of the simpler model, and this view is supported by the results of experiments reported in Chapter 8.

The introduction of these extra equations has the cost of making the system more complex. The gain is the explicit modelling of various effects suggested by economic theory, for example the fall in the ratio of consumption to income when inflation rises. This is not possible when a single equation is used for GDPE. Explicit modelling of effects suggested by theory has several advantages. It usually makes the model easier to understand. During forecasting it facilitates the choice of sensible judgemental adjustments, when necessary. During estimation it can provide a warning that an equation is invalid.

Extra equations: consumer income

The expansion of the model to include the five equations for expenditure components means that it is necessary also to add extra equations to explain consumer post-tax incomes, which are one of the items in the equation for consumers' expenditure. This is done by specifying a total of three extra equations: for average wages, for numbers employed, and for consumers' incomes. (Wages have an effect on investment as well as consumption.) The measure used for wages is an index of average wages and salaries in the whole economy, denoted WSI. Equations for wages are very difficult to specify and estimate; the approach adopted here is to specify a simple equation in which growth in average wages tends always to equal growth in consumer prices plus the trend rate of productivity (assumed to be 2.3 per cent per annum, see above, page 62). There is a slow adjustment towards this relationship between growth rates, which could be interpreted as reflecting both the effect of fixed contracts and the impact of backward-looking expectations of prices. The equation for prices causes price inflation to slow when UK competitiveness is poor; since poor competitiveness is usually associated with unemployment, this means that the prices equation has the properties of a Phillips curve. Since wages depend on prices, they too will exhibit Phillips curve properties, but there is no direct impact of unemployment on wages in this specification. From the earlier discussion about testing alternative models, the best procedure would be to specify a more general model that included a direct unemployment effect in the wages equation, but this has not been done because of limited resources. There are many other factors, such as the rate of unemployment benefit and the strength of unions, that may in theory provide part of the explanation of how wages are determined (see for example Nickell and Andrews, 1983). These have also been left out of the specification, because in the model-builder's judgement the more restricted specification will perform adequately for forecasting and for analysis of some types of policy (though not for analysis of policies involving changes in unemployment pay or in union power). This is an example of the type of judgement that model-builders have to make when few resources are available for constructing a macro-econometric model with many equations; this judgement must be based as far as possible on the work of other economists who have tried out more general specifications. An example of the more satisfactory approach to model-building, in which a general version of the equation is specified and tests are carried out to see if restrictions are valid, is given in Section 4.5.

In the second of the equations needed to build up consumer post-tax incomes, the total number of people employed in the whole economy (denoted ET) has a constant long run level, but it will tend to be below this level when GDPE is lower than implied by its trend growth rate or when wages are above their trend relationship with prices. The assumption of a constant long run level of employment ignores any tendency for the supply of labour to vary over time (e.g. due to changes in the population of working age or because of increased female participation) and this equation also ignores other possible variables that may affect employment, such as the rate of unemployment pay. As for the wages equation, ideally a general specification including all these extra effects would be used.

Total personal sector receipts of wages and salaries (defined as the wages index times the number employed and thus written WSI × ET) are added to persons' receipts of grants from the government and of net interest (both obtained from simple equations shown in the full listing of the model); taxes and social security contributions are subtracted from this total to give personal sector disposable (post-tax) income. This is denoted YD in the model and unlike all the variables discussed so far (except MO) it is measured in current prices. This means that before it can be used in the equation for consumer spending, it must be divided by the consumer prices index (denoted PC) to convert it to constant prices.

Extra equations: the balance of payments

To complete the specification of the model, two further important areas must be described. These are the balance of payments and government finances. The balance of payments current account is equal to non-oil export volume times non-oil export prices, plus net oil trade times oil prices measured in sterling, minus non-oil import volume times non-oil import prices measured in sterling, plus interest, dividend and transfer payments from abroad to the UK, net of those from the UK to overseas. The equations for non-oil exports and imports, X and M, have already been discussed and as noted earlier trade in oil, denoted O, is exogenous. Export prices are denoted PX and are modelled by a simple equation that allows them to diverge somewhat from world prices (measured in sterling) when UK wage costs are abnormally high or low; this equation specification relies on the assumption that UK exporters have some limited monopoly power in world markets. Non-oil import prices, measured in sterling, are taken as the exogenous world prices variable WWPI (which is in foreign currency) divided by the exchange rate EER to convert it to sterling. Similarly, oil prices in sterling are calculated as the exogenous oil price variable POILWC (again in foreign currency) divided by EER. The net flow of interest, dividends and transfers are modelled crudely as a world interest rate (denoted RSW, exogenous) times the net stock outstanding of foreign debt held by UK residents. This stock is denoted OJ in the model. (There is no separate variable for the flow of interest etc.; this flow is included in the equation for the current account balance.) The current account balance is denoted BAL.

The capital account balance of the balance of payments is by definition equal and opposite to the current account balance, although in practice recording errors and omissions mean there is a large residual between identified capital account flows and the current account. This problem, and also the problem caused by capital gains and losses that cause continual adjustments to the value of the overseas assets held in this country (and of UK assets held abroad) are assumed away in the model presented here. This is done by defining a single variable, denoted OJ, as equal to the cumulated sum of all past current account surpluses (measured as a positive number) plus all deficits (measured as negative numbers). This is a crude measure of the net outstanding stock of overseas assets held in the UK, but it is easy to compute and to forecast and it allows a simple link, during both forecasting and policy analysis, between the current account in early periods of the forecast and interest flows to or from abroad, which affect the current account in later periods. In the model, this net stock of debt is simply set equal to its own lagged value plus the current period's value of the current account, less any change in the reserves.

Extra equations: the PSBR and its financing

In modelling government finances, the amount that the government needs to borrow (the PSBR) and the way that this borrowing requirement is financed (in particular, the split between bonds and money) are both of interest. In simple theoretical models, the PSBR is usually written as exogenous government spending minus an average tax rate times GDP; many theoretical models also allow for payments of debt interest on outstanding government debt. The equation in the model used in this book (which is a technical equation, i.e. it is constructed from conventional assumptions and not estimated) follows the same pattern as these theoretical models, but with more detail. Government spending on goods and services at constant market prices (exogenous variable G) is multiplied by a price index to convert it to current prices. From this are subtracted taxes on wages and salaries (calculated as an average tax rate times average wages times employment), and taxes on spending (calculated as the adjustment to factor cost at constant prices multiplied by an average indirect tax rate); government receipts of rent and of taxes on interest payments and company incomes, all derived from simple technical equations, are also subtracted. To the resulting total are added payments of grants to the personal sector (which was also one of the components of personal sector income) and also debt interest payments, which depend on the total of government debt outstanding (this stock of debt is denoted GOVTB in the model).

In dealing with the financing of the PSBR, the problems of errors and omissions, and of revaluations, are again encountered. As for the balance of payments, they are assumed away by appropriate definition of variables. By identity, the PSBR in any period equals the government's financing transactions. These are the issue of high powered money (mainly notes and coin), any change in foreign currency reserves, and all other financing transactions which consist mainly of sales of bonds (usually called gilts) and of other forms of government debt (the most important of which are national savings). A further complication is caused by government sales or purchases of short-term bills in an attempt to influence interest rates (open market operations). In the model presented here, short-term interest rates are entirely determined by the government's exogenously chosen supply of high powered money (MO) and so the impact of bill transactions is ignored (they are treated as if they had the same effect as sales of bonds or national savings). The government's transactions in reserves and foreign currency are treated as an exogenous variable, DRESV, in the model; this variable has little effect, except to alter the outstanding stocks of other government debt and of UK private holdings of foreign assets and is included only for completeness and to show the link between the government's finances and the balance of payments capital account. With the PSBR determined as an endogenous variable as described above, and with the government's issue of money (denoted by the change in MO) and its change in reserves (DRESV) both exogenous, the change in other forms of debt (mainly bonds, and national savings, as noted above) is determined by identity. The outstanding stock of this debt is denoted GOVTB and so, since revaluations and omissions are ignored by assumption, this gives:

$$\text{GOVTB}_t - \text{GOVTB}_{t-1} = \text{PSBR}_t - (\text{MO}_t - \text{MO}_{t-1}) + \text{DRESV}_t$$

As for the variable OJ, the importance of the variable GOVTB in the model is that it means large PSBRs early in a forecast will result in increasing debt interest payments later in the forecast (unless a significant proportion of the PSBR is financed by issue of money MO, which is unlikely). This may provide the forecaster with a warning that an unsustainable policy is being pursued. Maintaining the outstanding stock of government debt at or below some proportion of gross domestic product could be an objective of policy.

It must be emphasized that the definition of money supply being used here is MO, which consists almost entirely of notes and coin held both by banks and by the public; the only other items included are the very small bankers' operational deposits held at the Bank of England. This measure is used because it is entirely non-interest bearing and is entirely held for transactions purposes, not saving, so it is in line with the type of money envisaged in theoretical models of the type shown in Box 4.1. However, because MO in total is fairly small (about £12 billion outstanding at the start of 1984), only a limited amount of the PSBR can be financed through issue of this type of money; the PSBR was about £8 billion in 1984 and MO was rising at about 5 per cent per annum, implying that it was providing about £600 million of finance. The proportion of the PSBR financed in this way could be increased by raising the growth of MO, but even if the growth rate were raised to 10 per cent, the contribution to financing the PSBR would only have risen slightly, to about £1.2 billion (to anticipate the results of Chapter 8, this increase would also lead to a similar rise in inflation). Another point about this definition of money is that, in contrast to the broad measure sterling M3, it includes only money issued by the government, and no money issued by the banks. Hence the identity linking MO to the PSBR (which is the equation shown just above) does not include bank lending, while the identity linking sterling M3 to the PSBR does include this.

This concludes the description of the specification of the model. The next stage in deriving a macro-econometric model is to obtain estimates for the parameters contained in this specification, and to carry out tests both to exclude some variables from general forms of equations, and to check that the specification is not an invalid description of the historical data. This is the process of estimation and is described in the next section.

4.4 Estimation

Estimation is the use of statistical techniques to analyse historical data and so quantify relationships among economic variables, with testing of theories about the size of those relationships and about whether they exist at all. Estimation starts from the equations derived during specification and obtains quantitative estimates of the parameters in those equations. Tests applied during estimation usually allow the model to be simplified, i.e. some variables are excluded and the equation(s) re-estimated. Sometimes tests can suggest that the equations specified are inconsistent with the historical data. When this happens, the model-builder has to reconsider the specification.

Econometrics includes both specification and estimation; in practice these two stages are not distinct. This section explains some of the simpler statistical techniques used during estimation (this discussion is brief and readers requiring a more detailed treatment should consult one of the econometrics textbooks referred to in the final section of this chapter). To illustrate the techniques described here, Section 4.5 contains a detailed worked example.

All the equations in Section 4.2 had one variable on the left hand side and many on the right hand side. The former is known as the *dependent* variable and the latter are called *explanatory* variables. Where a lagged value of the dependent variable appears on the right hand side of an equation, it is one of the explanatory variables but is also often called a *lagged dependent* variable.

Ordinary least squares

The equations discussed in Section 4.2, including the first three of those given in Box 4.1, had an error term denoted by an epsilon, e.g. ϵ_{M_t}. It was explained that these error terms were unobservable and varied over time, containing all the effects not captured by the explanatory variables included in the equation. That section also explained that these error terms were dealt with by treating them as if they were random variables, assumed to have an average value of zero and with some probability of falling a greater or a lesser distance on either side of that average value.

Given that the error terms represent all the unobserved factors not captured by the explanatory variables, an intuitively attractive idea is to choose estimated values for the parameters in the equation that will make the error terms as small as possible over the historical period for which there are data on the variables. This suggests that it might be desirable to try to minimize the sum of all the error terms over the data period, but in a straightforward sum, there would tend to be a mix of large negative and large positive errors cancelling one another out. The sum of the squares of the error terms is not subject to this problem and so a possible strategy is to choose parameter values that imply the minimum sum of squares of the error terms over the estimation period.

It can be shown that under certain conditions, minimizing the sum of squares of the error terms is not merely an intuitively attractive idea, but also gives *unbiased* estimates of the parameters. This means (except under very special circumstances) that the true values of the parameters are equally likely to lie above or to lie below the estimated values. Under certain extra assumptions, minimizing the sum of squares of the error terms can also be shown to give the *best unbiased estimates* of the parameters, where best is defined in the statistical sense of having least variance. This means that on average the estimates obtained in this way will be at least as close to the true values as the estimates obtained in any other way. The estimates derived by minimizing the sum of squares of the error terms are known as *ordinary least squares* estimates.

How are the values of the parameters that minimize the sum of squares of the error terms found? One way would be to use a computer program to try out many different values for the parameters until it found those that appeared to give the smallest sum of squares. This method is used for certain complicated estimation problems, where this is the only way that the problem can be solved, but for the simple equations under discussion here a direct method is available using calculus. In the equations of Section

4.2, the dependent variable is expressed in terms of the parameters, the explanatory variables, and the error terms. These equations can easily be re-arranged to give an expression in which the error term depends on all the variables and on the parameters. This expression is squared, summed over all periods for which historical data are available, and then differentiated with respect to the parameters. From elementary calculus, setting the resulting derivatives to zero will give the parameter values that minimize the sum of squares. Box 4.3 shows how this is done.

Box 4.3   Ordinary least squares

Consider an equation:

$$y_t = b_0 + b_1 x_t + \epsilon_t$$

where historical data on y and x are available for many time periods; b_0 and b_1 are unobservable parameters that have to be estimated, and ϵ is an unobservable error term. Ordinary least squares (OLS) estimates, described in the text, are obtained by choosing b_0 and b_1 to minimize:

$$\sum_{t=1}^{T} \epsilon_t^2$$

where T is the total number of observations. This implies minimizing:

$$\sum_{t=1}^{T} (y_t - b_0 - b_1 x_t)^2$$

The first derivatives of this expression, with respect to b_0 and b_1, are set to zero as a necessary condition for this minimum:

$$-2 \sum_{t=1}^{T} (y_t - \hat{b}_0 - \hat{b}_1 x_t) = 0$$

$$-2 \sum_{t=1}^{T} [(y_t - \hat{b}_0 - \hat{b}_1 x_t) x_t] = 0$$

where the ˆ indicates that $\hat{b}_0$ and $\hat{b}_1$ are the estimates that satisfy these equations. Re-arranging, we obtain:

$$\hat{b}_1 = \left[\sum_{t=1}^{T} x_t^2 - \left(\sum_{t=1}^{T} x_t \right)^2 \Big/ T \right]^{-1} \left[\sum_{t=1}^{T} x_t y_t - \left(\sum_{t=1}^{T} x_t \sum_{t=1}^{T} y_t \right) \Big/ T \right]$$

$$\hat{b}_0 = \left[\sum_{t=1}^{T} y_t \Big/ T \right] - \hat{b}_1 \left[\sum_{t=1}^{T} x_t \Big/ T \right]$$

These are the OLS estimates of b_0 and b_1. The properties of these estimates (e.g., whether they are unbiased) depend on the properties of the error term. For a full discussion of these properties, and for generalization of these expressions to the case where there are many variables on the right hand side of the equation, see one of the references to econometric textbooks given in the final section of this chapter.

An important feature about the results is that each estimated parameter depends on data for all of the variables in the equation, for all of the historical data periods. This implies that including extra variables in the equation or adding data for one or more extra time periods will usually alter all the parameter estimates. Adding an extra variable has no effect on the existing parameter estimates only when data on the new variable are *orthogonal* to data on the existing variables; intuitively this means that there is no overlap between the information in the new variable and that in the existing variables.

It is possible to obtain measures of how close each estimated parameter value is likely to be to the true parameter value. These measures are known as the *standard errors* of the parameter estimates and, like the parameter estimates, they depend only on the observed historical data. These standard errors are used for testing hypotheses about the estimated parameter values. This is illustrated in the worked example later in this section.

Instrumental variables

It was noted above that the method of ordinary least squares gives best unbiased parameter estimates, but only under certain assumptions. It is important to consider what happens when some of these assumptions fail to hold. One of the most important assumptions is that the error terms are independent of the explanatory variables. This means that there must, for example, be no tendency for the error terms to be positive when one of the explanatory variables is large. Typically, this assumption is violated when one of the explanatory variables is endogenous. For example, in the equation for money supply MO in Box 4.1, the short-term interest rate RLB is one of the explanatory variables. Since the government is assumed to be supplying an exogenously fixed supply of money, when the unobservable factors contained in the error term are positive, tending to push demand for money up above the exogenously fixed level, then interest rates will have to rise above the level they would have taken had the unobservable factors been zero, in order to choke off the extra demand for money.

Violation of the assumption of independence of the error term and the explanatory variables means that the method of ordinary least squares is no longer unbiased. Instead, it produces estimates that are more likely to lie to one side of the true parameter value than the other. Such estimates are described as *biased* and are highly undesirable. This problem can be avoided by the use of *instrumental variables*. This is an alternative to ordinary least squares and can be applied by a two stage process. In the first stage, a new equation is specified in which the explanatory variable that is not independent of the error term (RLB in the above example) is the dependent variable. On the right hand side of this new equation are a series of variables called instruments. These instruments must have the property of being independent of the error term on the original equation but must also be able to explain movements in the dependent variable of the new equation. In the above example, the new equation has RLB as dependent variable and world interest rates (RSW), UK tax rates and government spending, and the variable RLB lagged one period as instruments on the right hand side. Ordinary least squares is used to estimate the parameters of this new equation. Using the resulting parameter estimates, *fitted values* are calculated for RLB. Fitted values are the values for the dependent variable obtained by setting the error term to zero, multiplying each of the right hand side variables by its estimated parameter, and summing these products. Finally, the original equation (i.e. the equation for MO in the example being used) is estimated by ordinary least squares, using the fitted values for RLB instead of the historical data values. Where there is more than one explanatory variable in the original equation that is not independent of the error term, then fitted values derived in the same way must be used for all such variables. The parameter estimates obtained through this method of instrumental variables are unbiased but they are not best in the statistical sense of least variance; for the best estimates, a systems method, in which all the equations of a model (or at least several of the equations) are estimated together, must be used.

Autocorrelation

There are many other problems and issues arising in estimation; of these, only one other, important, one is mentioned here. This is the problem of *autocorrelation,* which arises when the error terms in different time periods are related, for example when there tend to be a series of positive error terms occurring in successive time periods. Autocorrelation violates the assumptions on which ordinary least squares is based and when it is present, that method will not yield the best parameter estimates, although they will be unbiased. Usually of more importance, the presence of autocorrelation may indicate that the entire specification of the equation is incorrect.

There are a variety of tests designed to indicate whether autocorrelation is present. The most widely used is the Durbin-Watson statistic (although this is only valid under certain circumstances; when the equation includes a lagged dependent variable, for example, this statistic will tend to indicate no autocorrelation even when it is present). A value of this statistic close to two suggests that first-order autocorrelation (i.e., a relation between errors one time period apart) is not present. Tables in econometrics textbooks, such as those mentioned in Section 4.7, give the precise values at which the hypothesis of first-order autocorrelation can be rejected; this varies according to the number of explanatory variables and the number of historical data periods used in estimation. There exist alternative tests against autocorrelation. That used in the practical example of estimation given below is a test against autocorrelation of up to fifth order. This test uses a statistic that is distributed χ^2 with five degrees of freedom. From tables for the χ^2 distribution (also found in statistics and econometrics texts), the hypothesis that autocorrelation of up to fifth order exists cannot be rejected at a five per cent confidence level if this statistic exceeds 11.07. The use of this is demonstrated below in the practical example of estimation, which occupies the next section.

4.5 Estimation in practice: an equation for consumers' expenditure

This section contains a step by step example of estimation in practice, using the consumers' expenditure equation suggested in Section 4.3. The dependent variable in this equation is total consumers' expenditure, on durable and non-durable goods, at constant 1980 market prices. Quarterly data for this variable will be found in the CSO's *Monthly Digest of Statistics* or *Economic Trends* (both published monthly). A long run of quarterly data, back to the mid-1950s, is available in the *Economic Trends* annual supplement. Full details of the sources of this and all the other variables used in this equation are given in Appendix 4.

Outline of the estimation strategy

In its general form, the specification for this equation suggested by the discussion in Section 4.3 states that consumers' expenditure depends on its own lagged value, on lagged values of consumers' real take-home incomes, on lagged values of the rate of inflation, and on lagged values of short-term interest rates. For this to be a general form, several lags of each of these variables must appear (in principle, all lags which might possibly be relevant should be included; in practice some reasonably large number of lags must appear). In its more specific form, which it is hoped can be justified by tests carried out during estimation, the equation suggested in Section 4.3 would contain fewer explanatory variables and would have a long run solution in which consumers' expenditure was a given proportion of real take-home incomes; this proportion would be high when inflation was low, and vice versa.

The strategy starts with the estimation of the general specification, using ordinary least squares. Tests are then applied, to see whether it is possible to exclude some of the variables and hence simplify the equation. These tests are usually carried out on one variable at a time. Once these exclusions have been made, the next stage is to test the additional restrictions needed to give the desired long run solution. If the estimates pass these tests, the final part of the estimation strategy is to carry out a further batch of tests; in the example given in this section, two will be applied. One checks whether the error terms are random, and the other examines whether the equation, using the estimated parameter values, is able to produce acceptable forecasts for consumer spending over an historical period, the data from which were not used in estimation.

In statistical terms, the earlier stages of the estimation process involve tests of restrictions against a well-defined alternative hypothesis (the hypothesis that the general form, without the restrictions, is valid). By contrast, the final part of the estimation process involves tests against no particular alternative hypothesis, because what is being tested is simply the vague assertion that the error terms are not random, or that the equation does not forecast outside its estimation period. These two types of test are sometimes described as tests of *specification* and of *mis-specification*, respectively. The entire process, starting from the general form of the equation and ending with the final tests, is usually known as *specification search*.

It must be noted that a wide range of issues in econometrics are encountered in this section, and for reasons of space these can only be considered briefly. For full details of specification searches, and full discussion of the issues raised here, see the references in the final section of this chapter. Note also that the precise way in which specification searches are carried out can vary. For example, different or additional tests may be used, and also precise criteria for determining whether or not to exclude variables are usually laid down at the start of the procedure.

Testing restrictions

The most general form of the equation that was tried is shown in Box 4.4. All the variables are in natural logarithms. Consumers' expenditure is the dependent variable and there are twelve explanatory variables, plus a constant term. These twelve variables are the first, second and fourth lags on consumers' expenditure itself(C), consumers' real take-home incomes (YD/PC), short term interest rates (RLB), and the rate of inflation (for inflation we use the change in prices PC, plus trend real growth – see below). The first and second lags on these variables have to be included because almost all of them are needed to give the desired long-run solution, as will shortly be explained. The inclusion of lags of any other length is decided by judgement and is inevitably an arbitrary choice. The fourth lags have been included to pick up any seasonal effects not already removed by the use of seasonally adjusted data. (A far more satisfactory way to deal with seasonal patterns is to use unadjusted data and include dummy variables to capture seasonal movements, but the procedure adopted here is to use seasonally adjusted data because this is in line with the practice in all large quarterly UK macro-econometric models and makes conjunctural analysis easier.)

The values shown in brackets under the coefficients are the standard errors. For each of the four fourth-lag variables, these standard errors are about twice as large as the coefficient, or even bigger. This information is shown in a different way by the figures labelled '$t =$', which are the *t-values*. Each of these is the ratio of the coefficient to the standard error, so a low value indicates that the coefficient is small relative to its standard error. It can be shown that these *t*-values follow a known distribution, tabulated in econometrics and statistical texts, that varies with the number of historical data periods. When there are a large number of historical data periods, as here (quarterly data from 1957 to the end of 1980), this

Box 4.4 'Unrestricted' regression

$\log(C_t) =$

$0.614 \log(C_{t-1})$	$+ 0.305 \log(C_{t-2})$	$+ 0.0687 \log(C_{t-4})$
(0.120)	(0.133)	(0.1250)
$t = 5.13$	$t = 2.29$	$t = 0.55$

$+ 0.170 \log(RPDI_{t-1})$	$- 0.0867 \log(RPDI_{t-2})$	$- 0.0465 \log(RPDI_{t-4})$
(0.095)	(0.1050)	(0.0822)
$t = 1.80$	$t = -0.82$	$t = -0.57$

$- 0.00340\ RLB_{t-1}$	$+ 0.00127\ RLB_{t-2}$	$+ 0.00015\ RLB_{t-4}$
(0.00149)	(0.00175)	(0.00110)
$t = -2.28$	$t = 0.73$	$t = 0.13$

$- 0.250[\log(PC_{t-1}/PC_{t-2})$	$- 0.0239[\log(PC_{t-2}/PC_{t-3})$	$+ 0.0491[\log(PC_{t-4}/PC_{t-5})$
$(0.269) \qquad + 0.0057]$	$(0.269) \qquad + 0.0057]$	$(0.201) \qquad + 0.0057]$
$t = -0.93$	$t = -0.09$	$t = 0.24$

$- 0.224$
(0.179)
$t = -1.25$

$R^2 = 0.996$ *Sums of squares*
$\overline{R}^2 = 0.995$ Total $= 2.573$
               Explained $= 2.562$
               Residual $= 0.0115$

Standard error $= 0.0119$
Percentage standard error $= 1.19$ per cent
82 degrees of freedom, from 1957 Q2 to 1980 Q4

Note: Throughout this and Boxes 4.5 to 4.9, RPDI is used to represent real personal disposable income. Since real income equals income at current prices divided by the price level, we can write RPDI in terms of variables used in the model, as: RPDI = YD/(PC/100).

---

distribution is approximately the same as the normal distribution. The hypothesis that one of the estimated coefficients is zero cannot be rejected at the 5 per cent level of significance unless the t-value for that coefficient is greater than about 1.96 in a sample of this size. This means that the hypothesis that each of the coefficients on the fourth-lag variables is zero cannot be rejected at this significance level, because the t-values for all of them àre well below 1. Strictly, this test must only be carried out on the coefficient on one variable at a time, and for all the later stages of this example that rule will be adhered to, but for these four variables there was only a weak case for including them in the specification. Also, their t-values are so small that it is almost certain that carrying out the correct procedure in which they are excluded one by one would also suggest that they should all be left out. For these reasons, all four of these fourth-lag variables are dropped from the specification and the equation re-estimated, again using ordinary least squares. The results are shown in Box 4.5.

Box 4.5   Regression with preliminary restrictions

$\text{Log } C_t =$

$$0.628 \log(C_{t-1}) \qquad\qquad + 0.315 \log(C_{t-2})$$
$$(0.112) \qquad\qquad\qquad\quad (0.118)$$
$$t = 5.62 \qquad\qquad\qquad\quad t = 2.67$$

$$+ 0.165 \log(RPDI_{t-1}) \qquad - 0.0879 \log(RPDI_{t-2})$$
$$(0.089) \qquad\qquad\qquad\quad (0.089)$$
$$t = 1.86 \qquad\qquad\qquad\quad t = -0.98$$

$$- 0.00365 \, RLB_{t-1} \qquad\quad + 0.00161 \, RLB_{t-2}$$
$$(0.00131) \qquad\qquad\qquad (0.00138)$$
$$t = -2.77 \qquad\qquad\qquad t = 1.17$$

$$- 0.255[\log(PC_{t-1}/PC_{t-2}) + 0.0057] \quad - 0.0111[\log(PC_{t-2}/PC_{t-3}) + 0.0057]$$
$$(0.244) \qquad\qquad\qquad\qquad\qquad\quad (0.217)$$
$$t = -1.05 \qquad\qquad\qquad\qquad\qquad t = -0.05$$

$$- 0.196$$
$$(0.151)$$
$$t = -1.29$$

$R^2 = 0.996$

$\overline{R}^2 = 0.995$

Sums of squares
Total = 2.780
Explained = 2.769
Residual = 0.0116

Standard error = 0.0115
Percentage standard error = 1.15 per cent
88 degrees of freedom, from 1956 Q4 to 1980 Q4

This form of the equation includes a coefficient on the second lag of the inflation rate that is almost exactly zero. The hypothesis that this coefficient is zero cannot be rejected and it is excluded from the next version of the equation, shown in Box 4.6. Notice that its exclusion has had very little effect on any of the other estimated parameters.

Box 4.6 contains two further estimated equations. These appear different from the first, but closer examination reveals that they have the same coefficients on the interest rate and inflation terms. All that has happened is that the variables have been re-arranged. This type of re-arrangement is very important in estimating dynamic equations. The first equation in Box 4.6 has the level of consumer spending as the dependent variable, and all the explanatory variables are also levels, not differences. (Note that all the variables, except RLB, are in logs and these references to levels and to differences refer to levels of the logarithms and differences in the logarithms.) In the second equation in that box, the dependent variable has been changed to a difference, i.e. it equals (the log of) consumer spending in the current period minus (the log of) consumer spending in the previous period. The explanatory variables have not been changed. The estimated coefficient on consumer spending lagged once is exactly one higher in the first equation than in the second. This is because consumer spending lagged once has been subtracted from the right hand side of the second equation by the change of dependent variable.

The third equation in Box 4.6 is again identical to the previous two, except for a re-arrangement, this time among the explanatory variables. For consumer spending, the two levels have been replaced by one level and by a difference (the variable lagged once minus the variable lagged twice). For consumer incomes, the two levels have been replaced by a difference (income lagged once minus income lagged two periods) and also by a variable formed by subtracting income (lagged once) from spending (also lagged once). This is simply a re-arrangement. No new variables have been added nor existing ones removed, as can be judged from the coefficients on interest rates and the inflation rate, which are the same in all these equations. It is possible to confirm that the changes in the coefficients on the lagged consumer spending and lagged income variables are exactly what is needed to offset the effect of the re-arrangement.

Note that the re-arrangement has the effect of drastically reducing the equation R^2. (The R^2 measures the proportion of the variation in the dependent variable that is explained by the equation and so it can be interpreted as an indication of how well the equation fits the data.) This illustrates the dependence of the R^2 on the form of the equation, and shows that it can be misleading. It should only be used in conjunction with other statistics, preferably as part of a specification search such as that being described here.

The purpose of this re-arrangement is to make it possible to test the restrictions on this general form of the equation that are needed to give an equation that has the long-run form suggested in Section 4.3. To obtain that long-run form, the equation has to contain most of the variables from the third of the equations in Box 4.6, but not the first variable from that equation. A test can now be carried out to see if exclusion of that first variable is justified by the data. This test simply involves considering whether the t–value on that variable exceeds 1.96. Since it is only 1.37, the hypothesis that the coefficient on that variable is zero cannot be rejected and it is dropped from the specification. The equation is re-estimated without that variable, giving the version shown in Box 4.7.

In the long-run version of the equation, the growth rates of real consumer spending and real consumer incomes, and the level of interest rates and the inflation variable, are by assumption constants. (See Section 4.2 for explanation of an equation's long run.) Calling these constants k, k, r and p respectively (spending and incomes are assumed to rise at the same rate k), the long-run version of the equation is:

$$k = (-0.237 + 0.074)\,k - 0.148\,(\log C - \log (YD/PC))$$
$$+ (-0.00351 + 0.00164)\,r - 0.179\,p + 0.00960$$

Since k, r and p are by assumption constants, this long-run solution states that there is a constant difference between log C and log (YD/PC), i.e. a

Box 4.6   Rearrangement of the regression

First version of the equation   Second version of . . .

$\text{Log}(C_t) =$ $\text{Log}(C_t) - \log(C_{t-1}) =$

$0.628 \log(C_{t-1})$	$+ 0.316 \log(C_{t-2})$	$- 0.372 \log(C_{t-1}) \ldots$
(0.111)	(0.117) . . .	(0.111)
$t = 5.65$	$t = 2.70$	$-t = -3.35$

$+ 0.164 \log(RPDI_{t-1})$	$- 0.0869 \log(RPDI_{t-2})$	$+ 0.164 \log(RPDI_{t-1}) \ldots$
(0.084)	(0.0863) . . .	(0.084)
$t = 1.95$	$t = -1.01$	$t = 1.95$

$- 0.00364 \, RLB_{t-1}$	$+ 0.00159 \, RLB_{t-2}$	$+ 0.00364 \, RLB_{t-1} \ldots$
(0.00129)	(0.00130)	(0.00129)
$t = -2.82$	$t = 1.22$	$t = -2.82$

$- 0.263[\log(PC_{t-1}/PC_{t-2})$	$- 0.263[\log(PC_{t-1}/PC_{t-2})$
$+ 0.0057]$	$+ 0.0057]$
(0.195)	(0.195)
$t = -1.35$	$t = -1.35$

$- 0.196$	$- 0.196$
(0.150)	(0.150)
$t = -1.30$	$t = -1.30$

$R^2 = 0.996$	*Sums of squares*	$R^2 = 0.263$
$\overline{R}^2 = 0.996$	Total $= 2.780$	$\overline{R}^2 = 0.205$
	Explained $= 2.767$	
	Residual $= 0.0116$	

Standard error $= 0.01143$ Standard error $= 0.01143$
89 degrees of freedom, from   89 degrees of freedom, from
1956 Q4 to 1980 Q4   1956 Q4 to 1980 Q4

constant average propensity to consume. This constant ratio is low at high values of p, which is in line with the argument (mentioned in Section 4.3) that more savings are needed at high inflation rates in order to top up the real value of financial asset holdings.

There are two further changes to be made before this equation is in the form used in the macro-econometric model. These are included for completeness and do not illustrate any further methods of estimation. The changes are difficult to understand and readers who are not especially interested in the consumption equation can turn without loss of continuity to page 81, where there is a description of the tests applied at the end of the estimation procedure.

In addition to topping up financial assets to allow for inflation, it seems

Box 4.6 *continued*

. . . the equation	Third version of the equation
	$\log(C_t) - \log(C_{t-1}) =$
. . . $+ \ 0.316 \log(C_{t-2})$	$0.0211 \log(C_{t-1})$
(0.117)	(0.0154)
$t = 2.70$	$t = 1.37$
	$- \ 0.316[\log(C_{t-1}) - \log(C_{t-2})]$
	(0.117)
	$t = -2.70$
. . . $- \ 0.0869 \log(RPDI_{t-2})$	$+ \ 0.0869[\log(RPDI_{t-1}) - \log(RPDI_{t-2})]$
(0.0863)	(0.0863)
$t = -1.01$	$t = 1.01$
	$- \ 0.0772[\log(C_{t-1}) - \log(RPDI_{t-1})]$
	(0.0881)
	$t = -0.88$
. . . $+ \ 0.00159 \ RLB_{t-2}$	$- \ 0.00364 \ RLB_{t-1} \ + \ 0.00159 \ RLB_{t-2}$
(0.00130)	$(0.00129) \qquad (0.00130)$
$t = 1.22$	$t = -2.82 \qquad\quad t = 1.22$
	$- \ 0.263[\log(PC_{t-1}/PC_{t-2})$
	$\qquad\qquad + \ 0.0057]$
	(0.195)
	$t = -1.35$
	$- \ 0.196$
	(0.150)
	$t = -1.30$

Sums of squares	$R^2 = 0.263$	*Sums of squares*
Total $= 0.0158$	$\overline{R}^2 = 0.205$	Total $= 0.0158$
Explained $= 0.00415$		Explained $= 0.00415$
Residual $= 0.0116$		Residual $= 0.0116$

Standard error $= 0.01143$
89 degrees of freedom, from 1956 Q4 to 1980 Q4

likely that consumers tend to raise their asset holdings to allow for real growth in income. If they failed to do this, then over time their holdings of financial assets would become a very low, or very high, proportion of income. We therefore assume that, in the long run, nominal asset holdings grow at the same rate as nominal incomes. On this assumption it can be shown that, in the long run, the average propensity to consume equals a constant times the sum of the inflation rate and the trend real growth rate.

This assumption implies further restrictions on the equation. Recall that the 'inflation' variable in the equation was constructed to equal inflation plus trend growth. Thus, on our assumption, all the other items in the long-run form of the equation should sum to zero. We test this restriction in two stages. In the first stage, the steady state growth rate (2.3 per cent

Box 4.7   Restrictions imposed on the regression

$\log(C_t) - \log(C_{t-1}) =$

   $- 0.237[\log(C_{t-1}) - \log(C_{t-2})]$
   (0.102)
   $t = -2.32$

   $+ 0.0735[\log(\text{RPDI}_{t-1}) - \log(\text{RPDI}_{t-2})]$
   (0.0862)
   $t = 0.85$

   $- 0.148[\log(C_{t-1}) - \log(\text{RPDI}_{t-1})]$
   (0.072)
   $t = -2.05$

   $- 0.00351\,\text{RLB}_{t-1}$
   (0.00129)
   $t = -2.71$

   $+ 0.00164\,\text{RLB}_{t-2}$
   (0.00131)
   $t = 1.25$

   $- 0.179\,[\log(\text{PC}_{t-1}/\text{PC}_{t-2}) + 0.0057]$
   (0.186)
   $t = -0.96$

   $+ 0.00958$
   (0.00418)
   $t = 2.29$

$R^2 = 0.248$	*Sums of squares*
$\overline{R}^2 = 0.198$	Total $= 0.0158$
	Explained $= 0.00391$
	Residual $= 0.0119$

Standard error $= 0.01148$
90 degrees of freedom, from 1956 Q4 to 1980 Q4

per annum, or 0.57 per cent per quarter) is subtracted from the dependent variable and from the right hand side consumption and income growth variables. The resulting equation is shown in Box 4.7. Since no extra variables have been added, nor any excluded, all the coefficients are unchanged; only the constant term is altered. The first stage of the restrictions is now tested by checking the t-value on the constant term to see if it is less than 1.96, which it is. This indicates that the restriction is not rejected by the data at the 5 per cent confidence level.

The final part of the restrictions implies that the two interest rate variables, lagged once and lagged twice, can be replaced by their difference. This is tested by the re-arrangement procedure. The two interest rate variables are replaced by one level, the exclusion of which is to be tested, and by the difference. The coefficient on the level has a t-value of 2.48 (see Box 4.8), indicating that the hypothesis that it is zero is rejected at the 5 per

Box 4.7 *continued*

$\log(C_t) - \log(C_{t-1}) - 0.0057 =$

$\quad - 0.237[\log(C_{t-1}) - \log(C_{t-2}) - 0.0057]$
$\quad (0.102)$
$\quad t = -2.32$

$\quad + 0.0735[\log(RPDI_{t-1}) - \log(RPDI_{t-2}) - 0.0057]$
$\quad (0.0862)$
$\quad t = 0.85$

$\quad - 0.148[\log(C_{t-1}) - \log(RPDI_{t-1})]$
$\quad (0.072)$
$\quad t = -2.05$

$\quad - 0.00351\, RLB_{t-1}$
$\quad (0.00129)$
$\quad t = -2.71$

$\quad + 0.00164\, RLB_{t-2}$
$\quad (0.00131)$
$\quad t = 1.25$

$\quad - 0.179[\log(PC_{t-1}/PC_{t-2}) + 0.0057]$
$\quad (0.186)$
$\quad t = -0.96$

$\quad + 0.00295$
$\quad (0.00410)$
$\quad t = 0.72$

$R^2 = 0.248$	*Sums of squares*
$\overline{R}^2 = 0.198$	Total = 0.0158
	Explained = 0.00391
	Residual = 0.0119

Standard error = 0.01148
90 degrees of freedom, from 1956 Q4 to 1980 Q4

---

cent significance level (although not at the 1 per cent level). Strictly, this implies that the level of interest rates should be retained in the final version, but in view of the need to keep the form of the equations as simple as possible, and to keep the long run form simple, and given that the restriction is not rejected at the 1 per cent level, this variable has been excluded. The final version of the equation, with this extra, not strictly justifiable restriction, is shown in Box 4.9.

The final stage: tests of mis-specification

Before this equation can be approved for inclusion in the macro-econometric model that is to be used for forecasting and policy analysis later in this book, it must be subjected to the tests against mis-specification mentioned earlier. There are two such tests used here (a range of other tests are also possible). The first of these is a test against autocorrelation of

Box 4.8   Further restrictions on the regression

$\log(C_t) - \log(C_{t-1}) - 0.0057 =$

     $- 0.215[\log(C_{t-1}) - \log(C_{t-2}) - 0.0057]$
       (0.097)
       $t = -2.21$

     $+ 0.0547[\log(RPDI_{t-1}) - \log(RPDI_{t-2}) - 0.0057]$
       (0.0819)
       $t = 0.67$

     $- 0.182[\log(C_{t-1}) - \log(RPDI_{t-1})]$
       (0.053)
       $t = -3.42$

     $- 0.00369\ RLB_{t-1}$
       (0.00127)
       $t = -2.92$

     $+ 0.00183\ RLB_{t-2}$
       (0.00128)
       $t = 1.44$

     $- 0.211\ [\log(PC_{t-1}/PC_{t-2}) + 0.0057]$
       (0.180)
       $t = -1.17$

$R^2 = 0.244$	*Sums of squares*
$\overline{R}^2 = 0.202$	Total $= 0.0158$
	Explained $= 0.00384$
	Residual $= 0.0119$

Standard error $= 0.01145$
91 degrees of freedom, from 1956 Q4 to 1980 Q4

up to fifth order; although this is designed as a test against the apparently specific alternative hypothesis of up to fifth order autocorrelation, it is really just a general test to check that the error terms are random and that the equation is not mis-specified, because there is no particular reason to believe that autocorrelation is present. The computed value of the statistic for this test is 5.16. This is distributed χ^2 with 5 degrees of freedom which, as noted earlier, means (from tables in statistical texts) that we reject the hypothesis of no autocorrelation only when this statistic is over 11.07 (assuming a 5 per cent significance level). Thus this test provides no evidence of mis-specification.

The other type of test against mis-specification carried out here is a post-sample forecast test. This involves taking data for the explanatory variables for as many quarterly periods as possible beyond the end of the historical period used to calculate the parameter estimates (the *sample period*). These post-sample data for the explanatory variables are then used to compute forecasts for the dependent variable, on the assumption that the error term is zero in all these forecast periods. The resulting fore-

Box 4.8 *continued*

$\log(C_t) - \log(C_{t-1}) - 0.0057 =$

$\quad - 0.215[\log(C_{t-1}) - \log(C_{t-2}) - 0.0057]$
$\quad (0.097)$
$\quad t = -2.21$

$\quad + 0.0547[\log(RPDI_{t-1}) - \log(RPDI_{t-2}) - 0.0057]$
$\quad (0.0819)$
$\quad t = 0.67$

$\quad - 0.182[\log(C_{t-1}) - \log(RPDI_{t-1})]$
$\quad (0.053)$
$\quad t = -3.42$

$\quad + 0.00186\ RLB_{t-1}$
$\quad (0.00075)$
$\quad t = -2.48$

$\quad - 0.00183\ [RLB_{t-1} - RLB_{t-2}]$
$\quad (0.00128)$
$\quad t = -1.44$

$\quad - 0.211[\log(PC_{t-1}/PC_{t-2}) + 0.0057]$
$\quad (0.180)$
$\quad t = -1.17$

$R^2 = 0.244$
$\overline{R}^2 = 0.202$

Sums of squares
Total $= 0.0158$
Explained $= 0.00384$
Residual $= 0.0119$

Standard error $= 0.01145$
91 degrees of freedom, from 1956 Q4 to 1980 Q4

casts of the dependent variable are then compared with the actual historical data that is available for these periods. If the forecasts are close to the actual, then the equation passes the forecast test, and if they are far away from the actual, then the equation fails. The results of doing this for ten quarterly periods for the consumers' expenditure equation are shown in the table on page 97. In order to perform this test, it was of course necessary to restrict the sample period so that it ended ten quarters before the actual end of the available historical data series. It is possible to carry out a formal test of whether the forecast values are close to the actual; this test involves computing a statistic which is distributed as χ^2 with as many degrees of freedom as periods are being forecast, ten in this example. The computed value of this statistic is 5.35; it would have to exceed 18.31 to imply rejection of the hypothesis that the difference between forecast and actual was due merely to random errors (at the 5 per cent significance level). Thus this test, like the previous one, implies no evidence of misspecification.

This test has the drawback that it is based on the estimated size of the

Box 4.9   Last restrictions on the regression

$\log(C_t) - \log(C_{t-1}) - 0.0057 =$

    $- 0.239[\log(C_{t-1}) - \log(C_{t-2}) - 0.0057]$
    (0.099)
    $t = -2.40$

    $+ 0.110[\log(RPDI_{t-1}) - \log(RPDI_{t-2}) - 0.0057]$
    (0.081)
    $t = 1.36$

    $- 0.0806[\log(C_{t-1}) - \log(RPDI_{t-1})]$
    (0.0350)
    $t = -2.30$

    $- 0.00280 \, [RLB_{t-1} - RLB_{t-2}]$
    (0.00125)
    $t = -2.24$

    $- 0.419 \, [\log(PC_{t-1}/PC_{t-2}) + 0.0057]$
    (0.163)
    $t = -2.56$

$R^2 = 0.192$ *Sums of squares*
$\overline{R}^2 = 0.157$ Total $= 0.0158$
                         Explained $= 0.00304$
                         Residual $= 0.0127$

Standard error $= 0.01177$
92 degrees of freedom, from 1956 Q4 to 1980 Q4

variance of the error terms obtained from estimation over the historical sample period. Thus an equation that fits the historical data very badly may be likely to pass the post-sample forecast test, not because the forecasts are close to the actual data, but because the error terms have apparently been large in the past, and the post-sample forecast test statistic allows for this when indicating whether or not an equation has passed the test. When interpreting the results of post-sample forecast tests, it is advisable to check to see if this effect has occurred. In the example given here, the equation standard error is 0.01177 (which because the dependent variable is measured in logarithms implies about 1.2 per cent); this provides an estimate of the (square root of) the variance of the equation's error term. There is no formal measure of whether this is a large or small standard error, but a judgement of whether it is large or not can be made by comparing it with the average change in consumers' expenditure over the estimation period. This suggests that the standard error is neither exceptionally small nor very large, implying that the forecast test is a reasonably good guide to the forecasting ability of the equation.

A further drawback to this type of forecast test is that it uses data for the lagged dependent variable (and for all the other explanatory variables which, when an actual forecast is being made, will have to be predicted using the equations of the model). This type of forecast is called a static test, because of its use of data. When the forecast values are used instead of data for the lagged dependent variable, the test is known as *dynamic tracking* and the forecasts produced in such a test will almost certainly fit the data much less well than those produced by a static test. It is also possible to carry out a dynamic test of the whole macro-econometric model, in which predicted values, not data, are used for all endogenous variables.

4.6 Estimation of other equations in the macro-econometric model

The previous section described in detail the estimation of the consumers' expenditure equation, as an example of estimation in practice. No detailed description of the estimation of the other equations in the small macro-econometric model will be given, although their specification was discussed in Section 4.3, and full results for all the equations are included in Appendix 1, including standard errors and figures for the tests of mis-specification described in the previous section. For ease of reference the long run versions of the equations are given here, in Box 4.10.

All the equations were estimated using ordinary least squares with the exception of the money demand equation which, as noted in Section 4.4, was estimated using two stage least squares to allow for short term interest rates being endogenous. In many of the equations a detailed specification search like that carried out for the consumer spending equation was used, but this was not done for the less important equations.

Some of the equations shown in Appendix 1 have no standard errors or test statistics. These equations are either identities which are, of course, true by definition and are not estimated, or they are *technical* equations. Most macro-econometric models contain some technical equations, which instead of being estimated, are imposed by the model builder, usually because they reflect directly observable institutional arrangements. An example is given by the calculation of the adjustment to factor cost (working variable F) as a constant times each expenditure component. These constants are based on the proportion of net expenditure taxes allocated to each component of demand in 1980, which can be observed directly from published CSO statistics. This contrasts with the consumers' expenditure equation and other equations that reflect behaviour represented by unobservable parameters; such parameters have to be estimated.

4.7 Further reading

The four equation model used in Section 4.2 is based on the form of the small open economy model presented by Buiter and Miller (1981), and although this article demands a fair amount of mathematical ability, it contains a very clear description of the model's implications (note that

Box 4.10   Long run versions (1) of the model equations

The symbol '$\triangle$' indicates a rate of change. See note (2) for formal definition. Division is denoted by '/', '$\div$', or by a horizontal line. Notes are given on page 88.

1   UK prices   = world prices $\div$ the exchange rate
     PC   =   /WWPI $\div$ EER

2   Real demand for   =   effect   –   effect of   –   effect of   –   constant
     high-powered   of output   interest   structural
     money   rates   change
     log(MO/PC)   = $1.57 \times \log\text{GDPE}$ – $1.23 \times \text{RLB}$ – $0.0057 \times \text{TIME}$ –   11.6

3   Rate of change   = UK interest   –   world interest
     of exchange rate   rates   rates
     $\triangle$EER   = $\dfrac{\text{RLB}}{400}$ – $\dfrac{\text{RSW}}{400}$

4   Change in   = change in   +   productivity
     average earnings   prices   growth
     $\triangle$WSI   = $\triangle$PC   +   0.0057

5   Competitiveness   = UK wages divided by $\div$ world prices
                          trend productivity   in sterling
     COMP   =   (WSI/PROD) $\div$ (WWPI/EER)

6   Non-oil exports   =   effect of   –   effect of
     at constant prices   world trade   competitiveness
     log X   = $0.577 \times \log\text{XWM}$ – $0.476 \times \log\text{COMP}$

7   Export prices   =   effect of world   +   effect of UK
                             prices   costs
     log PX   = $0.639 \times \log(\text{WWPI/EER})$ + $0.405 \times \log(\text{WSI/PROD})$

8   Stock of private   = constant
     fixed investment at
     constant prices as a
     proportion of
     output
     log(KI/GDPE)   =   6.18

9   Stock of   = constant   –   effect of real
     inventories at   interest rates
     constant prices as a
     proportion of
     output
     log(KII/GDPE)   =   0.330   – $0.914 \times \left(\dfrac{\text{RLB}}{400} - \triangle\text{PC} \right)$

10   Change in   =   change in   –   productivity
     employment   output (GDP)   growth
     $\triangle$ET   = $\triangle$GDPE   –   0.0057

11   Personal   = Employment times   +   interest receipts
     disposable income   average earnings
     at current prices   (net of tax)
     YD   = $\text{ET} \times \dfrac{\text{WSI}}{100} \times (1 - T)$ + $\dfrac{\text{RLB}}{400} \times \text{GOVTB}$ + $\dfrac{\text{RSW}}{400} \times \text{OJ}$ (see note 4)

Box 4.10 *continued*

---

12 Real consumer = depends inversely on the
    spending as a   savings needed to top up
    proportion of   the fall in the real value
    real incomes   of assets due to inflation,
    $\log(C/(YD \times$ and on the savings
    $100/PC))$ needed to keep up with
                       real growth
                   = $-5.199 \times (\triangle PC + 0.0057)$

13 Non-oil imports =   effect of   +   effect of   – constant
    at constant prices   UK output   competitiveness
    log M   = $3.25 \times \log GDPE$ + $0.373 \times \log COMP$ – 27.3   (see
                                                                         note 3)

14 Current account = non-oil   –   non-oil   + net interest +   net oil
    balance   exports   imports   receipts   trade
    BAL   = $X \times \dfrac{PX}{100}$ – $M \times \dfrac{WWPI}{EER}$ + $\dfrac{RSW}{400} \times OJ$ + $O \times \dfrac{POILWC}{EER}$

15 Capital account:
    Change in private = current account – change in
    net foreign assets   balance   reserves
    $OJ - OJ_{t-1}$ =   BAL   –   DRESV

16 GDP, expenditure = Consumer + non-oil – non-oil + net oil + government
    measure   spending   exports   imports   trade   spending
    GDPE   =   C   +   X   –   M   +   O   +   G

                     + change in   +   net   +   investment
                        inventories   private   to offset
                                         investment   depreciation
                     + $KII - KII_{t-1}$ + $KI - KI_{t-1}$ + $4610 \times (1.009)^{TIME}$
                     –   factor
                          cost
                          adjustment
                     – $0.158 \times C$

17 Public sector = govern- +   debt   –   income
    borrowing   ment   interest   tax
    requirement   spending   payments   receipts
    PSBR   = $G \times \dfrac{PC}{100}$ + $\dfrac{RLB}{400} \times GOVTB$ – $T \times ET \dfrac{WSI}{100}$
                     – expenditure
                       tax
                       receipts
                     – $\dfrac{TREF}{100} \times 0.158 \times C$ (see note 4)

18 Government bond = borrowing – high-powered + change in
   issues   money issues   reserves
   $GOVTB - GOVTB_{t-1}$ =   PSBR   – $(MO - MO_{t-1})$ + DRESV

Box 4.10   *continued*

Notes: (1) These long run versions are conditional on the right hand side variables having reached their steady-state levels.

(2) The symbol '$\triangle$' indicating rate of change, is defined formally as:
$$\triangle X = \log X_t - \log X_{t-1}$$
which is almost exactly equal to:
$$(X_t - X_{t-1})/X_{t-1}$$

(3) The full import equation used in the model includes an additional term, not shown here, which allows for import penetration into the UK increasing in line with the ratio of OECD trade to OECD output. Also, the coefficient for COMP shown here is the average of the coefficients for world prices and UK costs that appear in the model equation.

(4) Unemployment and other social security benefits, which affect both personal disposable income and the PSBR, are allowed for in the full model but are omitted here.

Other minor simplifications, e.g. to the factor cost adjustment, have also been made in order to simplify the presentation in this box.

many of the properties of the model are discussed in Chapter 8, not in this chapter). The IS and LM curves used in that model are covered in almost every introductory macro-economics textbook; see for example Begg, Fischer and Dornbush (1984), Chapter 24. That text (Chapter 28) also deals briefly, in a non-mathematical way, with some of the effects of the exchange rate equation introduced in this chapter.

For econometrics, dealt with in the later sections of this chapter, a good introduction for non-specialists is Stewart (1976). A standard introductory mathematical treatment of much of the relevant theory appears in Johnston (1972), which avoids the use of matrix algebra in presenting some of the basic results. A similar, widely used text is Maddala (1977), and Theil (1971) provides a more advanced treatment. However, none of these covers explicitly the specification search technique illustrated in Section 4.5. For this, see Harvey (1981). While most of these textbooks include some worked examples, the choice of textbooks devoted exclusively to applied econometrics is relatively limited; Wallis (1979) is a standard text.

5

Preparing a forecast

This chapter describes how economic forecasts are prepared. As illustration, a forecast is built up using the macro-econometric model derived in Chapter 4. At every stage judgement is necessary, and information from conjunctural analysis is of importance.

5.1 Forecasts with one equation

To illustrate the process of forecasting with a macro-econometric model, we start with a single equation. This is the equation for the consumer price index, variable PC. The long-run version of this equation is shown at the top of Box 4.10. The full version of the equation, which is needed for forecasting, is shown near the beginning of the model listing in Appendix 1, and is reproduced in Box 5.1.

To demonstrate the use of this equation, assume that we have full historical data for all variables up to and including 1983 third quarter, and no information for later periods; the equation is to be used to produce a forecast for the consumer prices index in 1983 fourth quarter. This assumption implies a sudden move from a period of full data to a period of no data. Chapter 3 demonstrated that a clean break of this type does not occur in practice, but the assumption will be useful in this section to help demonstrate how forecasts are made. It is abandoned in Section 5.3,

---

Box 5.1 The consumer prices equation

$$
\begin{aligned}
PC_t = \exp [&\log(PC_{t-1}) \\
&+ 0.636 \log(PC_{t-1}/PC_{t-2}) \\
&+ 0.0600 \log(TREF_t) \\
&- 0.0750 \log(TREF_{t-1}) \\
&+ 0.0199 \log(TREF_{t-4}) \\
&- 0.0275 \log (PC_{t-1}/(WWPI_{t-1}/EER_{t-1})) \\
&+ 0.1144 \log(GDPE_{t-1}/(1.0057^{(TIME_t - 32)})) \\
&- 1.08] \\
&+ \text{error term}
\end{aligned}
$$

Note: 'log' indicates logarithms to base e (natural logarithms). 'exp' indicates an exponent, i.e. e is to be raised to the power of the value in the brackets following 'exp'.

Table 5.1   Data for consumer prices forecast

Year	Quarter	PC	TREF	GDPE	EER	WWPI	TIME
1982	1	117.3	138.8	49234	94.9	115.5	109
	2	119.8	131.9	49475	94.0	117.1	110
	3	121.3	134.7	49438	95.2	118.8	111
	4	122.7	134.3	50861	92.7	119.9	112
1983	1	124.7	136.9	51591	83.9	121.5	113
	2	125.8	133.6	50627	87.7	123.2	114
	3	127.4	134.2	50941	88.3	124.9	115

which shows how the information from conjunctural analysis is incorporated into the forecast.

To use this equation for forecasting, a value is needed for each of the items on the right hand side. The first item, log PC_{t-1}, is the logarithm of the consumer prices index in the quarter previous to that for which we are preparing the forecast. In our example, this means the logarithm of the index in 1983 third quarter. From Table 5.1, the index was 127.4 in that quarter, and use of a pocket calculator gives its natural logarithm as 4.847. For the second item, log (PC_{t-1}/PC_{t-2}), two values of the index are needed. Reading these from Table 5.1 gives log (127.4/125.8), which equals 0.0126.

The third item on the right hand side of the equation is log $TREF_t$. The variable TREF is an index of the value of indirect tax receipts, i.e. revenue from VAT, duty on petrol and beer, etc. The subscript t indicates a current period value, which in this example means 1983 fourth quarter. By assumption, historical data for this quarter are not available so a forecast value for TREF must be used.

Because indirect tax rates are fixed as part of government policy making and not as a direct result of private sector behaviour, TREF is treated as an exogenous variable. There is no fixed rule about the determination of forecasts of exogenous variables. In some cases forecasters use a formal model, treated separately from the main macro-econometric model; in other cases they rely on judgement and extraneous information. The use of a separate model is particularly common for world variables. For example the London Business School uses a small model containing about five variables to predict world output, prices etc.; these projections are then fed into the UK macro-econometric model as exogenous variables. For tax rates, a more eclectic approach is often used, taking account of information about the broad stance of government policy, about particular prejudices (e.g. governments have been reluctant to reduce mortgage interest tax relief), and about administrative delays in implementing tax changes.

In forming a prediction for TREF, an economist with full information up to 1983 third quarter and none beyond then would note than no announcement of any tax change had been made, nor was there any obvious pressure on the government's announced targets to suggest that any change might be necessary. So there would be a reasonably high probability that indirect tax rates in the fourth quarter would be the same as in the third quarter, and a forecast could be prepared on that assumption.

The indirect taxes indexed by TREF fall into two broad categories: the *ad valorem* taxes such as VAT, revenue on which rises automatically in line with inflation; and specific duties, like the taxes on beer and wine, receipts from which respond only to volume changes. The specific duties are usually raised once a year, in the budget, to ensure that revenue from them keeps up with inflation. This produces an irregular pattern of receipts over the year, with roughly the same pattern repeated annually. This pattern is reflected in the movements of TREF. To allow for this, it is convenient to use a simple technical equation for this exogenous variable:

$$TREF_t = TREF_{t-4} \times PC_{t-1}/PC_{t-5}$$

Noting from Table 5.1 that TREF had a value of 134.3 in 1982 fourth quarter and also reading off the relevant values for PC, this expression gives a prediction for TREF of 134.3 × 127.4/121.3 which equals 141.1. This is our forecast for TREF in the fourth quarter of 1983; its logarithm is 4.950. It must be emphasized that the most important stage in preparing this forecast for TREF was the decision to assume that tax rates would be unaltered. Having made that decision, the equation is a convenient way of allowing for the irregular path taken by TREF between quarters. Were a change in indirect taxes expected (other than the usual annual uprating in line with inflation), this equation would be invalid and some other way of forecasting TREF would be needed.

We have carried out calculations for the first three items on the right hand side of the equation for the consumer prices index PC. The next two items, $\log TREF_{t-1}$ and $\log TREF_{t-4}$, refer to the logarithms of TREF in 1983 third quarter and in 1982 fourth quarter respectively. These can be computed from the historical data given in Table 5.1. The following two items also depend only on historical data (and on the variable TIME, which simply increases by one every quarter), and so can be calculated using the information given in Table 5.1. The final item is a constant term which involves no variables. The results of all these calculations are shown in Box 5.2.

One item in the equation remains to be dealt with. This is the error term. In Chapter 4 the error term was described as including many unobservable factors. Their combined effect can be treated as random with an average value of zero. To prepare a forecast of PC in 1983 fourth quarter, a projection for the error term in 1983 fourth quarter is needed, just as a prediction was needed for TREF. Since the error term has an average value of zero, the obvious forecast for it is zero. It must be emphasized that this forecast is a best guess made from a state of ignorance. The actual value for the error term, when full data for PC and all other variables become available, is almost certain to be non-zero. Despite this, zero is the best

Box 5.2   Forecasting with the consumer prices equation

	Computed value
$PC_t = \exp[\log(PC_{t-1})$	4.847
$+ 0.636 \log(PC_{t-1}/PC_{t-2})$	$+ 0.636 \times 0.0126$
$+ 0.0600 \log(TREF_t)$	$+ 0.0600 \times 4.950$
$- 0.0750 \log(TREF_{t-1})$	$- 0.0750 \times 4.899$
$+ 0.0199 \log(TREF_{t-4})$	$+ 0.0199 \times 4.900$
$- 0.0275 \log(PC_{t-1}/(WWPI_{t-1}/EER_{t-1}))$	$- 0.0275 \times 4.501$
$+ 0.1144 \log(GDPE_{t-1}/(1.0057^{(TIME_t - 32)}))$	$+ 0.1144 \times 10.361$
$- 1.08]$	$- 1.08$

Sum	4.8625
Exponent of sum	129.3
+ error term	?

Note: 'log' indicates logarithms to base e (natural logarithms). 'exp' indicates an exponent, i.e. e is to be raised to the power of the value in the brackets following 'exp'.

guess that can be made because the assumptions about the error term imply that positive values are just as likely as negative ones.

Under certain special circumstances, these arguments will not hold. In particular, information from conjunctural analysis will sometimes provide a strong reason for choosing a non-zero value for the error term. The cases which require non-zero values are considered in Section 5.3; here we complete the calculation of the forecast for PC on the assumption that the error term is zero.

Adding up all the figures shown in Box 5.2, we obtain a total of 4.8625. On the first line of the equation for PC, the characters 'exp' appear, indicating that e must be raised to the power of the value given in the brackets that follow. (The notation exp is short for 'exponent', because the item in brackets is the exponent to which e is being raised.) This is equivalent to taking the (natural) antilog of the value in brackets. Use of a pocket calculator shows that e raised to the power 4.8625 is 129.3. To this must be added the forecast for the error term, but for the moment this has been taken as zero. Thus 129.3 is our forecast for the consumer prices index, PC, in 1983 fourth quarter.

This completes the forecast for one variable, one period ahead. Two key issues remain: the problem of predicting further into the future, and the difficulties of forecasting several (or many) interrelated variables. The second of these issues is postponed to the next section, but the first is considered here.

We retain the assumption that there are no historical data for 1983 fourth quarter. This appears to cause a problem, for these data are needed to prepare a projection for PC in 1984 first quarter. (Recall that when making a forecast for 1983 fourth quarter we drew heavily on historical data for the previous quarter.) This problem is solved readily, by using forecast values for 1983 fourth quarter in place of data values. Similarly, projections for 1984 first quarter can then be used to make a forecast for the second quarter. This process can be continued into the indefinite future and is fundamental to forecasting with macro-econometric models.

---

1. Start with historical data.
2. Predict one quarter ahead (or one year if using an annual model).
3. Use that prediction as if it were data to forecast the next quarter, and so on.

5.2 Forecasts using many equations

This section explains how forecasts of many variables are generated from a macro-econometric model containing many equations. The small macro-econometric model presented in Chapter 4 is used to illustrate the methods. We continue to assume that full data are available up to 1983 third quarter with no data beyond then, and we assume that all forecasts of error terms are zero. These assumptions are relaxed in the next section.

All the equations referred to are shown in the full listing of the model given in Appendix 1, and the long-run versions of the equations are shown in Box 4.10 at the end of Chapter 4. The preparation of a forecast for PC, using the first equation in the model, was described above. In the second equation, which is for interest rates RLB, the only current period variable appearing on the right hand side is MO_t. This variable is treated as exogenous in the model and a judgemental forecast for it is prepared by assuming that it grows in line with the government's announced targets for the growth of money supply. All the other variables on the right hand side, such as PC_{t-2}, are lagged variables and so historical data for them are available. (There are also quarterly 'dummies' in this equation. The dummy Q1 takes a value of 1 in the first quarter of the year and zero in other quarters; Q2 and Q3 are defined analagously.) Using the exogenous forecast for MO and historical data for other items, the forecast for RLB can be computed on a calculator or by computer.

The next equation is for the effective exchange rate, EER. On the right hand side of this equation is RSW_t (world interest rates), which is exogenous, and $XEER_t$ (the expectation of the value to be taken by the exchange rate one quarter into the future), which we are also treating as exogenous for the moment. Forecasts of these exogenous variables are, as above, obtained by separate equations or by judgement (Section 5.4 gives further details). One further item is needed : a value for RLB_t, i.e. a projection of interest rates in 1983 fourth quarter. Continuing to assume there is no partial information available from conjunctural analysis, there is an obvious source for this projection : the forecast of interest rates in 1983 fourth quarter already obtained from the previous equation. This is the value that would be used, allowing calculation of the forecast for EER.

The next equation, for the average wages and salaries index WSI, has only lagged variables on the right hand side. It therefore needs only historical data in order to generate a forecast for WSI in 1983 fourth quarter. By contrast the following equation, for competitiveness (variable COMP), depends on current period variables WSI_t and EER_t, and also on the current period exogenous variable $WWPI_t$ (world wholesale prices in foreign currency). As for the EER forecast, it is necessary to use the projections of WSI and EER that have already been made, plus an exogenous forecast of WWPI, in order to calculate a forecast for COMP in 1983 fourth quarter.

A pattern is now beginning to emerge. Each of the equations in the model has up to three different types of variable on the right hand side: lagged variables; current period exogenous variables; and current period endogenous variables for which projections have already been obtained from earlier equations. A method of forecasting 1983 fourth quarter with the whole macro-econometric model is thus to use each of the equations in turn to produce a forecast for the variable on the left hand side. That forecast is then available for use on the right hand side of another equation, later on in the process.

The whole of the macro-econometric model set out in Chapter 4 can be used for forecasting in this way. This process is known as *solving* the model. There is one equation for each of the endogenous variables in the model. When forecasts for 1983 fourth quarter have been obtained for all the endogenous variables, it is possible to return to the start of the model and to produce a forecast for 1984 first quarter. When doing this, the forecasts previously obtained for 1983 fourth quarter are used as if they were historical data. After this a projection can be made for 1984 second quarter, and so on into the indefinite future, just as was outlined in the previous section when only one equation was being used. For every quarter being forecast, projections of exogenous variables are needed, obtained using the methods outlined above.

This process for preparing forecasts can be applied to any starting point, provided historical data are available up to that starting point. Later in this chapter the forecast beginning in 1983 fourth quarter is described in more detail and there is a description of the method for generating your own forecasts, using the macro-econometric model of Chapter 4 but starting from a later date. Here, we consider a complication present in most macro-econometric models (but avoided by the model of Chapter 4) and in the next section we discuss circumstances when error terms are not set to zero.

The remainder of this section is slightly more difficult than the earlier parts and can be omitted without losing the continuity of the discussion.

In the process described above for solving the macro-econometric model of Chapter 4, the forecasts produced from some of the equations at the beginning of the model were used on the right hand side of equations later in the model. To be able to do this, it was necessary to use the equations in a certain order. For example if we tried to use the equation for EER before the equation for RLB, there would be no forecast for RLB available for use on the right hand side of the EER equation.

For some macro-econometric models the solution method given earlier cannot be used whatever the order of the equations. For example, suppose one of the items on the right hand side of the RLB equation was the current period value of the exchange rate, EER_t. Since the current period value of interest rates RLB_t appears on the right hand side of the EER equation, no amount of re-ordering would make it possible to use one equation, then the next, and obtain a solution.

All macro-econometric models in which some endogenous variables depend on others are known as *simultaneous*. When it is possible to find an order for the equations that allows use of the solution method described earlier, a model is said to have the special property of being *recursive*. Where no such ordering exists, a macro-econometric model is sometimes called *fully* simultaneous. The model of Chapter 4 is recursive, while all the models used by the main forecasting groups are fully simultaneous.

To solve fully simultaneous macro-econometric models, various methods are available but a technique called 'Gauss-Seidel' is in almost universal use. Under this method, solution of the model starts just as for a recursive model. When an endogenous variable appears on the right hand side of an equation and no forecast for it has yet been generated from an earlier equation, a preliminary guess is used – usually the value from the previous quarterly time period. In this way, all the equations in the model are used to produce forecasts, as in the recursive case. However, where it has been necessary to use a preliminary guess for a variable, this will not be the same (except by sheer chance) as the forecast value produced later in the process by the equation for that variable. The next stage is to repeat the process, again computing forecasts from each equation, but this time instead of using preliminary guesses for right hand side endogenous variables, the forecasts just obtained from the equations are used. This generates a new set of forecasts. The process is then repeated again, using the new set of forecasts on the right hand side. This repetition, using the latest set of forecasts each time, carries on until the results are altered very little by repeating the process. 'Very little' might mean 0.1 per cent, or some other amount chosen by the forecaster – this is a matter for judgement, and different values may be used for different variables. The number of times the process has to be repeated depends on the model, on the ordering of the equations, and on the forecaster's choice of the 'little' percentage. In the LBS model of some five hundred variables, between eight and twenty repetitions are typical during forecasting. These are called *iterations*.

Once this iterative process is complete, a forecast has been obtained for all the variables for a single time period. These forecast values are then used as if they were historical data to allow a similar process to be used for

computing a forecast for the next time period, and so on into the future.
To produce a forecast for five years, i.e. twenty quarters, into the future
with an average of say twelve iterations for each quarter means re-
calculating each equation in the model two hundred and forty times.
Together with associated reading to and from files, this can take an appre-
ciable amount of computer time and, if carried out on-line, of actual time
depending on the size and type of the model and the computer. The
rational expectations and optimal control methods described at the end of
this chapter and in Chapter 8 usually involve repeated generations of such
forecasts and can thus take much longer.

5.3 Reasons for non-zero forecasts of error terms

In Section 5.1 it was argued that the best guess for the future value of error
terms equalled the average value, zero, unless there were special circumstances. This section explains some of those special circumstances.

Conjunctural analysis provides a very important reason for choosing
non-zero error terms. Non-zero error terms chosen because of information from conjunctural analysis have a justification in statistical theory
because there is extra information available, additional to that provided
by the items in the equation. By contrast it is often difficult to reconcile
other reasons for choosing non-zero error terms with statistical theory.

We will use the example of an economist in mid-December 1983 preparing a forecast for 1983 fourth quarter. Earlier in this chapter we assumed
that historical data were available up to and including the third quarter,
with nothing beyond. Chapter 3 indicated that in practice, an economist in
mid-December 1983 would have a considerable amount of extra information, and we now discuss how this is used to choose non-zero values for
error terms. (Note that strictly there are not full historical data available
even for the third quarter, but data or good estimates are available for all
variables by mid-December and this complication is ignored.)

The forecast for the consumer prices index PC in the fourth quarter of
1983, calculated in the first section of this chapter, was 129.3. This was
based on information up to the third quarter only. The estimate for the
fourth quarter obtained from the conjunctural analysis described in
Chapter 3 was 128.8. This suggests that a negative error term, of about
– 0.5 per cent, should be added to the model forecast of PC, instead of the
zero error term used earlier in this chapter. Using this non-zero error term,
the forecast produced by the equation becomes identical to the estimate
derived from conjunctural analysis.

The justification for choosing an error term not equal to the average,
zero, is that conjunctural analysis has provided information about the
fourth quarter, based on the retail prices index and other sources, which
is not contained elsewhere in the equation. Conjunctural analysis also
suggests non-zero error terms in the fourth quarter of 1983 for two other
variables, consumers' expenditure and imports. (See Chapter 3.) There is

no information from the conjunctural analysis to suggest non-zero error terms on these or any other variables in 1984 first quarter or in any later quarters. In spite of this, the information from conjunctural analysis continues to have an effect in all the later quarters. This is because the projections for future quarters depend on the forecast for 1983 fourth quarter. For example, because PC in that quarter has been lowered, the projection for PC in 1984 first quarter will be reduced significantly.

In addition to use of information from conjunctural analysis, there is another common reason for using non-zero values for error terms. This is when the forecaster is aware that, had an equation been used to produce forecasts a year or so earlier, it would have tended to underpredict or over-predict. As illustration, consider again an economist in mid-December 1983, using the macro-econometric model of Chapter 4 to produce a fore-cast. This economist has historical data or good estimates for all the model variables up to 1983 third quarter. A sensible check on the equations is to pretend that data for the dependent variables are only available for the periods used during estimation (which ended on 1980 fourth quarter); to produce 'forecasts' for the quarters from then up to 1983 third quarter; and to subtract those 'forecasts' from the observed, historical data for those quarters. These differences are known as *residuals*. For an equation performing well residuals should be small with a mixture of positive and negative values; a badly performing equation would give large residuals tending to be mainly positive or mainly negative. The residuals in the table below are computed using outturn data for all right hand side variables, including the lagged dependent variable. Chapter 6 gives details of alternative ways to compute the residuals.

Typically, forecasting groups test the randomness of residuals both during estimation, as described in Chapter 4, and again before the start of each forecast. The usual reason for doing the test twice is that extra histori-cal data generally become available in between estimation and forecasting, allowing a larger number of post-sample residuals to be tested. (There may

Quarter	Consumers' expenditure, variable C £m. 1980 prices	Stock of inventories, variable KII £m. 1980 prices
1981 1	− 88	− 93
2	− 342	− 862
3	− 214	+ 374
4	− 95	− 210
1982 1	− 213	− 160
2	− 121	− 74
3	+ 257	− 1031
4	+ 294	− 766
1983 1	− 551	+ 104
2	+ 359	− 1331

also be data revisions.) In principle, it is desirable to re-estimate a model on the latest data before each forecast; in practice limited resources prevent this.

A simple inspection of the residuals in the table gives little guidance as to whether these equations are performing well or badly. However, formal test statistics, described in Chapter 4, suggest that the residuals on the consumers' expenditure equation can be attributed to random factors, while those on the stock of inventories equation cannot. An intuitive inter-pretation can be placed on this evidence from the formal tests. The level of consumer spending in 1983 was about £36,000m. a quarter at 1980 prices, so all of the residuals except that in 1983 first quarter are less than 1 per cent of the variable being forecast, and many of the residuals are a much smaller percentage. By contrast, four of the residuals on the equation for the stock of inventories are more than 1 per cent of the variable being forecast – the level of KII was about £65,000m. at 1980 prices in each quarter of 1983. All four of these big residuals (in 1981 second quarter, 1982 third and fourth quarters, and 1983 second quarter) are of the same sign, which adds to the doubt about their randomness.

Given the formal tests, a forecaster examining these residuals would probably conclude that the equation for consumers' expenditure was per-forming satisfactorily, while that for the stock of inventories was unsatis-factory. Since the residuals (particularly the large ones) on the inventories equation mainly seem to be negative, i.e. the forecast has been too high, a forecaster might consider using negative error terms when calculating the forecast, instead of zero values. In Section 5.1 it was argued that use of non-zero error terms in a forecast can only be justified in special circum-stances. Does some special circumstance apply here?

It is possible to find reasons why the equation for KII has overpredicted over the period from early 1981 to mid-1983. The equation is specified in a way that tends to return inventory levels to a given proportion of GDP (with the proportion being higher when real interest rates are low and vice versa; see Chapter 4). This proportion was estimated using data prior to 1981. It seems that with the widespread introduction of new computer-based stock-keeping techniques, many companies are now able to operate at a much lower stock:sales ratio than was possible in the past. There is evidence to support this view from newspaper articles and from discus-sions with those involved in business. In addition changes in the corpora-tion tax regime in 1980 and again in early 1984 have made stockholding less attractive. This suggests that the equation is likely to overpredict the level of inventories and to go on doing so indefinitely.

On this analysis, the equation is unsatisfactory because it omits two factors – one due to technology and one due to taxation – neither of which was present during the period covered by the data used for estima-tion. This suggests that a new equation should be specified and estimated, incorporating these extra two factors. It is tempting for the forecaster in such circumstances to argue that the period from early 1981 up to mid-1983 provides the only information about these new factors, and this is too short to give sensible estimates for the two extra parameters. An alternative to re-estimating the equation would be to use judgement to guess the size of the effect from these two factors, and to set the error term in future periods equal to this guess.

Using a non-zero error term in these circumstances can be defended because it is quick and easy. Moreover, it could be argued that the use of judgement to choose this non-zero value was the only action open to the forecaster in this case, because of the short number of data periods available since the change occurred and because technological change is always difficult to quantify.

It is not always impractical to re-specify and re-estimate an equation in these circumstances. For example, many of the equations for flows of financial assets in the Treasury model were estimated prior to abolition of exchange controls and required considerable judgemental adjustment after the controls were removed. The London Business School, using only a short run of data for the period after the abolition of the controls, has estimated a formal model of behaviour in the absence of the controls by assuming that people and institutions regard foreign assets in an analogous way to their view about risky domestic assets.

When it is possible to use formal re-specification and re-estimation to replace an equation that is performing badly because of changed circumstances, then this is the statistically efficient method and should be used in preference to judgemental choice of non-zero error terms. However, even in the largest forecasting organizations this is not always done, because resources are limited and other activities may take priority.

It sometimes occurs that equations are found to perform badly over the recent past, even though there is no apparent institutional, technological or other change that is relevant. In such circumstances, it may simply be that the equation is an unsatisfactory representation of the way the economy works, even though it was successfully specified, estimated and tested. When this occurs, a new specification (and/or estimation method) needs to be chosen and used to generate a replacement equation, although in the absence of any obvious change it may not be clear why the original specification was unsatisfactory. As before, the claims on resources from other projects may prevent such an equation being replaced as soon as the unsatisfactory performance is observed, particularly if its role in the model is relatively unimportant. In such cases, the forecaster will again choose judgementally non-zero future error terms, perhaps using some rule of thumb such as averaging the last ten residuals observed over the recent past.

We have discussed two main reasons for using non-zero future error terms: information from conjunctural analysis; and bad performance over the recent past, which may or may not be attributable to some change. A third reason also sometimes causes forecasters to impose non-zero error terms in their forecasts. This is when the projections from the equations are inconsistent with the forecaster's prior beliefs about the future.

The use of non-zero error terms to bring results from the equations – which are based on formal analysis of historical data – into line with a forecaster's own beliefs is very difficult to justify. Nevertheless it is done fairly often. One possible justification is that the forecaster feels that the equations, even if they are properly estimated and pass appropriate econometric tests, may have some implausible properties which show up only when they are used to forecast some way into the future. In this case, re-specification and re-estimation of the equations to bring them into line with the forecaster's view of plausible properties, while retaining their ability to explain the past, would be better than imposition of non-zero error terms by the forecaster. However, it is always quicker to impose a non-zero error term than to replace an equation.

One further reason for using non-zero error terms occurs when fore-casters wish to overcome *internal* inconsistencies in the results from a macro-econometric model. For example, there is no mechanism in the model of Chapter 4 to prevent company spending (on investment and stocks) from continually outgrowing company income (from profits, rent etc.). All the company equations have been derived and tested, and as individual equations they appear satisfactory (apart from the problem with the stocks equation, which is dealt with as described above). In spite of this they could produce inconsistent results when taken together. If this happened, the forecaster might use non-zero error terms to keep spending growing in line with income. A more satisfactory approach is to specify groups of equations such as these in a way which prevents inconsistent forecasts being produced.

The projections of error terms used for forecasting are known by several alternative names. They are sometimes called *constant adjustments*, or *con adjustments*, or simply *adjustments*. In the following section we refer to them as constant adjustments because this name is used commonly by forecasters in the UK, although the projections of error terms are often not constant over time.

5.4 The forecast

The earlier sections of this chapter have indicated three types of information required to make a forecast, in addition to the macro-econometric model itself. The first type of information consists of historical data up to the latest available date; the second consists of projections of exogenous variables for every period covered by the forecast; and the third consists of constant adjustments (predictions of error terms) for all those periods.

To make a forecast, the latest historical data is loaded to the computer, either by hand from press releases and other CSO publications, or from data tapes. Projections of exogenous variables, obtained using equations separate from the main model or by eclectic methods (as described earlier) are also loaded. If no computer is being used, all this information must be tabulated. This is done in Table 5.2 for historical data and in Table 5.3 for projections of exogenous variables.

Using this information, one-period ahead forecasts are computed on the assumption that all constant adjustments are zero, as described in Section 5.2. Comparing the results with estimates from conjunctural analysis gives constant adjustments for this one period, as described in Section 5.3. These adjustments, together with those for later periods (derivation of which was also discussed in Section 5.3) are loaded on to the computer, or tabulated. The model is now used to compute predictions for all the periods for which a forecast is required. The results from doing this are shown in Table 5.4.

Typically at this stage the forecasters examine the results, alter some of the constant adjustments and re-compute the forecast. They do this because the results do not conform to their prior beliefs or perhaps because internal inconsistencies appear in the predictions from the model, as discussed in Section 5.3. Often the process of examining the results, altering the adjustments and re-computing is repeated many times before a forecast is finalized. It is difficult to justify this procedure, although it is widely used by forecasters. (It has not been used for the forecast presented in this chapter.) As well as changing constant adjustments, the forecasters often alter the projections of exogenous variables. They may, for example, adjust government policy because the impact on the economy of the assumed policy appears to be unsustainable. Given that exogenous variables are by definition meant to be unaffected by developments in the economy, this process is apparently hard to justify, although it may not be as strange as it appears. As mentioned in Chapter 4, it is common practice to treat policy variables as exogenous in macro-econometric models, even though they are known to be influenced by the economy. The forecaster, by altering them in reaction to the model's predictions, is using judgement to provide the missing equations, and in effect making these variables endogenous.

The forecast shown in Table 5.4 covers the period up to the end of 1988 and is computed from historical data up to 1983 third quarter, with estimates from conjunctural analysis for the last quarter of 1983. The remainder of this section describes this forecast, starting with some detailed notes on the preparation of the historical data, forecasts of exogenous variables, and constant adjustments.

Historical data for endogenous variables

Data for all quarters from the mid-1950s or early 1960s, up to 1980, were used to estimate the equations in the macro-econometric model, with data beyond 1980 used in the post-sample tests. For forecasting, it is vital to have the latest available data but there is no need for a long run of past data. The minimum requirement is sufficient data to provide information for the longest lag on each variable. For example, examination of the

Table 5.2   Historical data

		GDP (exp. measure)	Consumer spending	Public spending	Fixed capital stock	Stock of invent- ories	Non-oil exports	Non-oil imports	Net oil trade
		GDPE	C	G	KI	KII	X	M	O
1981	1	49.1	34.4	14.8	392.7	67.5	13.2	11.7	0.6
	2	48.0	34.4	14.7	393.9	66.2	13.4	12.3	0.6
	3	48.2	34.3	14.6	395.2	66.0	13.7	13.5	0.5
	4	49.1	34.4	14.5	396.4	65.9	14.0	13.2	0.5
1982	1	49.2	34.2	14.7	397.8	65.9	13.8	13.2	0.5
	2	49.5	34.6	14.6	399.1	66.2	13.9	13.5	0.7
	3	49.4	35.1	14.7	400.5	65.6	13.0	13.0	1.0
	4	50.9	35.7	15.0	401.9	64.9	13.6	13.2	1.3
1983	1	51.6	35.5	15.5	403.4	65.5	13.5	13.9	1.2
	2	50.6	36.1	15.2	404.8	65.4	13.3	13.9	1.0
	3	50.9	36.4	15.3	406.6	65.4	13.3	14.0	1.2

Note: All figures are in £billion at 1980 prices unless indicated. These units have been used for ease of presentation, but actual calculations with the forecasting model should use the data in £million shown in Appendix 2. All data are seasonally adjusted except for the interest rate and exchange rate. For sources see Appendix 4.

Table 5.3   Exogenous variables

		World short-term interest rates	World exports of manufactures	World whole- sale prices	World GNP	World oil prices	Money supply M0	Expected exchange rate
		% p.a.					£m., current prices	
		RSW	XWM	WWPI	WGNP	POILWC	MO	XEER
		Annual values						
	1979	8.7	95	87	99	57	9852	94
	1980	11.9	100	100	100	100	10630	102
	1981	12.7	103	110	102	124	11201	96
	1982	11.4	100	118	101	132	11512	91
	1983	8.6	99	124	104	122	12710	87
	1984	9.0	104	132	108	121	13845	88
	1985	9.0	109	141	110	121	14956	88
	1986	9.0	114	151	112	121	16087	88
	1987	9.0	118	162	115	121	17155	88
	1988	9.0	123	173	117	121	18184	88
		Quarterly values						
1983	1	9.1	100	122	102	128	12098	88
	2	8.2	100	123	103	119	12554	88
	3	8.7	98	125	104	121	12587	87
	4	8.5	100	127	106	121	13599	87
1984	1	9.0	102	130	106	121	13275	88
	2	9.0	104	131	107	121	13683	88
	3	9.0	105	133	108	121	13677	88
	4	9.0	106	135	109	121	14746	88

Note: All series are indices, based at 1980 = 100, unless stated. For data sources, see Appendix 5.

Table 5.2 *continued*

		Consumer price index	Personal disposable income	Short-term interest rates	Exchange rate index	Average earnings (whole economy)	Employment
		Index 1980 = 100	£bn. current prices	%p.a.	Index 1980 = 100	Index 1980 = 100	000s
		PC	YD	RLB	EER	WSI	ET
1981	1	106	42.5	13.6	106	107	24521
	2	110	42.9	12.0	102	109	24298
	3	113	43.8	12.3	94	113	24204
	4	115	45.1	15.2	93	116	24081
1982	1	117	46.1	13.8	95	118	24027
	2	120	46.8	12.9	94	121	23921
	3	121	47.1	11.3	95	122	23817
	4	123	48.2	9.7	93	125	23715
1983	1	125	49.0	10.8	84	129	23699
	2	126	49.6	10.0	88	130	23717
	3	127	50.6	9.5	88	132	23681

Table 5.3 *continued*

	Average income tax rate	Average indirect tax rate	Change in reserves etc.	Time trend, 1955 Q1 equals 1	Council house sales	Public spending	Net oil trade
	ratio		£m. current prices		£bn. 1980 prices		£bn. 1980 prices
	T	TREF	DRESV	TIME	ICHS	G	O
Annual values							
1979	0.20	80	1576	98.5	0.6	60.8	– 1.5
1980	0.20	100	940	102.5	1.0	60.6	– 0.5
1981	0.22	121	– 1128	106.5	1.1	58.6	2.1
1982	0.22	135	– 1056	110.5	2.3	59.0	3.4
1983	0.22	136	– 431	114.5	1.8	61.4	4.4
1984	0.22	143	0	118.5	1.5	62.4	4.1
1985	0.22	154	0	122.5	1.2	63.3	4.5
1986	0.22	165	0	126.5	1.0	64.2	4.8
1987	0.22	176	0	130.5	1.0	64.9	4.8
1988	0.22	186	0	134.5	0.9	65.7	5.0
Quarterly values							
1983 1	0.22	137	– 176	113	0.5	15.5	1.2
2	0.22	134	– 288	114	0.4	15.2	1.0
3	0.22	134	33	115	0.4	15.3	1.2
4	0.22	141	0	116	0.4	15.4	1.0
1984 1	0.22	144	0	117	0.4	15.5	1.0
2	0.22	140	0	118	0.4	15.6	1.0
3	0.22	141	0	119	0.4	15.6	1.0
4	0.22	149	0	120	0.3	15.7	1.1

Table 5.4 Summary of the forecast made on the assumption of exogenous expectations

	GDP (exp. measure)	Consumer spending	Public spending	Fixed capital stock	Stock of inventories	Non-oil exports	Non-oil imports
	GDPE	*C*	*G*	*KI*	*KII*	*X*	*M*
	Annual values						
1979	201.4	138.0	60.4	380.0	70.9	56.8	52.0
1980	196.4	137.3	60.6	388.8	70.2	56.8	50.8
1981	194.4	137.6	58.6	394.6	66.4	54.2	50.6
1982	199.0	139.6	59.0	399.8	65.6	54.3	52.9
1983	205.1	144.7	61.4	405.9	65.4	54.0	56.0
1984	211.3	149.5	62.4	414.6	65.4	58.7	61.9
1985	215.5	152.3	63.3	425.4	66.4	61.6	67.1
1986	218.1	155.6	64.2	436.5	67.8	63.3	70.6
1987	220.8	159.6	64.9	447.2	68.7	64.9	73.2
1988	224.4	163.7	65.7	457.4	69.7	66.7	76.4
	Quarterly values						
1983 1	51.6	35.5	15.5	403.4	65.5	13.5	13.9
2	50.6	36.1	15.2	404.8	65.4	13.3	13.9
3	50.9	36.4	15.3	406.6	65.4	13.3	14.0
4	51.9	36.8	15.4	408.6	65.4	13.9	14.3
1984 1	52.4	37.1	15.5	410.9	65.3	14.2	14.8
2	52.6	37.3	15.6	413.3	65.3	14.6	15.4
3	53.0	37.5	15.6	415.9	65.4	14.8	15.7
4	53.3	37.6	15.7	418.5	65.6	15.0	16.0

Note: For full details of this forecast, see Appendix 2.
All figures are £billion at 1980 prices, unless indicated, and all data are seasonally adjusted except for the interest rate and the exchange rate. For sources, see Appendix 4.

Table 5.4 *continued*

	GDP (exp. measure)	Consumer spending	Public spending	Fixed capital stock	Stock of inventories	Non-oil exports	Non-oil imports
	Annual percentage changes						
1979	1.7	5.0	0.8	2.6	3.6	0.5	12.2
1980	− 2.5	− 0.5	− 0.3	2.3	− 1.0	− 0.1	− 2.3
1981	− 1.0	0.2	− 3.3	1.5	− 5.4	− 4.6	− 0.3
1982	2.3	1.4	0.7	1.3	− 1.2	0.2	4.5
1983	3.1	3.7	4.0	1.5	− 0.4	− 0.4	5.9
1984	3.0	3.3	1.6	2.2	0.0	8.5	10.5
1985	2.0	1.9	1.6	2.6	1.5	5.1	8.4
1986	1.2	2.1	1.4	2.6	2.1	2.7	5.2
1987	1.3	2.6	1.1	2.4	1.4	2.5	3.8
1988	1.6	2.6	1.3	2.3	1.4	2.9	4.4
	Quarterly percentage changes						
1983 1	4.8	3.6	5.8	1.4	− 0.7	− 2.1	4.7
2	2.3	4.2	3.8	1.4	− 1.1	− 3.9	2.6
3	3.0	3.8	3.9	1.5	− 0.3	2.2	7.8
4	2.1	3.1	2.4	1.7	0.7	2.3	8.7
1984 1	1.5	4.5	− 0.2	1.9	− 0.3	5.3	6.7
2	3.9	3.5	2.7	2.1	− 0.2	9.3	10.8
3	4.1	3.2	2.0	2.3	0.1	11.5	12.4
4	2.7	2.2	2.1	2.4	0.4	8.1	12.0

Table 5.4 *continued*

	Consumer price index	Personal disposable income	Short-term interest rates	Exchange rate index	Average earnings (whole economy)	Employment
	Index 1980 = 100	£bn. current prices	%p.a.	Index 1980 = 100	Index 1980 = 100	000s
	PC	YD	RLB	EER	WSI	ET
	Annual values					
1979	86	135.9	13.7	91	83	25367
1980	100	160.7	16.3	100	99	25121
1981	111	174.3	13.3	99	111	24276
1982	120	188.3	11.9	94	121	23870
1983	127	201.0	9.8	87	131	23679
1984	134	216.7	10.1	88	140	23489
1985	144	236.4	11.2	88	154	23383
1986	154	259.4	11.5	88	169	23305
1987	164	282.0	10.9	88	185	23152
1988	173	303.8	10.6	88	200	22953
	Quarterly values					
1983 1	125	49.0	10.8	84	129	23699
2	126	49.6	10.0	88	130	23717
3	127	50.6	9.5	88	132	23681
4	129	51.8	9.0	87	134	23619
1984 1	131	52.8	8.9	88	136	23558
2	132	53.6	8.8	88	139	23504
3	134	54.6	11.1	88	142	23462
4	137	55.7	11.5	88	144	23434

Table 5.4 *continued*

	Consumer price index	Personal disposable income	Exchange rate index	Average earnings (whole economy)	Employment
	Annual percentage changes				
1979	13.4	20.0	7.2	15.2	1.3
1980	16.5	18.2	10.1	20.3	– 1.0
1981	11.1	8.5	– 1.2	11.7	– 3.4
1982	8.3	8.0	– 4.7	9.3	– 1.7
1983	5.3	6.8	– 8.0	8.1	– 0.8
1984	5.5	7.8	1.6	6.9	– 0.8
1985	7.4	9.1	0.3	9.4	– 0.5
1986	7.4	9.7	0.1	10.2	– 0.3
1987	6.4	8.7	– 0.1	9.2	– 0.7
1988	5.6	7.7	– 0.1	8.2	– 0.9
	Quarterly percentage changes				
1983 1	6.3	6.4	– 11.6	8.9	– 1.4
2	5.0	5.9	– 6.6	7.8	– 0.9
3	5.0	7.4	– 7.2	8.2	– 0.6
4	5.0	7.4	– 6.6	7.5	– 0.4
1984 1	4.8	7.6	4.6	5.8	– 0.6
2	5.3	8.1	0.0	6.8	– 0.9
3	5.5	7.8	– 0.1	7.0	– 0.9
4	6.4	7.6	2.0	7.9	– 0.8

macro-econometric model (see Appendix 1) shows that the stock of fixed investment appears only with no lag, written KI_t, or with one lag, KI_{t-1}. This means that its longest lag is one and so we need only one period's historical data for it in order to calculate the forecast. In the illustrative forecast used in this chapter, this means that we need historical data on variable KI for the period 1983 third quarter only. Some other variables, such as the current balance (variable BAL) or the PSBR, do not appear as lagged variables anywhere in the macro-econometric model and so we can make a forecast without any historical data for them, although it is useful to have available for comparisons. By contrast the longest lag for variable WSI (wages and salaries index) is six, in the equation for imports. The minimum requirement for WSI is thus data for all quarters from 1982 second quarter up to 1983 third quarter.

Exogenous variables

Historical data for exogenous variables are shown in Table 5.3. As for endogenous variables, the historical data must provide sufficient information for the longest lag used in the model. Projections for the exogenous variables are also shown in Table 5.3. Because of their importance we will describe their derivation in some detail, illustrating the use of the eclectic methods referred to earlier in this chapter.

The exogenous variables, as in large macro-econometric models, fall into two main categories: those describing the world economy and those reflecting government policy. There is also a time trend (which rises by one every period) needed to allow for productivity growth. In addition UK net oil sales are taken as exogenous and, for the moment, expectations about the exchange rate are treated as exogenous.

Five exogenous variables describe developments in the world economy. The gross national product of the OECD countries (Organization for Economic Co-operation and Development, comprising the major industrialized nations) is denoted WGNP and OECD exports of manufactures are XWM. Of these, XWM is an important determinant of UK exports, while the ratio of XWM to WGNP gives a ratio of trade to output in foreign countries which in the model affects import penetration in the UK. In addition to these two measures of the volume of world economic activity, there are two measures of prices in the world economy. These are WWPI and POILWC, which measure OECD wholesale prices and oil prices, respectively. Both are denominated in 'world currency'. WWPI affects competitiveness and import costs in the model, while POILWC affects the current account and government revenue. Finally, RSW measures foreign short term interest rates.

A variety of methods are used by UK forecasters for predicting world variables. As noted earlier the LBS uses a small formal econometric model and the Treasury has a formal model. However, both these organizations also make considerable use of other sources of information including the forecasts prepared by specialists who devote substantial resources to analysing the OECD nations. One of the most important of these forecasts is prepared by the economists employed by the OECD office in Paris. They produce a biannual forecast covering the economies of all their member countries.

The forecasts in Table 5.3 for the exogenous variables describing the world economy are based on the short-term projections to mid-1985 set out in the OECD's December 1983 *Economic Outlook*, with forecasts beyond then based on the London Business School's world economy projections. Unlike the Treasury or the London Business School models, the macro-econometric model used in this book does not include even a simple formal system giving world economy forecasts for comparing against the OECD projections. However, we can check that the world economy forecasts in Table 5.3 are consistent with our views about economic theory, and with conclusions based on casual observation of past events. (Note that it has also been necessary to apply judgement to gauge the quarterly values in that table from the OECD's annual or half-yearly data.) Had we disagreed with any of the major policy assumptions underlying the OECD projections, a significant adjustment would have been necessary. This would clearly be based on judgement if we had no formal model of the world economy.

The projections show output of the OECD countries, WGNP, rising by about 4 per cent in 1984. This is similar to the 1983 figure, reflecting some slowdown in US growth being offset by an acceleration in European growth. Because the European economies are more open than the US, i.e. they have a higher tendency to trade per unit of output, there is a distinct increase in trade growth between 1983 and 1984. No increase in inflation is envisaged in 1984, reflecting in part continued tight monetary policies world-wide. This also reflects world interest rates which remain high relative to inflation during 1984.

There are four main exogenous government policy variables in the model and two less important policy variables. The major variables are the average income tax rate, T, the value of indirect taxes, TREF, the volume of current and capital spending on goods and services, G, and the money supply (wide monetary base), MO. An apparently simple way to treat these variables is to assume unchanged policies. This assumption is not unambiguous and since the mid-1970s uncertainty about its interpretation has been increased by higher inflation and by the shift in emphasis from fiscal to monetary policy. We will describe the interpretation that has been used by forecasters in the past and demonstrate in detail how it can be implemented; then various objections and alternative interpretations will be considered.

The interpretation of unchanged policies used by NIESR and the Treasury, with minor variations, includes the following assumptions: the income tax system is adjusted to insulate it from the effects of inflation, which means raising allowances and bands in line with inflation (this is often called 'Rooker-Wise' after the MPs who successfully proposed it in a

Finance Bill amendment); indirect taxes are similarly adjusted; government spending on goods and services follows announced plans; pension and social security benefit and contribution rates rise in line with price inflation; and money supply growth is within announced target ranges. Each of these policy assumptions can be allowed for in the macro-econometric model of Chapter 4.

Income tax revenue is calculated in the macro-econometric model as T times the wage and salary bill, and times interest receipts. Thus the assumption that allowances and bands are raised to keep the tax take a constant proportion of income is implemented easily by holding T constant. (To smooth out the impact of recent quarterly fluctuations, future values of T should be equal to the average of the last four historical data observations.) The value of indirect taxes, net of subsidies, is given by the variable TREF. The assumption of unchanged policies states that this rises in line with inflation, which is done by using the formula in Section 5.1.

For government spending, the apparently simple assumption of following government plans is difficult to implement, because the published plans do not give information in the appropriate form. Most obscure of all are the figures in the annual public expenditure White Paper, which require complex adjustments. The most useful figures appear in the Financial Statement published on budget day and updated at the time of the autumn statement. The table showing forecasts of GDP components (Table 3.9 in the March 1984 edition) gives half-yearly data at constant prices for current spending on goods and services and for capital spending by general government (quarterly data have to be guessed). The sum of these two almost gives our variable G, except that we also need to add public corporations' capital spending. A figure for this is obtained for the financial year as a whole by taking the current price figure shown in the PSBR components table (at the back of the financial statement) and dividing by a guess at the price index being used. This is a tedious procedure, giving only an approximate result. A quicker alternative is to make a guess about the path of G that is consistent with the broad stance of government policy announcements. This means falling as a per cent of GDP under the Thatcher administration and probably implies rising as a proportion of GDP under a Labour administration. This guessed path can be compared with the White Paper and the Financial Statement to ensure broad consistency.

Pensions and other grants to persons are fixed at a constant rate in real terms in the equations of the macro-econometric model, thus implementing automatically the unchanged policies assumption. Money supply MO is assumed to grow at a rate near to the top of the government's target ranges. These ranges allow for a gradual reduction in the rate of growth, which falls in the forecast from about 8 per cent in the financial year 1984/5 to about 6 per cent by 1988. (This variable follows an irregular quarterly pattern and exogenous forecasts must be calculated by applying the desired growth rate to its level a year earlier.)

Before discussing some objections and alternatives to the use of an unchanged policies assumption, we consider the two minor exogenous policy variables in the macro-econometric model of Chapter 4, ICHS and DRESV. The first of these represents council house sales and is important because these sales are treated in the national accounts as negative public sector investment. The rapid increase in ICHS, which occurred after 1981 when council tenants were given the right to buy their houses, thus caused a significant fall in the variable G and raised KI. This is an example of a problem caused in practical forecasting when the government introduces new policy instruments. It is reasonable to assume the ICHS declines gradually as the pent-up demand, released when the scheme began, is satisfied. After 1985 this variable is assumed to settle at a fairly low constant level. The other minor policy variable DRESV is the change in foreign currency reserves. As noted in Chapter 4, this is included for completeness but has no impact on the exchange rate and the simplest assumption is that it is zero over the forecast period.

For the illustrative forecast, we assume unchanged policies and base our projections for the exogenous policy variables on the above analysis. These projections are shown in Table 5.3. Before discussing the forecast calculated from these projections, we consider some objections and alternatives to the interpretation of unchanged policies adopted above.

Mrs Thatcher's government has committed itself to the reduction of public borrowing and monetary growth. An unchanged policies forecast that yielded results inconsistent with those aims would implicitly assume abandonment of the government's stated objectives. This would force the forecaster to make a judgement. Either the forecast is accepted, so the government is assumed to abandon its aims, or one or more of the exogenous policy variables must be altered and the forecast re-computed. For example, if the PSBR is above target, tax rates could be raised or public spending cut. In the Liverpool University macro-econometric model, the need for this judgement is avoided by treating the PSBR (relative to gross domestic product) as an exogenous policy variable and making taxes and public spending endogenous, so they adjust to achieve the exogenous public borrowing target. This is a different way of interpreting the assumption of unchanged policies.

A different type of problem arises when a government commits itself to some objective not under its direct control. For example a Labour administration might aim to cut unemployment by a certain amount over a certain period. Suppose that certain fiscal policies are announced to achieve this aim, but the model's forecast suggests that unemployment does not fall far or fast enough. If the forecaster believes that the government is determined to reach its objective, then some policy change must be assumed to take place. The forecaster might try to find the appropriate policy by trial and error but the rigorous method is to use the optimal control techniques described in Chapter 8. These will either select the best policy or indicate that the target is unobtainable – at least according to the model.

Another problem arises when the chosen combination of policy variables leads to an unsustainable path for some of the items in the model. A typical example is when expansionary fiscal policy leads to accelerating growth in the outstanding stock of government debt. The forecaster can deal with this judgementally by guessing the point at which the policy has to be reversed. Alternatively the requirement that the stock of government debt must not grow without limit can be treated as part of an optimal control problem (see Chapter 8).

One final problem arises when the forecast period includes a likely election date. One way to deal with this is to take an 'average' of likely post-election policy regimes, but this means little. A more sensible approach is to make a clear assumption about which party will win the election and about its policies. The alternative outcomes under other administrations can be calculated, using a different set of projected exogenous variables, and presented as a separate forecast. This is called a *policy simulation* and is discussed further in Chapter 8.

This concludes the discussion of exogenous policy variables. Three exogenous variables remain to be considered. Variable TIME is a time trend with value 1 in 1955 first quarter, 121 in 1985 first quarter and so on. Variable O is oil exports net of oil imports, at constant 1980 prices. The projections for this item shown in Table 5.3 are based on the government's forecasts of likely North Sea oil output. See Department of Energy (1983) or a later issue. (The UK's oil output exceeds its consumption, but the output is of high quality and much of it is therefore exported, making it necessary to import lower quality oil for UK use. These imports depend on GDP and oil prices but any variation is likely to be small and is neglected.) Variable XEER represents expectations about the value of the exchange rate one period ahead. This is a vital item and a formal way of forecasting it is discussed in Section 5.5 For the forecast in this section, we assume little change from current levels.

Constant adjustments

In addition to historical data and projections of exogenous variables, constant adjustments are also needed for calculating a forecast. For the forecast presented in this section, some constant adjustments are needed in 1983 fourth quarter to reflect information from conjunctural analysis, and an adjustment to variable KII is needed in later periods. These adjustments were discussed above in Section 5.3.

The short-term outlook

The results of the forecast are shown in Table 5.4. The forecast shows growth in GDP (expenditure measure) in 1984 at 3 per cent, the same rate as is estimated for 1983. This is a rapid rate of growth by the standards of the 1970s. The growth rate *through the year*, i.e. 1984 fourth quarter compared to 1983 fourth quarter, is slightly slower at 2.7 per cent. Among the components of demand, consumers' expenditure rises by 3.3 per cent year on year, almost as much as the fast growth of 3.7 per cent estimated for 1983. However through the year consumption growth is significantly slower, at only just over 2 per cent. Even this reduced growth requires some fall in the savings ratio, because personal disposable income rises 7.6 per cent through the year while consumer prices grow 6.4 per cent. This means real incomes rise only 1.2 per cent, so by the end of 1984 the savings ratio must fall by about 1 percentage point from its end 1983 level. A possible reason for this is that it is a delayed response to declines in inflation that occurred in earlier years and is occurring despite the pickup in inflation in 1984, which is small relative to earlier falls.

Turning to other demand components, there is a sharp rise in exports in 1984 following the weak figure for the previous year. This is partly in response to a turnaround in world trade, which was little changed in 1983 and is expected to grow by almost 5 per cent in 1984 as the European economies recover from recession. It also reflects a delayed reaction to the improvements in competitiveness (falls in the real exchange rate) that took place since late 1982.

The level of inventories rises only slowly during the year, despite the rapid rise in output. This reflects the high level of real interest rates. Fixed investment increases fairly rapidly during 1984, in line with the CBI and Department of Trade investment intentions surveys. This is partly in response to the increase in output in 1983 and 1984 and is also due to the substantial rise in profits that occurred in 1983 and which continues, at a slower rate, in 1984. Profits are not a variable in the model but their share in GDP must be rising. This is because during 1984 the rise in consumer prices plus the rise in GDP is considerably larger than the rise in personal incomes and at the same time the terms of trade are improving, since export prices are rising faster than the rise in world prices minus the exchange rate change.

In response to the increases in domestic demand, import volume grows rapidly in 1984. Even though imports rise more than export volume, the current account remains broadly in balance because of the terms of trade improvement.

Taking these projections for demand components together, we have rapid increases in export and fixed investment, and a fairly large rise in consumer spending partly offset by higher imports. Together these give the forecast for 3 per cent GDP growth in 1984 compared to 1983, with a 2.7 per cent rise through the year. Although this increase is higher than the 2.3 per cent trend productivity growth (output per employee) built into the model, it is not sufficient to prevent a fall in employment during the year. This is partly because the model generates some cyclical increase in productivity in a year of rapid output growth and partly because real wages are still at a high level compared to the level which the estimated equation regards as an equilibrium figure. Some rise in unemployment during 1984 is implied by the employment projection, but since unemployment is affected by demographic changes and economic factors such as benefit changes as well as by employment, it is not possible to give a good estimate of it without an equation.

The rate of price inflation rises slightly during 1984, to just under 6½ per cent. This partly reflects the pickup in output and also the decline in sterling during 1983. It seems likely that the government would not be prepared to accept this level of inflation, given its policy announcements. This suggests that we should alter one or more of the policy variables. This is not done here, but the effect of relevant policy changes is discussed in Chapter 8.

The medium-term outlook

Table 5.4 also summarizes the forecast for years up to 1988. Gross domestic product growth follows a cycle, with the first year of the forecast, 1984, showing the peak growth rate of 3 per cent. The growth rate declines in later years to 1.2 per cent in 1986 and then rises slightly in the last two years. Productivity growth (output per employee) varies with the cycle, being faster in years of high output growth, but its average over the forecast period is close to its trend rate of 2.3 per cent per annum. With GDP growth averaging slightly below this trend rate, numbers employed decline slowly over the forecast period. By the start of 1988 employment is more than half a million lower than its level when the forecast began. Unemployment, which is not included as a model variable, will tend to rise by the same order of magnitude as the fall in employment. The rate of consumer price inflation rises from 5 per cent at the end of 1983 to about 8 per cent in 1985 and then falls back to about 6 per cent by the end of the forecast.

5.5 A rational expectations forecast

This section explains and illustrates rational expectations forecasts. Much of the material in this section is more complex than that in earlier parts of this chapter, and some readers may wish to omit it on first reading.

The *rational expectations hypothesis* asserts that people do not make systematic mistakes when forming expectations (as defined in Begg, 1982). Since the model itself is in principle a description of how the economy has behaved in the past and will continue to behave, this hypothesis is usually interpreted to mean that expectations are consistent with the projections made by the model itself. Rational expectations do not simply mean self-justifying circularity, in which any set of expectations is consistent with a set of forecasts from the model. Instead, it can be shown that under certain conditions, there is only one set of expectations that is consistent with projections from the model (discussion of this uniqueness property is postponed to Chapter 8).

The first part of this section considers various ways to model expectations, and explains the attractions of assuming rational expectations. Next there is a discussion of the computer techniques used to ensure consistency between expectations and model forecasts; and the section concludes with a description of a forecast prepared using rational expectations. Note that the illustrative macro-econometric model used here only includes one explicit expectations term, for the exchange rate. This is a simplification; in practice, it is likely that expectations of other variables influence peoples' behaviour, and ideally, in a larger model, these would also be included explicitly.

Alternative ways of forming expectations

The forecast described in the previous section took expectations about the exchange rate as exogenous. These expectations have a powerful effect (see the exchange rate equation in Box 4.2) and taking them as exogenous is almost like taking the exchange rate itself as exogenous. This is not unusual, for most of the main forecasting groups have had little faith in their exchange rate forecasting systems and have frequently (see Chapter 7) overridden their own models, forecasting the rate by judgement and thus removing one of the most important links in the economy. Fixing expectations exogenously involves less of a departure from the model than fixing the exchange rate itself, because some use is made of the equation. The fixing of expectations can be justified for projections a few periods ahead when the forecaster has information about the view of the future held by foreign exchange markets, which would not otherwise be used by the model. However, exogenous expectations are difficult to justify for forecasts far into the future (and can produce implausible results in simulations, as demonstrated in Chapter 8). For such forecasts, the economist needs to derive expectations (and hence the exchange rate itself) in the way that financial markets have formed them in the past.

One possible way to do this is to estimate a single equation for exchange rate expectations. This might depend on, for example, interest rates and on indicators of likely future government policies, or it might be an adaptive system depending only on past values of the exchange rate itself. The forecaster could use this equation to predict financial market expectations. This approach has been widely used in the past, as described in Chapter 7. A drawback is that expectations formed in this way could lie systematically to one side or the other of the exchange rate actually being predicted by the model. For example, if agents formed expectations by using the simple rule, 'Next period's rate equals the current rate', then they would be systematically overpredicting the rate when it was falling; and if they used the rule, 'Next period's change in the exchange rate equals this period's change', they would obtain correct predictions when the exchange rate was falling at a constant rate but would systematically over-predict if the exchange rate was declining at an accelerating rate. Of course, it is possible to assume that people make systematic mistakes when forming expectations but, as Begg comments, this is not an appealing assumption. By contrast, the hypothesis of rational expectations asserts that people do not make systematic mistakes when forecasting the future.

Applying the rational expectations hypothesis to macro-econometric models

As explained at the start of this section, when economists apply the rational expectations hypothesis to macro-econometric (or to theoretical) models, they almost always interpret it to mean that people's expectations are consistent with the forecasts generated by the model. This does not mean that economists are assuming that everyone knows about the model and uses it to form expectations (this is possible, but is not necessary). Instead they are assuming that people use some way of forming expectations which, if the model is a true description of the real world, would not produce systematic forecasting errors. This assumption, turned around, implies that if the projections from the model are used as estimates of people's expectations, then those estimates will not be systematically incorrect.

We will now explain two of the methods used in computer programs to ensure that the forecasts produced by non-linear macro-econometric models are consistent with expectations. The first method, as applied to the macro-econometric model of Chapter 4, involves trying out in a systematic way many different values for the expectation term XEER, in each of the time periods being forecast, until the minimum value is found for:

$$\text{Sum over all forecast periods of: } (\text{XEER}_{t-1} - \text{EER}_t)^2$$

Of course, as different values for XEER are tried out, the model's forecasts for EER itself will change, and this is taken account of by the computer program. Ideally, the values that are finally chosen for XEER should make this expression indistinguishably close to zero for all the time periods of the forecast, but since the search procedure can take a considerable amount of computer time, the forecaster is in practice content when it is very small.

This method of choosing expectations says nothing about the figure for the last quarter of the forecast period. This point is illustrated by a forecast made for the period up to 1988 fourth quarter. No projection is made for EER in 1989 first quarter, so there is no figure to compare with the 1988 fourth quarter value of XEER. This does not mean that the choice of XEER in that quarter is unimportant – on the contrary, given the exchange rate equation, it plays a significant role in determining the 1988 fourth quarter level of EER, which in turn affects XEER in 1988 third quarter, and so on back to the figures for EER in the earliest quarters of the forecast. This indicates that some rule is needed to determine XEER in the last quarter.

There are various possible rules that might be used. One rule would state that XEER in the last period equals the value it took in the previous quarter. Another possibility is to make the rate of change of XEER between the second to last and last quarters equal to the rate of change between the third to last and second to last quarters; and other rules could be invented. In practice the second of the suggested rules is typically used when forecasting the nominal exchange rate. This is because it implies that the nominal rate is settling down to a constant rate of change; this is an attractive property because it is at least approximately consistent with the path for the exchange rate in the distant future suggested by the theoretical rational expectations model on which this macro-econometric model is based (provided projections for exogenous variables are at roughly constant growth rates by the end of the forecast period). See Chapter 8. This rule for determining XEER in the last period is known as a *terminal condition* or *tranversality condition* and, as explained in that chapter, it plays a vital role in ensuring that rational expectations forecasts are unique.

Combining this terminal condition with the rule for the other periods suggested earlier gives a complete problem for the computer to solve. This is to choose values of XEER, for every quarter of the forecast period, to minimize:

Sum over all forecast periods of $(XEER_{t-1} - EER_t)^2$
Plus for the last period $(XEER_t/XEER_{t-1} - XEER_{t-1}/XEER_{t-2})^2$

The computer solves this problem numerically, trying out in a systematic way many different values of XEER for each period until it finds the smallest value for the above expression. The method used to carry out this type of minimization is useful for other applications to macro-econometric models and is described in Holly and Zarrop (1983), and summarized in Section 4 of Chapter 8. Even with a small model such as that described in Chapter 4, many attempts may have to be made by the computer before the solution is found. (Between ten and twenty attempts were needed for the results reported later in this section.) Each attempt involves one complete forecast for the whole model over the whole forecast period, which means that it is not practical to carry out this exercise by hand.

There is an alternative method for finding rational expectations forecasts that does not involve minimizing the sum of squares shown above (although it should produce the same results). This alternative method begins with the production of a forecast, in which expectations are treated as if they were fixed exogenously at some guessed values (the forecast using exogenous expectations, reported in the previous section, would be an example of this). Next, a new set of expectations is calculated, by taking the original guesses and altering them to bring them some fraction (for example 0.7) of the way towards the model's forecasts for the exchange rate with which they are meant to be consistent. For example, if the original guess for XEER in 1984 fourth quarter is 88, and the model's forecast for EER in 1985 first quarter is 89, then the new estimate for

XEER in 1984 fourth quarter will be 88.3. Using this new set of expectations, the forecast is re-computed; the resulting values for the exchange
rate should be closer to the expectations than they were before, but they
will not yet be equal. Next, another new set of expectations is computed, in
the same way as before, and the process continues until the expectations
and the model's exchange rate forecasts are very close (for the last period
of the forecast, a terminal condition is imposed in an analagous way to
that described above). This method, based on the *Hall algorithm* (see
Fisher *et al.*, 1985) is relatively new but preliminary results suggest that
it may use considerably less computer time than the method described
earlier.

Example of a rational expectations forecast

Table 5.5 shows projections of the exchange rate EER obtained on the
assumption of rational expectations. These projections were prepared
using the model of Chapter 4 and using the same exogenous assumptions
and adjustments as for the forecast described in Section 5.4, except that
XEER was determined using rational expectations methods. For all
periods, the expectations variable XEER is very close to the level of EER
itself in the following quarter, the difference generally being 0.1 per cent
or less. The terminal condition has also been satisfied. The rational expectations forecasts for GDPE and other main variables are shown in

Table 5.5   Rational expectations projections of the
exchange rate

	Exchange rate index	Expected exchange rate
	EER	*XEER*
1984 1	90.9	91.0
2	91.0	91.1
3	91.2	90.9
4	91.0	90.5
1985 1	90.8	90.5
2	90.5	90.4
3	90.5	90.3
4	90.4	90.2
1986 1	90.2	89.9
2	89.9	89.7
3	89.8	89.6
4	89.6	89.5
1987 1	89.5	89.3
2	89.3	89.1
3	89.1	88.9
4	88.8	88.6
1988 1	88.6	88.3
2	88.3	88.2
3	88.1	87.9
4	87.8	87.6

Table 5.6. Compare these results with the projections shown in Table 5.4, which assumed exogenous expectations. The difference in the exchange rate forecasts is not large, ranging from about 1 per cent up to 3 per cent. This is sufficient to alter the prediction of GDP by up to about ¼ per cent between the forecasts. The reasonably small size of these differences indicates that sensible choice of exogenous expectations can give similar results to those obtained through the less arbitrary, but more complex, method of rational expectations forecasts. However it will be shown in Chapter 8 that holding expectations exogenous when deriving policy simulations can cause very great differences compared to the assumption of rational expectations.

This section has considered briefly the application of the rational expectations hypothesis to macro-economic forecasting. A more formal discussion of this area is given in Holly and Hughes-Hallett (forthcoming). Its application when macro-econometric models are used for policy analysis is discussed in Chapter 8, and a discussion of other applications, and of many of the issues and problems that it raises, is given in Begg (1982).

5.6 Do-it-yourself forecasting

It is possible to prepare your own up-to-date forecast, using the macro-econometric model described in Chapter 4. This model is recursive (see Section 5.2). This means that each equation needs to be solved just once for each time period, and so it is possible to prepare a forecast using only a pocket calculator. However, for repeated use or for projections a long way ahead, it is easier to use a microcomputer. (Note: rational expectations forecasts require calculation of repeated forecasts and are impractical without a computer.)

The steps in preparing your own forecast are as set out in Section 5.4. Three types of information must be tabulated: the latest historical data, projections for exogenous variables, and constant adjustments. To assist you, there are blank tables in Appendix 5. These can be photocopied and filled in, first with the latest historical data and projected exogenous variables, and then with forecasts as they are computed. Full details of variable definitions and sources are given in Appendix 4. All the data are obtained from readily available official publications. For many variables, data can be copied directly from the publication onto the working sheet. For other variables, simple calculations are required. These are explained fully in the notes on definitions and sources.

For preparing projections of exogenous variables, see the discussion in Section 5.4. In particular, it is important to follow the procedure given for predicting money supply MO. This must be calculated as the desired percentage increase on its own value a year earlier, in order to give predictions of the irregular quarterly pattern observed in past data. If this is not done, large errors will appear in the forecast for interest rates.

The production and use of economic forecasts

Table 5.6 Summary of the forecast made on the assumption of rational expectations

	GDP (exp. measure)	Consumer spending	Public spending	Fixed capital stock	Stock of inventories	Non-oil exports	Non-oil imports
	GDPE	C	G	KI	KII	X	M
	Annual values						
1984	210.8	149.6	62.4	414.6	65.4	58.1	61.8
1985	215.5	153.1	63.3	425.3	66.3	61.1	67.2
1986	218.2	156.6	64.2	436.3	67.8	63.1	71.1
1987	221.3	160.4	64.9	447.1	68.9	64.9	73.8
1988	225.0	164.1	65.7	457.5	70.0	67.1	76.8
	Quarterly values						
1984 1	52.3	37.1	15.5	410.9	65.3	14.2	14.8
2	52.5	37.3	15.6	413.3	65.3	14.4	15.4
3	52.9	37.6	15.6	415.8	65.3	14.7	15.7
4	53.2	37.7	15.7	428.5	65.5	14.9	16.0

Note: For full details of this forecast, see Appendix 3.
All figures are £billion at 1980 prices, unless indicated, and all data are seasonally adjusted except for the interest rate and the exchange rate. For sources, see Appendix 4.

Table 5.6 *continued*

	GDP (exp. measure)	Consumer spending	Public spending	Fixed capital stock	Stock of inventories	Non-oil exports	Non-oil imports
	Annual percentage changes						
1984	2.8	3.4	1.6	2.2	− 0.1	7.5	10.3
1985	2.2	2.3	1.6	2.6	1.5	5.1	8.6
1986	1.3	2.3	1.4	2.6	2.2	3.3	5.9
1987	1.4	2.4	1.1	2.5	1.7	3.0	3.7
1988	1.6	2.3	1.3	2.3	1.5	3.3	4.1
	Quarterly percentage changes						
1984 1	1.3	4.5	− 0.2	1.9	− 0.3	4.7	6.7
2	3.6	3.5	2.7	2.1	− 0.2	8.3	10.7
3	3.8	3.3	2.0	2.3	− 0.0	10.3	12.2
4	2.5	2.5	2.1	2.4	0.2	6.9	11.6

Table 5.6 *continued*

	Consumer price index	Personal disposable income	Short-term interest rates	Exchange rate index	Average earnings (whole economy)	Employment
	Index 1980 = 100	£bn. current prices	%p.a.	Index 1980 = 100	Index 1980 = 100	000s
	PC	YD	RLB	EER	WSI	ET
	Annual values					
1984	133	216.5	9.6	91	140	23484
1985	142	234.5	9.9	91	152	23354
1986	152	255.7	9.9	90	166	23269
1987	161	277.5	9.8	89	182	23134
1988	171	299.8	10.0	88	197	22966
	Quarterly values					
1984 1	131	52.8	8.9	91	136	23558
2	132	53.6	8.6	91	139	23502
3	134	54.6	10.4	91	141	23456
4	136	55.6	10.4	91	144	23419

Table 5.6 *continued*

	Consumer price index	Personal disposable income	Exchange rate index	Average earnings (whole economy)	Employment
	Annual percentage changes				
1984	5.2	7.7	5.1	6.8	– 0.8
1985	6.5	8.3	– 0.6	8.6	– 0.6
1986	6.9	9.0	– 0.7	9.4	– 0.4
1987	6.4	8.5	– 0.8	9.0	– 0.6
1988	6.0	8.0	– 1.1	8.5	– 0.7
	Quarterly percentage changes				
1984 1	4.8	7.6	8.4	5.8	– 0.6
2	5.1	8.1	3.8	6.8	– 0.9
3	5.2	7.7	3.3	6.9	– 1.0
4	5.8	7.4	5.1	7.6	– 0.8

6

Limitations of forecasts

Forecasts rarely turn out correct and are often very inaccurate. The first section of this chapter examines the size of past forecasting errors, by looking at the track record of the main UK forecasting groups. The second section discusses the sources of these errors and the final section considers ways in which these errors can be reduced and their effects mitigated.

Throughout this chapter, standard statistical terms such as 'mean', 'variance', etc., are used without definitions being given. Readers unfamiliar with these terms may find it useful to refer to a statistical textbook for their definitions.

6.1 How accurate have forecasts been?

This section compares the forecasts made by three of the main UK forecasting groups with the events that actually occurred, which are known as *outturn*, and explains that this comparison is not as straightforward as it might seem.

Forecast errors are defined as the difference between forecast and outturn (they will often be referred to simply as *errors*; they are distinct from the error terms on the end of equations, denoted ϵ throughout this book, although they are partly caused by those error terms). For long-established groups such as the Treasury and NIESR, forecast errors can be calculated for every year back to the mid-1960s or earlier. The convention of calculating the errors by subtracting the outturn from the forecast is used here, so that a positive error indicates that the forecast was too high.

Bias

When there is a tendency for forecasts to lie to one side or the other of the outturn there is said to be *bias*. When there is no such effect, the forecasts are said to be *unbiased*. It is usually thought desirable for forecasts to be unbiased, although under exceptional circumstances users might be content with biased projections if some other advantage offset this drawback. It is possible for forecasts of one variable to be unbiased while those of another item are biased.

For each of the variables predicted by a forecasting group, it is possible to check for bias by examining the average of past errors (an alternative is to analyse mathematically the forecasting process; this is impractical for economic forecasts). When this average is close to zero, then the sum of all the overpredictions has been approximately balanced by under-predictions, providing strong evidence that the forecasts are unbiased. When the average is far from zero, there is evidence of bias. In principle, it should be possible to quantify how far the average must be from zero for it to be regarded as evidence of bias, by using information about how spread out the errors are (see below), but in practice this can be done only very approximately (because with only a small number of past errors, little is known about their distribution).

The first row of Table 6.1 shows the averages of the errors for Treasury, NIESR and LBS forecasts of GDP growth made for the five years 1978 to 1982 (this relatively short run of years is used because the LBS only has records for its more recent forecasts). The Treasury tended on average to underestimate GDP growth slightly (a negative average error), the LBS overpredicted slightly, and the NIESR overpredicted on average by rather more. A formal test suggests that none of these average errors is far enough from zero to provide evidence of bias, although this is a very uncertain conclusion particularly given the very small number of past errors used to calculate the averages. Intuitively, the LBS and Treasury figures seem reasonably close to zero while the NIESR average error is sufficiently far away to suggest that bias may be present.

Had the forecasters believed, when preparing their projections, that bias existed, they could have tried to eliminate it by replacing the part of their model thought to be causing the bias. Chapter 7 gives examples of such changes. Alternatively, as a short-term expedient they could try to obtain an unbiased projection by correcting the published forecasts by the extent of the bias. For example the NIESR might have adjusted their predictions for one or more of the components of GDP so as to reduce their forecasts for GDP by 1.4 percentage points. In Chapter 5, the use of this type of adjustment was discussed in detail, using the example of an inventories equation that was found to exhibit bias.

Average absolute errors

Whether forecasts are unbiased or not, it is useful to examine the extent to which they spread out around their mean. The usual statistical measures of

Table 6.1 Forecast errors in 1978–82 GDP growth forecasts (forecasts made in February or at budget time for the current year)

Type of error	LBS	NIESR	Treasury
Average error, percentage points	0.6	1.4	− 0.3
Average absolute error, percentage points	1.0	1.5	1.2

Sources: Published forecasts of LBS, NIESR and Treasury. No allowance is made for policy changes. Forecasts are compared with the latest available data.

Note: These figures refer to forecasts made for the current year. For example, they include the projection made in February 1982 for the percentage growth in GDP, at constant prices, between 1981 and 1982.

this are the variance and its square root, the standard deviation. The larger these measures, the greater the tendency for the errors to fall a long way from the mean. In practice, an estimate of the size of the standard deviation is given (for unbiased forecasts) by calculating the *root mean square error*, which is the square root of the average of the squares of past errors. A very similar figure, used widely in the analysis of forecast errors, is the *average absolute error*. This is the average of the positive past errors and of the numbers obtained when all the negative past errors are multiplied by minus one (on certain assumptions this can be shown to be an estimate of 0.8 times the standard deviation – see Box. 6.1).

The second row of Table 6.1 shows average absolute errors for Treasury, NIESR and LBS projections of GDP growth, calculated using forecasts made for each of the years from 1978 to 1982. The average absolute errors vary, from 1.0 percentage points for LBS to 1.5 percentage points for NIESR.

The sizes of these average absolute errors mean little unless we have some yardstick to measure them against. One possibility is to consider how the results compare with those that could have been obtained from some

Box 6.1   Relation between average absolute error and the distribution of the error terms

Assuming that the errors (written x) are distributed normally, with mean zero and variance σ^2 (see below for discussion of this assumption), then the density of the absolute values of the errors is:

$$\frac{2}{\sqrt{(2\pi\sigma^2)}} \exp(-x^2/2\sigma^2) \text{ over the range } 0 \text{ to } \infty$$

The average of this, i.e. the average absolute value of the underlying population of errors, is:

$$A = \frac{2}{(2\pi\sigma^2)} \int_0^\infty x \exp(-x^2/2\sigma^2) dx$$

$$= \sqrt{\left(\frac{2\sigma^2}{\pi}\right)}$$

so $\sigma = \sqrt{\left(\frac{\pi}{2}\right)} A$

(which means that A is approximately 0.8 times σ), so the 95 percent confidence interval for x is:

$$-1.96 \sqrt{\left(\frac{\pi}{2}\right)} A, \ +1.96 \sqrt{\left(\frac{\pi}{2}\right)} A$$

or approximately $-2\frac{1}{2}A, \ +2\frac{1}{2}A$.

We only have a small sample estimate of A, which should be corrected for the number of observations. The results shown here assume normally distributed errors; in practice the distribution may often be very different, particularly because exogenous variables may not always follow unimodal distributions, e.g. oil prices may be expected either to stay roughly where they are, or to rise sharply, with a low probability that they take an intermediate value.

very simple forecasting formula, for example 'GDP growth equals its average of the last twenty years'. Such formulae are often called *naive models*. Noting that GDP growth averaged about 2.3 per cent per annum over the last twenty years (this is the trend growth rate in the model of Chapter 4), we can calculate that the average absolute error from using this particular naive model to predict GDP growth in 1978 to 1982 would have been 2.0 percentage points. This is higher than for any of the forecasting groups, which is what we would expect given the substantial resources, the economic theory and the econometric analysis used to generate their projections. Note that we could try using other naive models, which might tend to perform better than the one suggested above.

Another way to interpret the size of the average absolute errors shown in Table 6.1 is to use them to construct a confidence interval. On certain assumptions (that the calculated average absolute error equals the true one, and that the errors are normally distributed with mean zero), it can be shown that there is a 95 per cent probability of the outturn lying in a range 2.5 average absolute errors either side of the forecast. (Box 6.1 shows that this is just a re-statement of the usual confidence interval based on the standard deviation.) The assumptions are likely to be only approximately correct, at best, but they allow us to place some interpretation on results which would otherwise mean little. We can say, for example, that the LBS projections implied that there was approximately a 95 per cent chance of the outturn falling in a range from 2.5 percentage points below the published forecast, up to 2.5 percentage points above. Intuitively, this seems a wide range, although it is not as wide as the range needed to include all the outturn growth rates for GDP over this period, which varied from + 3.1 per cent to – 2.6 per cent.

The need to make doubtful assumptions in order to deduce a confidence interval indicates that more research is needed in this area. Until this has been done, the information about past errors published by the forecasting groups will be of only limited use.   •

Difficulties when comparing forecasts with outturn

So far we have assumed that the calculation of forecast errors by subtracting outturn from forecast is straightforward. In practice, there are considerable difficulties. It is not clear whether the figure used for the outturn should be the first published figure, or the latest available at the time when the errors are being computed, or some intermediate figure. As explained in Chapter 2, data revisions mean that these may differ significantly. A typical approach is to use the latest available figure, because this includes all available information about what actually happened.

A further problem is that the base year used to calculate national accounts constant price data is changed every five years or so. This has a particularly big effect on the calculation of errors for forecasts of 1978, made in 1977. The forecasts were at 1970 prices, in line with the national accounts historical data. However, the government statisticians never produced figures for GDP in 1978 at 1970 prices. Instead the first constant prices data for GDP in 1978 used 1975 prices. Because of the enormous change in oil prices, relative to other prices, between 1970 and 1975, and because of the increasing importance of oil production in the UK economy, the GDP growth figure in 1978 was significantly higher at 1975 prices than it would have been on the old basis. A similar but less severe problem exists for forecasts of 1984 produced during 1983.

The change of price basis is sometimes ignored, sometimes tackled by excluding the affected years from the analysis, and sometimes dealt with by a crude adjustment. None of these approaches is fully satisfactory, and the choice of method can have a considerable effect on the apparent performance of a forecasting group.

Another problem is that examining growth rates may give a different result from an examination of levels. For example, a prediction of a 2 per cent rise in GDP between 1984 and 1985 may turn out correct, but data revisions (or any difference between estimates from conjunctural analysis and the actual official data) may mean that the figure for GDP in 1984, on which this projection was based, was 1 per cent too low. Thus the level predicted for GDP in 1985 would be 1 per cent below the outturn. The usual convention is to ignore levels and examine forecasts of growth for most variables, looking at the level only in a few cases such as the PSBR and the current account of the balance of payments. This is intended to reflect the form in which the forecasts are mainly used.

A related problem arises because projections for growth between the whole of one year and the whole of the next, prepared around the end of the first year, are made using historical data for that first year. For example a forecast for growth between 1983 and 1984, made in December 1983, makes use of information about events during most of 1983. Such projections are thus made with the help of reasonably firm data for half of the period which they aim to forecast. This contrasts with projections for growth between the quarter when the forecast is made and the same quarter a year later, for example a projection of growth between 1983 fourth quarter and 1984 fourth quarter, made in December 1983. Forecasts of this second type use no historical information about events during the forecast period and examination of them therefore generally provides a more stringent test of forecasting performance, although it is done relatively rarely.

Adjustments for government policy changes

Government policies often turn out to be different from those in the forecasts. For most business users, who are interested in knowing about the total amount of error from whatever source, this particular cause of forecast error should be treated no differently from others. For the government, which controls those policies (with some limits on its actions), it may be useful to examine forecast errors that have been adjusted to remove effects from this particular source. This is done using either a crude

Table 6.2 Forecast errors (forecasts made in February or budget time for current year)

Type of error	NIESR	Treasury
	GDP growth forecasts	
Average error, percentage points	0.2	n.a.
Average absolute error, percentage points, no allowance for policy changes	1.4	n.a.
Average absolute error, percentage points, adjusted for effect of policy changes	1.2	1
Calculated using forecasts made in years	1959–1982	1965–1980
	Inflation forecasts	
Average error, percentage points	– 2.0	n.a.
Average absolute error, percentage points, no allowance for policy changes	2.5	n.a.
Average absolute error, percentage points, adjusted for effect of policy changes	2.1	2
Calculated using forecasts made in years	1964–1982	1970–1980

Source: Articles in *National Institute Economic Review*, no. 105, August 1983, and no. 107, February 1984; and Treasury (1983).
Note: NIESR predict consumer prices, Treasury predict the RPI.

amendment or a complete recalculation of the whole forecast. The Treasury usually publishes forecast errors that have been adjusted in this way.

Table 6.2 shows the average absolute error in NIESR forecasts of GDP and inflation, unadjusted and after adjustments of this type. For comparison the table also shows the adjusted figures for Treasury predictions. (This table uses information from many more years than Table 6.1, because the LBS, which has records of only its recent forecasts, is excluded.) The effect of the adjustments is to reduce the average absolute error, because one of the sources of uncertainty has been removed. However, the reduction is only from 1.4 percentage points to 1.2 percentage points for GDP, and from 2.5 to 2.1 for inflation, indicating that there are other important sources of error. In the next section we consider what these other sources are.

6.2 The sources of forecast errors

Figure 6.1 shows some of the many factors contributing to the total forecast error. In this section we explain what these various sources are, and discuss whether it is possible to calculate how much each contributes to the total. In the following section we examine ways of reducing the errors or mitigating their effects.

The error terms

The most obvious sources of error are the error terms themselves. In the single equation shown in Fig. 6.1 the error term is written ϵ. Recalling

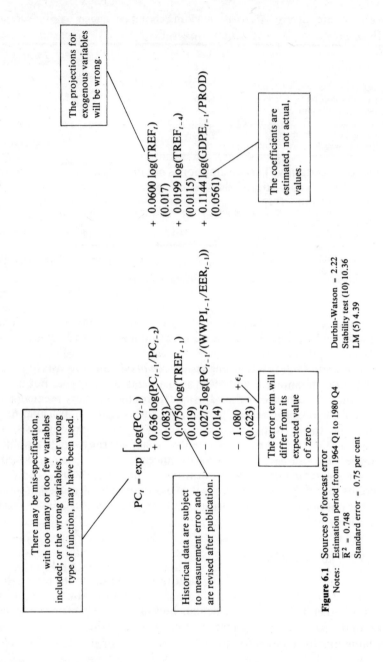

Figure 6.1   Sources of forecast error

Notes: Estimation period from 1964 Q1 to 1980 Q4   Durbin-Watson = 2.22
        $\bar{R}^2 = 0.748$ Stability test (10) 10.36
        Standard error = 0.75 per cent   LM (5) 4.39

The following content appears within the figure:

The projections for exogenous variables will be wrong.

The coefficients are estimated, not actual, values.

There may be mis-specification, with too many or too few variables included; or the wrong variables, or wrong type of function, may have been used.

Historical data are subject to measurement error and are revised after publication.

The error term will differ from its expected value of zero.

$$PC_t = \exp\left[\log(PC_{t-1})\right.$$
$$+ 0.636 \log(PC_{t-1}/PC_{t-2})$$
$$(0.083)$$
$$- 0.0750 \log(TREF_{t-1})$$
$$(0.019)$$
$$- 0.0275 \log(PC_{t-1}/(WWPI_{t-1}/EER_{t-1}))$$
$$(0.014)$$
$$+ 0.0600 \log(TREF_t)$$
$$(0.017)$$
$$+ 0.0199 \log(TREF_{t-4})$$
$$(0.0115)$$
$$+ 0.1144 \log(GDPE_{t-1}/PROD)$$
$$(0.0561)$$
$$\left. - 1.080 \right] + \epsilon_t$$
$$(0.623)$$

Chapter 4, this can be treated as a random variable with an average value of zero, provided that the equation is well specified. A measure of the variability of the error term is its standard deviation, larger values of which indicate a tendency for errors to fall a long way from zero. This cannot be observed, but an estimate of its value known as the *equation standard error* is obtained at the same time that the equation coefficients are estimated.

The equation standard error shown in the figure is 0.75 per cent, expressed as a percentage of PC. Using this value, we can compute a confidence interval for the forecast, assuming that there are no other sources of uncertainty. This assumption is not in general true, but is often approximately valid for a one period ahead forecast. Making the additional assumption that the error term is normally distributed, there is a 95 per cent probability of the outturn lying within a range from 1.96 × 0.75 (which is 1.47) per cent below the forecast, up to 1.47 per cent above.

Because the lagged value of PC itself appears on the right hand side, we have to use a forecast value for lagged PC when making projections two or more periods into the future, as explained in Chapter 5. This forecast value is of course subject to error, which we must take account of in calculating confidence intervals. A similar complication (not present in this equation) is that other endogenous variables often appear on the right hand side, and we must allow for the errors in projections of them.

This implies that a forecast for two periods ahead is generally subject to greater uncertainty (i.e. wider confidence intervals) than one for only one period ahead, because the effect of the error term is augmented by uncertainty about the values of other items on the right hand side. In general, the total uncertainty continues to increase for forecasts further into the future. However, provided the equation is stable (see Chapter 4 for definition of stability) it can be shown that the rate at which the uncertainty is growing becomes smaller as the forecast goes further into the future, and after some while it will be rising so slowly that it is effectively constant.

This important result is valid for entire macro-econometric models as well as for single equations. This means that we must look elsewhere to find a source of error that explains our intuitive belief that things become more and more uncertain as we look further ahead, or we must abandon that belief. Before considering other sources of uncertainty, a technique for computing the combined effect of all the error terms in the model will be considered.

Quantifying uncertainty through stochastic simulations

To compute by hand the effect of all the interactions between error terms in a large macro-econometric model, both within single equations over time and between equations, would be an enormous task and is usually impractical. Instead, a computer-based method known as *stochastic simulation* can be used.

This involves generating many values for each of the random variables in each of the time periods; these values are consistent with the information that is known or assumed, i.e. they have an average of zero, they tend to be close to zero for random variables whose standard error is small, and far from zero when the standard error is large. For each set of values of the random variables, a forecast is computed for each of the endogenous variables. This technique therefore produces a large number of slightly different forecasts, with the variation entirely attributable to different realizations of the random variables. The mean and standard deviation of this set of slightly different forecasts can then be calculated, thus giving the combined impact on the endogenous variables of all the error terms.

This method is attractive, although for large macro-econometric models it can take up a great deal of computer time. Ideally, it could make allowance for interrelations (covariances) among error terms on different equations, although in practice this is rarely done. An example of a practical exercise of this type is reported in Corker (1983).

The exogenous variables

The exogenous variables also contribute to the forecast errors. It is difficult to draw firm conclusions about their effect because, as explained in Chapter 5, forecasters predict the exogenous variables by a variety of different methods and use a considerable amount of judgement. Economists investigating forecast errors sometimes estimate a very simple macro-econometric model for the exogenous variables, and combine this with the model under investigation to give a larger model that has no exogenous variables. The new equations would all have their own error terms, with equation standard errors, and this information could be used to calculate confidence intervals for all the variables in the original model.

An objection to this procedure is that it does not necessarily capture the way in which the forecasting groups actually predict the exogenous variables, particularly given that investigations of this type sometimes use only a very simple model for the exogenous variables, perhaps expressing them only in terms of their own lagged values. If a procedure of this type is to be used, it should be done by, or in close co-operation with, the forecasting groups so that the equations for the exogenous variables reflect the techniques that are actually used for forecasting.

It is possible that the exogenous variables are forecast in such a way that they contribute a source of ever-increasing uncertainty to the forecast error. This would imply that, if we were able to write down an equation describing the way they were forecast, then it would be unstable. One example of such an equation is a *random walk*, in which a variable equals its own lagged value plus an error term.

Uncertainty about coefficients

The coefficients used in the macro-econometric model are estimates of the true values believed to exist in the real world. During estimation, measures of the likely closeness of the estimates to the true values is obtained. These are the coefficient *standard errors*, shown in Fig 6.1 in brackets under the coefficients themselves. Analagous to the equation standard errors, on certain assumptions it is possible to use these to construct a confidence interval indicating how close to the true values the estimates are. From this it is also possible, in principle, to calculate the impact of this type of uncertainty on total forecast error. In practice, this can be rather tedious. Another possibility is to extend the method of stochastic simulation described above to allow for the errors in the estimates of the coefficients, and for errors in forecasts of exogenous variables.

Mis-specification

Mis-specification means that the macro-econometric model is an inappropriate description of the real world. A simple type of mis-specification is the omission from the model of some exogenous variable that ought to have been included. For example, oil prices appeared in few models prior to 1973. This was because over the period for which data were used to estimate those models, oil prices had not moved far out of line with other indices of world prices. This both made it unnecessary to use oil prices to explain what had happened in the past, and meant that it would have been difficult to use econometrics to disentangle the effect of oil price movements from changes in other variables. After the large rise in oil prices in 1973, it became clear that models without a separate oil price term were badly mis-specified.

Another form of mis-specification occurs when an endogenous variable is formed by adding together two or more items that in reality move in different ways. For example an important variable in the early 1984 version of the LBS model was an index of average earnings in public corporations plus private services. This variable spans the most highly unionized industries in the economy (coal, railways, etc.) and also the least unionized (retail trade, hotels and catering). In the Liverpool University model, the unionized and non-unionized sectors are treated separately on the grounds that the labour market is monopolistic in one and approximately perfect in the other; if the view on which the Liverpool model is based is correct, then that version of the LBS system was severely mis-specified.

A further type of mis-specification arises when an equation is of the wrong form. This usually means that it is linear, or linear in the logarithms of the variables, when a more appropriate form would be non-linear, or non-linear in the logarithms. The attractions of linear models are ease of estimation on widely available computer software, relative simplicity for analysis, and intuitive appeal. However, they are inappropriate in many cases because the endogenous variables in a linear model always respond by the same absolute amount (or same percentage, for a linear in logs model) to a change in an exogenous variable. Although this is a convenient property, it is often unrealistic. It implies that a policy which has desirable effects during high unemployment will have the same effects at full employment. Figure 6.2 shows an equation for consumption that is linear in logarithms. This is estimated over historical data on which it fits reasonably well, but it produces wildly inaccurate forecasts when a future value taken by real income (one of the explanatory variables) is much larger than any of the values taken during the estimation period.

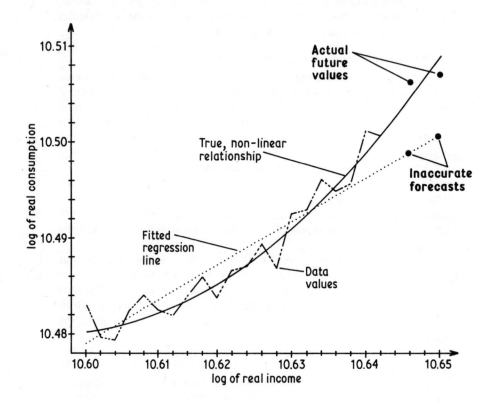

Figure 6.2   Inappropriate use of linear regression as a source of error
Note: The axes are labelled with the log of real consumption and real income to give an economic interpretation, but the data are imaginary.

Another form of mis-specification occurs when no allowance, or inadequate allowance, is made for the way that people take account of government policy when forming their plans. This problem is known as the *Lucas critique* and is discussed further in the final section of Chapter 8.

Even when appropriate variables and equation type are used, mis-specification can occur because an unsatisfactory estimation procedure has been used to obtain the coefficients of the model. A widespread example is the use of ordinary least squares to estimate equations that include current period endogenous variables on the right hand side. As explained in Chapter 4, this will give biased estimates and two stage least squares should be used instead.

Quantifying mis-specification is usually even more difficult, both in theory and in practice, than quantifying the effect on forecast errors of the other factors discussed earlier. It can in general be done only when we have in mind one alternative macro-econometric model, or possibly several, plus some idea of the likelihood of these alternatives.

Which items are most difficult to forecast?

The above analysis of the sources of forecast errors suggests an explanation of why some variables are apparently more difficult to forecast than others. To illustrate this diversity, Table 6.3 gives the average absolute errors for Treasury forecasts of ten important variables. These figures were computed from one year ahead forecasts made over about fifteen years up to 1980. The average absolute error for forecasts of GDP growth was 1 per cent, and for investment 2½ per cent was recorded. Of more concern to some users, the average absolute error for the PSBR was £4 billion, which seems very large in comparison with typical levels of the PSBR of about £6 to £10 billion. Projections for the current account also appear subject to errors that are large compared to the level of the balance itself.

The PSBR and the current balance are both small balances between two large numbers. The current account, for example, equals exports minus imports (plus interest, profits, dividends and transfers, which are relatively small). From elementary statistics, we know that the variance of the difference between two items equals the sum of their variances, minus

Table 6.3   Forecast errors: relative sizes of errors on different variables

Variable	Error in percentage points
Retail price index	2
GDP	1
Consumers' expenditure	1
General government consumption	1½
Fixed investment	2½
Exports of goods and services	2½
Imports of goods and services	2½
Change in stockbuilding (as per cent of level of GDP)	¾
	Error in £ billion
Current account balance	2
PSBR	4

Source: Treasury (1983).
Note: Forecasts made at budget time for coming year by HM Treasury, adjusted for policy changes.

any covariance; and standard errors are estimates of the square root of the variances of the error terms. Hence, the standard error of the current account equation depends positively on the standard errors of both the export and the import equations. Thus there is reinforcement rather than cancelling in the variability of the error terms. (There might be a covariance tending to offset or further reinforce this effect.) The current balance is at most a few billion pounds each year (positive or negative), while exports and imports are each around £80 billion per annum. Thus relatively small standard errors on the export and import equations can give a very large standard error on the balance.

6.3 Reducing the limitations

In this section we consider how forecast errors can be reduced, and how their effects can be mitigated.

Reducing forecast error

In Section 6.2, we identified several sources of error. In principle, it should be possible to derive a macro-econometric model that was capable of no further improvement in any of these areas; in practice, the models used by all the forecasting groups can be improved in all of them. Often, considerable resources may be needed to achieve only small reduction in the forecast errors, and also there can be doubt about whether the errors were lowered rather than increased. For these reasons, considerable judgement is needed when deciding the priorities for tackling the different causes of forecast error.

The first cause of forecast errors identified above was the error term itself, whose contribution was measured by the equation standard error. One way this can be reduced is by using extra information during estimation, which for macro-econometric models almost always means using observations for a larger number of time periods. Typically, all available observations are already used (except for those reserved for use in a post-sample forecast test, as described in Chapter 4), so there is usually no scope for improvement in this area, except perhaps for increasing the frequency of re-estimation as new data become available.

An alternative way to reduce the contribution from the error terms is to use an improved estimation procedure. Most equations in UK macro-econometric models are estimated one at a time using single equation methods, such as ordinary least squares and two stage least squares described in Chapter 4. In principle, improved estimates can be obtained for the whole model by using instead a *systems* estimation method, in which all the equations of the model (or at least all those in one section of the model) are estimated simultaneously. An example of such a method is three stage least squares (for this and other systems estimators, see one of the less elementary econometrics textbooks, for example, Theil, 1971).

In practice, relatively little systems estimation has been done. This is partly because the theory underlying systems estimation methods is more difficult than that needed to understand single equation techniques, and can only be understood with the use of complex matrix algebra. A further drawback to the use of systems estimation is that it may require a considerable amount of computer time. Another reason sometimes given is that mis-specification in one equation can adversely affect the estimates in another, well-specified equation, which cannot occur under single equation estimation. This reason seems irrelevant for equations that are to be included in a macro-econometric model, because mis-specification in one equation, even if all the others are correctly specified and estimated, will affect the properties of the whole model.

The second source of forecast errors identified above was from forecasts of exogenous variables. Given the eclectic methods used, it is difficult to suggest a clear procedure for improvements in this area. For the third source of error, uncertainty about coefficients due merely to estimation errors and not due to mis-specification, the use of more observations and of systems estimation will usually produce improvements.

The fourth source of error was mis-specification. Several ways of reducing error from this source are possible. Greater use can be made of tests of specification and mis-specification, such as those suggested and illustrated in Chapter 4. One of those tests was a post-sample forecast test, which analysed the ability of the equation to predict values of the dependent variable, over periods not used in estimation. In the form described in Chapter 4, this was a static test, because actual values of the lagged dependent variable and of all other right hand side variables were used, so the equation was never having to rely on forecast values. An alternative, more stringent test is known as *dynamic tracking*. It uses forecast values of the dependent variable on the right hand side of the equation. Dynamic tracking can also be carried out for the whole macro-econometric model, with model forecasts being used for all current and lagged endogenous variables. Such tests are usually much more likely to detect mis-specification when carried out over data periods not used in estimation, in the same way that the static test of Chapter 4 used post-sample data.

Another way to check for mis-specification is to confirm that the macro-econometric model is consistent with economic theory and has sensible long-run properties. This is not an econometric test, but a check against the forecaster's prior beliefs based on economic theory. It is done by carrying out simulations, which are described in Chapter 8. Often, the forecaster may have intended to impose these desired properties through the model specification and through the tests carried out during estimation, but a further check on the complete model is desirable.

Comparing forecast performance

The method of dynamic tracking can also be used as a means of comparing the models of different forecasting groups. In contrast to a straight-

forward comparison of their forecasts, which is subject to the problems of
data revisions mentioned in Section 6.1, and to other difficulties such as
different timing of publication and hence different information, a
dynamic tracking exercise offers the opportunity of a 'laboratory' experiment in which an identical set of historical data is supplied to the models of
all the groups. Against this, the treatment of exogenous variables presents
a considerable problem, because their number and importance may vary
among models. For example, if one of the models lacks an exchange rate
equation, because the forecasters typically predict it by judgement, then
some unsatisfactory procedure must be adopted. Either the outturn values
could be used (giving that group an unfair advantage), or some other
values such as those from a simple extra equation could be used (altering
the model that was being tested). Another problem is that if the model of
one group has been estimated over a longer time period than the others,
then it may have an advantage that is not due to that group's view of the
way the world works being a better description than the others. Reflecting
these problems, no large-scale comparitive dynamic tracking exercise has
been documented for the UK; a straightforward comparison of forecasts
is given in Artis (1982) and Wallis (1985), Chapter 3.

Mitigating the effect of errors

The combined effect of introducing all the improvements discussed above,
even if fully successful, would be to bring average absolute forecast errors
down to the minimum achievable value; given the very considerable,
irreduceable uncertainty about the future, this would still be a high figure.
Although this uncertainty cannot itself be removed, the adverse effects of
it can usually be lowered if the users of forecasts are aware of it, and of its
approximate size, and take account of it in forming their plans.

One way to take account of uncertainty involves carrying out
simulations, which are variants of the forecast in which one or more of the
exogenous variables is altered and the forecast re-computed. (The use of
simulations in which policy variables are altered, as a way of evaluating
government policy, is discussed in detail in Chapter 8.) Using such simulations, companies can work out the implications for their businesses of
various different outcomes for the economy, and can identify which
courses of action are likely to be the most risky. They may then, perhaps,
choose to act in a way that offers a lower return but carries less risk. Other
forecast users can, in principle, adopt a similar approach. This use of
simulations, sometimes known as *scenario planning* or *sensitivity
analysis*, is fairly widespread among the corporate planning departments
of large companies.

In theory, it should be possible for users to adopt an even more sophisticated approach, taking full account of all the sources of error described
in Section 6.2, working out the effect of all possible outcomes on their
future profits (or on any other objective at which they were aiming). They
could then weigh up the relative risks and returns of all available courses

of action, and act accordingly. This is impractical because it would require vast amounts of computer time, but the scenario planning described above can be regarded as an approximation to this more sophisticated approach.

7

Development of forecasting models in the UK

This chapter describes the development of the main macro-econometric models in the UK. We begin with the earliest versions of the National Institute (NIESR) and Treasury models, from the 1950s, and study changes in these and in models introduced later by other groups. Throughout the chapter, we emphasize that these changes, and sometimes the introduction of new models, were related to developments in economic theory, to the needs of users, and to external events that demonstrated inadequacies in the existing models.

To describe fully all the macro-econometric models of the UK, with complete details of the way they have evolved, is beyond the scope of this book, and would involve considerable duplication because changes in one of the models have often been followed by similar alterations in the others. The approach adopted here is to describe major developments in the form that they were first introduced by one of the groups, with only brief comments on the later adoption of similar systems by the others. The final section of this chapter gives sources for further, more detailed reading on the various models, and considers likely areas of further development by the forecasting groups.

7.1 The early income-expenditure models (1950s to early 1970s)

The macro-economic forecasts in the early issues of the *National Institute Economic Review*, which was launched in 1959, were prepared without the use of a formal macro-econometric model. Instead the forecasters had a set of relationships probably based on judgement and perhaps a limited amount of estimation, and not necessarily all written down. Worswick, in the introduction to Surrey (1971), states that an '. . .economic model. . .was always implicit, if somewhat informally, in the forecasting process. . .'. The structure of this informal model can be approximately reconstructed from details given by Worswick. It is likely that the forecasting methods used at this time in the Treasury were similar.

In the informal NIESR model, real average wages were inversely related to unemployment (a Phillips curve). Employment (and hence unemployment) was determined by past movements in output, and average wages times numbers employed gave personal incomes from wages and salaries. This was combined with projections of other sources of income and of taxes (both probably taken as exogenous) to give total personal disposable income. Real disposable income was obtained by dividing this by a forecast of consumer prices, which was dependent on past wages and on exogenous import prices. Real consumer spending was determined by current and past real disposable income and by current hire purchase controls.

Stocks and investment depended on the rate of change of output (an accelerator), and exports were determined by an exogenous projection for world trade and by competitiveness which, with the exchange rate fixed, depended on the relative movements of UK and foreign labour costs. Together with public spending, which was assumed to be an exogenous policy variable, these components of demand gave total domestic demand and this determined imports and hence GDP. As noted above, movements in GDP gave forecasts for employment. This informal model also included the important identity giving the balance of payments current account from trade volumes and prices.

All the calculations for forecasting had to be carried out by hand, without the aid of computers, but the techniques were the same as those described in Chapter 5. Starting from historical data and projections for the exogenous variables, a one period ahead forecast was prepared; this was used as the base for the following period, and so on. Even without the use of a computer, a certain amount of policy analysis was possible. This policy analysis involved studying how the forecast changed when exogenous policy assumptions were altered (and was therefore just like the policy simulations described in Chapter 8, except that the calculations had to be done by hand).

Measures designed to increase demand, such as tax cuts, higher public spending and relaxation of hire purchase controls, had the direct effect of raising domestic output and reducing unemployment. Against these beneficial effects, the model predicted some adverse results. Wage inflation, and hence price inflation, increased in response to the lower unemployment, and the current account deficit worsened (or the surplus fell) as some of the demand was met by imports. With the exchange rate fixed, the increase in wages implied reduced competitiveness, which gave further adverse movements in net trade and in the current account, and offset some of the gains in output.

When unemployment was high, wage increases low and the current account in surplus, Treasury and NIESR economists, working with this type of model, would typically advise measures designed to raise demand. As wage inflation accelerated and the current account deteriorated, they would change to advising contractionary policies.

Most contemporary criticism of policy-making accepted the broad structure of the models, arguing that the policy recommendations based on these models tended to come too late and to be of the incorrect magnitude. The forecasters responded to this criticism partly by improved modelling techniques. The use of estimated, rather than judgemental, equations appears to have increased in the early 1960s, with the general outline of the models remaining as set out above.

In 1966 the existing forecasting groups at NIESR and the Treasury were joined by a third group, at the London Business School (LBS). The first LBS model contained sixteen equations and was similar to the two existing models, but the calculations were carried out by computer instead of by hand. Computerization of forecasting by the other two groups followed in 1969 (for NIESR) and 1971 (for the Treasury), although both had carried out experimental computer forecasting before these dates. It seems that no major changes were made to the structure of the models at the time of computerization, both NIESR and the Treasury drawing on econometric work carried out earlier, much of which was already in use for forecasting.

Once the models were based on computers, it became easy to increase the number of items forecast, and to alter existing equations. The models expanded rapidly between 1969 and 1973. Larger models reduced the need for unrealistic aggregation, facilitated conjunctural analysis and increased the detail available to forecast users. Although they also offered the opportunity to improve the forecasting and policy analysis of the whole model, while retaining the broad structure set out at the start of this section, the emphasis at this time appears to have been on the development of individual equations. With restricted computing power it was not always easy to check the impact of a new equation on the whole system.

The Cambridge Economic Policy Group (CEPG), by contrast, concentrated at this time on the properties of their model as a whole. This group, which started publishing projections in 1971, was one of those receiving funds from the Social Science Research Council (SSRC) for macro-econometric model development (see Chapter 1). The CEPG argued that there was no need for a large number of equations which allowed, among other things, fiscal policy to influence consumption, consumption to influence imports, and imports to affect the current account. Instead, the CEPG suggested that changes in the current account deficit could be predicted to be approximately equal to changes in the government's financial deficit. No detailed modelling was needed no reach this conclusion, because the private sector (persons and companies) acted to keep its net financial position broadly unchanged, and by identity (see Section 2.3) the financial positions of government, overseas and private sectors sum to zero.

This was known as the *New Cambridge* view. It was supported by the CEPG's apparent success in forecasting that the current account would worsen substantially in response to the expansionary fiscal policy adopted by the Conservative administration in 1973; the other forecasters expected less deterioration. However, subsequent data revisions have made it less clear that the CEPG prediction was closest.

7.2 Exchange rate forecasting and associated developments (mid to late 1970s)

Until 1973, the forecasters treated the exchange rate as exogenous, even though it was understood that continuing current account deficits, due in part to lack of competitiveness, were major causes of the devaluations that occurred in 1968 and 1971. From 1973, the fixed parities agreed two years earlier (the Smithsonian agreement) became unsustainable and the UK and other major industrialized nations moved to a system of floating exchange rates. This made it necessary to devise some system for predicting the exchange rate.

At about the same time, public borrowing rose very rapidly, with large increases in all the years from 1972 to 1975, partly as a result of the expansionary fiscal policy pursued by the government in 1971–72. This was initially accompanied by a rapid rise in output (the 'Barber Boom'), but in 1974 and 1975 there were significant falls in GDP. All the forecasters underpredicted the severity of this recession. There were several other large changes in exogenous factors at about this time, including the very large rise in oil prices at the end of 1973 and structural changes in the banking system following the competition and credit control measures of 1971. However, it seemed likely that one of the most important causes of the failure to forecast the 1974–75 falls in output was that expansionary fiscal policy had not produced the beneficial effects predicted by the models.

In reaction to these events, the Treasury, LBS and NIESR all introduced exchange rate equations and made related changes, particularly to the modelling of the financial sector and the influence of monetary policy. In this section we describe these developments in detail, drawing partly on the description of the three models as at June 1977 given in Laury *et al.* (1978).

Treasury model

The Treasury model model in 1977 included an explicit equation for exchange rate expectations. These depended principally on UK money stock growth compared to that in the US, adjusted for discrepancies in the rates of change of output. The difference between the actual and the expected exchange rate determined private capital account flows. Government intervention, and other public capital flows, were taken as exogenous. The current account was determined in broadly the same way as in earlier versions of the model, implying that it depended indirectly on the exchange rate. The sum of private and public capital flows must be equal and opposite to the current account (apart from the residual error in the balance of payments accounts), and the exchange rate was forecast by choosing the value which ensured that this identity was satisfied.

This Treasury system recognized explicitly the role of expectations (which caused a jump in the exchange rate when monetary growth was altered) and incorporated the notion that the exchange rate was a price adjusting to equalize supply and demand for foreign exchange. In these respects it was similar to much more recent macro-econometric models, such as the 1984 version of the LBS model and also the model presented in Chapter 4. However, there was no mechanism to prevent the expected rate from differing systematically from the actual rate predicted by the model. Nor was there a formal way to capture market expectations of future (as opposed to current period) policy changes, although this could be done by adjusting the expected rate.

Related to the exchange rate forecasting system, the Treasury also experimented with a detailed model of the financial system. The supply of gilts (long-dated bonds) by the government rose either when the PSBR increased, or when monetary growth targets were reduced. Demand for gilts by the private sector was determined by the interest rates on alternative assets but not by expectations about future supply. The yield on gilts adjusted to equate supply and demand.

When either the new exchange rate forecasting system, or the financial equations, or both, were overridden, then an expansion of public spending led to a marked and sustained rise in GDP. This property was similar to that of the earlier versions of the model described in the first section of this chapter. When both the exchange rate and the financial equations were allowed to operate, the increase in GDP and reduction in unemployment from higher government spending was largely temporary. After five to six years, GDP returned almost to its starting point.

This result was due to a continual rise in gilts yields, which the new equations generated in order to sell the gilts needed to finance the higher public spending without raising taxes or money supply. This rise in the yield on one type of sterling asset raised the exchange rate, at a time when UK inflation was increasing in response to the initial fall in unemployment, thus worsening competitiveness and depressing output.

The continuing rise in gilts yields was implausible, because it implied that those purchasing gilts were making a continuing capital loss (gilts pay a fixed amount of interest, so their price must fall to raise the yield). Again, there was no mechanism to ensure consistency between market expectations and the predictions of the model.

Thus the new equations provided a possible, but rather implausible, explanation for the adverse effect on inflation of the 1974–5 expansion of public borrowing. These equations were regarded as experimental by the Treasury and were probably not used for regular forecasting. The next part of this section considers the LBS views about the impact of public borrowing and the determination of the exchange rate, which are related to the Treasury's but differ in many important respects.

The London Business School model

Between 1975 and 1977, the London Business School introduced radical alterations to the model which gave it properties based on the theory known as *international monetarism*. According to this theory, a rise in the

UK money supply relative to overseas money supply caused an immediate proportionate fall in the exchange rate (measured as usually quoted in the newspaper, i.e. as the value of sterling relative to other currencies), assuming that other things were unchanged.

This theory relied on the assumption that higher UK money supply led eventually to higher UK prices and wages. Since the real exchange rate had to return to some given level in the long run to prevent a growing trade imbalance (the theory of long-run *purchasing power parity*), this meant that the nominal exchange rate would eventually depreciate. This in turn was assumed to mean that markets would mark sterling down straight away, rather than take an anticipated capital loss later. When money supply growth was raised, this type of model gave a continuing depreciation.

Like the 1977 version of the Treasury model, this system had some similarities to much more recent macro-econometric models, but expectations of policy changes due to take place in future had no effect.

This new LBS model required not only a new exchange rate equation but also new wages and prices equations which ensured that changes in the exchange rate were followed by proportionate changes in the domestic price level. According to the estimated equations, most of this effect occurred within about two or three years. Thus a rise in money stock caused an instant exchange rate fall, and it also caused temporary increases in competitiveness and output that were gradually cancelled out as prices and wages rose. After two or three years, output reached the level it would have attained if money supply had been unaltered, but the price level was higher. Similarly an increase in the growth of the money supply raised inflation without having any long-run effect on output. This contrasted with the models described in the first section of this chapter, in which devaluation always caused some gain to competitiveness and hence to output, at the cost of some rise in prices.

Preliminary versions of this new LBS model took money stock as an exogenous government policy variable. Later versions had an endogenous money stock determined partly by government borrowing (the PSBR), so the direct boost to output from higher government spending or tax cuts was accompanied by a higher PSBR and hence a rise in money supply. Permanent changes in spending or taxes raised money supply growth. One of the side-effects of expansionary fiscal policy was thus a devaluation, leading before long to a higher price level or higher inflation through the routes described above.

There was one other change in some versions of this model. Consumer spending was made to depend inversely on the rate of inflation as people saved more to maintain the real value of their financial assets. This is now a feature of almost all macro-econometric models of the UK, including that presented in Chapter 4. With this additional effect, the higher inflation caused by fiscal expansion would reduce consumer spending, offsetting some of the direct beneficial effects on output from the higher government spending or lower taxes. The revised LBS model thus provided an explanation of the way that higher inflation, without higher output, had apparently resulted from the fiscal expansions of the early 1970s. An intermediate stage in the development of this model is given in Ball *et al*. (1977).

These fundamental changes to the LBS model were achieved by modifications to, or addition of, several important equations, with most of the model unaltered. In contrast to the period of development up to 1974, these equation changes were made with the intention of altering the properties of the whole model. It is interesting to note that, because only a few equations had been changed, little was needed to restore the former properties of the model. For example, it was often tempting to put constant adjustments on the exchange rate equation, or to override it completely by making the exchange rate exogenous, because this equation did not forecast well. When this was done, it removed one of the most important links needed to give the model its international monetarist properties, and made the model more like the 1960s versions, in which higher government spending raised output substantially. This demonstrates that interference with a single equation in a macro-econometric model can completely alter the whole system.

The National Institute model

In the 1977 version of the National Institute model, the exchange rate depended on UK prices relative to overseas prices, on the visible trade balance and on the covered differential between UK and US interest rates. This equation had the property that price competitiveness would eventually return to some given long-run level.

This property, of long-run purchasing power parity, was also present in the 1977 version of the LBS model, as noted above (and also now applies to many other models including that of Chapter 4). However, in the LBS model it was, and still is, imposed via terms in domestic price equations rather than through a term in the exchange rate equation. With both domestic prices and the exchange rate endogenous, this property can be imposed via either equation (or indirectly through other parts of the model).

Placing the long-run purchasing power parity term in the exchange rate equation did not imply that wages affected the exchange rate without any effect in the opposite direction. For example, if some exogenous factor caused an initial jump of, say, 5 per cent in UK wages, then the long run fall in the exchange rate, and the eventual rise in wages themselves, might both be rather more than 5 per cent. This is because a depreciation in response to higher wages generates increased domestic inflation, pushing up wages further, and causing another depreciation. In macro-econometric models, this type of interaction between equations is usually analysed most easily by simulation (i.e. by changing an exogenous assumption and preparing a new forecast; see Chapter 8).

The covered interest rate differential in the NIESR exchange rate equation was intended to capture the influence of exchange rate expectations. It is the difference between two alternative ways of holding 'forward' foreign exchange. When exchange controls existed, as in the UK in 1977, it sometimes temporarily became fairly large, reflecting market beliefs that the interest differential was insufficient to compensate for an expected parity change. In practice it always fell back rapidly to about zero as either interest rates or exchange rates changed. With the abolition of exchange controls in 1979, it ceased to provide any information about expectations, because arbitrage now ensures that it reflects only transactions costs, which are small.

This was not a satisfactory way to deal with exchange rate expectations, for it reflected anticipated interest rate changes as well as exchange rates, and because it only covered a very short way ahead. For forecasts more than one period into the future, these expectations would have to be predicted using judgement.

Related to the exchange rate forecasting equation, the National Institute introduced a simple financial system. Money stock depended on an exogenous interest rate, with the option to reverse this to have exogenous money supply determining interest rates. There were only weak links from interest rates on to real economic activity.

None of the three exchange rate systems performed well when used for forecasting. Brooks and Henry (1983), commenting on the 1977 NIESR model, say: 'Like so many other models of the exchange rate, it proved highly unstable. It completely failed to track the appreciation and subsequent depreciation of sterling over the period 1979 to 1982. . .'. With inadequate formal systems, the forecasters had to use eclectic, informal techniques, or conventional assumptions, for exchange rate forecasting.

In response to the events of the early 1970s, the forecasters had attempted to model both the determinants of the exchange rate and the possible adverse effects of high public borrowing, but there were clearly many limitations in the new versions of the models. A description of the models as they were in mid-1978 is given in Ormerod (1979). Before we discuss the next stage in the development of exchange rate forecasting in UK macro-econometric models, we will consider the treatment of supply factors in the models; over-simplified modelling of these may have been another cause of the forecasting errors in the early 1970s.

7.3 The supply side of goods and labour markets (late 1970s and early 1980s)

The LBS, NIESR and Treasury models, in all the versions described above, covered aggregate demand and its determinants in considerable detail. Changes in real income, real wealth (implicitly, via the inflation term in the consumption function), the exchange rate, government spending and interest rates had direct effects on one or more of the components of demand.

In principle, it should also be possible to treat supply explicitly and in detail, allowing for changes over time in relative factor prices, capital stock, technological progress and any other effects that alter the willingness of companies to supply goods and services. It is possible to assume that supply and demand are always brought into line with one another by movements in prices (instantaneous market clearing). Alternatively, it can instead be assumed that this equality of supply and demand applies only in the long run, and that prices adjust slowly towards the market clearing level, tending to fall when supply increases or when demand falls, and vice versa.

In the LBS, NIESR and Treasury models, supply factors were modelled in a simple way. There was assumed to be some shift over time in the supply curve, usually at a constant rate, reflecting technical progress and capital accumulation. This effect did not appear explicitly in an equation for the supply of goods and services, but typically entered the model implicitly through a term in the domestic prices equations. This term caused prices to rise when total demand was high relative to some reference level (as in a Phillips curve), with the reference level rising over time to reflect the trend shift in the supply curve. (This term itself was not always explicit; in the LBS model, and the model of Chapter 4, the effect was achieved indirectly through competitiveness terms.) This effect could be regarded as a shift in prices towards the long run level at which supply and demand were brought into line.

The main criticism of this approach was that supply factors should be modelled in greater detail, with explicit allowance for changes in energy, raw material and labour costs, and also for actual capital stock growth rather than the trend growth already implicitly included. The new City University Business School (CUBS) model, first used for published forecasts from 1983, was designed to do this. Unlike the existing models, it used annual data and contained only a relatively small number of equations. The first versions of this model included explicitly the determinants of aggregate supply noted above. However, an important limitation was that the model included much less detail about demand than existed in the LBS, NIESR and Treasury models.

In addition to modelling supply, demand and prices in the goods market, the CUBS model adopted a similar approach for the labour market. This was achieved by estimating an employment equation, which was interpreted as a demand curve that depended in part on wages, and also by estimating an equation for wages which depended in part on factors that influenced labour supply such as the rate of unemployment benefit.

This type of equation system can be interpreted as a description of a perfect market for labour, in which wages adjust to the level at which supply equals demand. It can alternatively be interpreted as a description of more sophisticated hypotheses about labour market structure, for example a model in which companies are assumed to take wages as given, but to have full freedom to choose employment, while unions fix wages, taking account of the impact on employment from companies' reactions.

The decisions made by companies about employment were another area in which inadequate modelling led to large forecasting errors. The next section describes the events that caused these errors, and the forecasters' reactions.

7.4 Modelling company behaviour (early 1980s)

During the year to mid-1980, average earnings in the UK rose by more than a fifth, partly in response to the substantial rise in VAT introduced in 1979 and partly because private sector pay agreements tried to keep up with the very large (typically 25 per cent) public sector awards made by the Clegg pay commission. The adverse effect on company finances was compounded by a rising exchange rate, high interest charges and (for companies not producing oil) increased oil prices. In export markets, the high exchange rate meant that UK companies had to hold or even reduce sterling prices, despite increased costs (by contrast, many importers allowed domestic producers to set prices, taking increased profit margins instead of cutting prices to gain volume). As a result, in the second half of 1980, real profitability fell to the lowest recorded level.

The immediate reaction of companies was to cut stocks, which were the only item that could be reduced rapidly and easily. This assisted cash flow, because goods sold from stock generated revenue but involved no further production costs. For 1980 as a whole, stock volumes fell by about 1 ½ per cent of GDP. This was one of the highest figures recorded and had a severe effect on demand because stocks had risen in the previous year. The fall in demand was most marked in manufacturing, where output fell about 15 per cent over the eighteen months to mid-1981.

In response to lower output, manufacturers were generally unable or unwilling to reduce employment immediately, because of statutory or negotiated procedures and redundancy payments. During 1981 manu-facturers appear to have taken the view that the reduction in demand would not be reversed rapidly, and they started to reduce their workforces. Many factories were closed and manufacturing employment fell by about 800,000 (13 per cent) over the two years to the end of 1982. Expenditure on investment was also reduced substantially.

The forecasters failed to predict the size of the cutbacks in company spending. The LBS and Treasury models contained identities which derived the company sector financial balance (the difference between companies' spending and their income). This provided an indication of the financial pressure on companies but the formal links in the model equations between this financial balance and company spending on stocks, employment or investment were weak or non-existent.

The Treasury dealt with this problem by using a simple interim solution. An equation was estimated for desired company gross liquid financial assets, i.e. readily encashable assets such as bank deposits. A separate calculation gave the liquid asset holdings implied by existing equations for company expenditure on stocks, employment and investment. If desired liquid asset holdings were higher than the level implied by the expenditure equations, then spending on stocks, numbers employed and investment were each reduced below the levels implied by their respective equations, the total value of the reduction being sufficient to halve the difference between desired and actual liquid asset holdings. The choice of halving and the allocation of the cuts among the three spending categories were arbitrary, based on the Treasury forecasters' judgement.

A significant limitation of the Treasury's approach was that companies were unlikely to choose separate, inconsistent targets for liquid assets, stocks and other items, and then adjust them by some arbitrary rule. It would be more plausible to assume that companies chose consistent targets for assets, employment and other items jointly, to maximize a discounted future stream of profits (or to maximize some other objective such as volume of sales). Because the maximization would be subject to the companies' budget constraint, no cuts below target levels would be needed, except when decisions were based on expectations that turned out incorrect. Both the LBS and NIESR carried out research using this general approach although at the time of writing (mid-1984) these new systems had not been used for practical forecasting work.

In principle, the company maximization problem described above could involve decisions not only about liquid assets, stocks, employment and investment; other items, including the volume and price of sales, could also be assumed to be chosen. The appropriate items depend on the market structure that seems the best approximate description for UK companies. For example, under perfect competition, companies would choose sales volume but not output prices, while a monopoly could choose any combination of sales and output prices that lay on its demand curves.

7.5 The exchange rate and rational expectations (early to mid-1980s)

Neither the exchange rate forecasting systems developed in the mid-1970s, nor the forecasters' eclectic techniques, were able to predict the sharp rise in sterling up to early 1981, which was then partially reversed. Developments in the theory of exchange rate determination during the second half of the 1970s, which used the assumption of rational expectations, offered a possible explanation for these sharp movements in the exchange rate.

The first regular forecasts made using this type of theory were prepared not by any of the existing teams, but by a new forecasting group at Liverpool University.

The Liverpool University model

The Liverpool model, first used for forecasting in 1980, was in many respects similar to the existing macro-econometric models of the UK economy. It incorporated a demand for money equation (LM curve) and equations for consumption, net exports and capital expenditure (on both fixed investment and stocks) which, together with the GDP identity, formed an IS curve.

However, the Liverpool model also included several developments in economic theory which were not in use in the existing macro-econometric models in 1980. The most important of these was the use of an uncovered interest parity exchange rate equation (for explanation of this, see the box on page 57 in Chapter 4) combined with the assumption that exchange rate expectations were rational. As demonstrated in Chapter 8, Section 8.3, using the model of Chapter 4, this way of modelling the exchange rate predicts a sudden jump, which may be followed by partial reversal of the initial movement, when tighter monetary policy is announced. This seemed to give an approximate description of the events of 1979–82, which the earlier exchange rate forecasting systems had failed to do.

Other major differences between the Liverpool model and the 1980 versions of the earlier models were: the inclusion of rational expectations of domestic prices, which allowed the sudden receipt of previously unexpected information about future prices to influence output; an explicit allowance for the impact of changes in wealth on consumption (although the LBS and other models had included an implicit effect of this sort since the mid-1970s, as described in Section 7.2 above); and the inclusion of factors affecting the supply of labour, in particular the rate of unemployment benefit. Increases in this were supposed to cut labour supply thus raising measured unemployment (a very strong effect according to this version of the Liverpool model) and pushing wages up. One other major difference between the Liverpool model and the NIESR, Treasury and LBS models was that the former was based on annual data and generally had simpler dynamic specifications.

In November 1980, the Liverpool University forecasting group predicted a sharp fall in inflation over the next few years, from almost 20 per cent at the time of the forecast to under 3 per cent in 1984. This projection relied on the assumption that expectations of both domestic prices and the exchange rate would take account of the government's medium term financial strategy (MTFS), which gave targets for a gradual reduction in monetary growth over the forecast period. The Liverpool projections also showed unemployment declining rapidly to under two million (excluding school leavers) in 1984.

The Liverpool group's forecast for inflation turned out to be closer to the outturn than the projections made by the other forecasting teams at that time, but their prediction for unemployment was too low by an even larger margin than the forecasts made by the LBS. As emphasized in Chapter 6, comparing forecasts with outturn is subject to many problems; the comparisons given here refer to only one single forecast out of the many made by all the groups and are included only to highlight the difference of approach and of results between Liverpool and the other groups at that time.

The London Business School model

During the early 1980s the London Business School model was expanded and modified to include a detailed financial sector in which the exchange rate was determined as a market-clearing price (i.e. it moved to bring supply and demand for foreign currency into equality), under the assumption of rational expectations. Improved modelling of the labour market and an explicit effect on consumption from changes in wealth were also introduced. The LBS model thus took account of many of the theoretical innovations incorporated in the Liverpool model, with the important contrast that the LBS tended to use a far more disaggregated approach throughout almost all of the model (except, at this stage, in the labour market). There were also many important differences in the order of magnitude of effects suggested by simulations.

In its 1984 version, the LBS model assumed that the choice among financial assets could be treated as if income and expenditure were given from the older sections of the model. The economy was divided into several sectors: personal, companies, government, banks, pension funds and overseas. For each sector, the difference between income and spending gave its net flow of new funds available for investment in financial assets, known as the financial balance. (Chapter 2 describes this identity in detail.) This balance might be positive, indicating that income exceeded expenditure and implying that net purchases of financial assets were possible, or negative, indicating that a shortfall of income below spending must be financed by an increase in financial liabilities (i.e. by net borrowing).

In the model each sector could buy a wide variety of financial assets including gilts, equities, bank deposits and foreign currency. Several liabilities were also available, for example bank loans and mortgages. (Each financial item is an asset to one sector and a liability to another, so for instance gilts are an asset to persons but a liability to government.)

In the LBS model, the decision about which assets and liabilities to acquire was determined, for each sector, by a series of portfolio choice equations. These were of a form which ensured that in total the sector's financial transactions summed exactly to the financial balance. This choice depended partly on the expected return on each asset (interest or dividend payment plus expected capital gain or loss, adjusted for tax), partly on the risk of that return not being realized, partly on the total sum available for investment, and also on the transactions and other benefits from asset-holding. This last item, which was assumed to decline as more of an asset was held, ensured that agents would hold an asset such as cash that offered little or no interest payment.

Because portfolio choice depended on expected returns, demand for the risky assets (gilts, equities and foreign exchange) was influenced by the current and expected prices of those assets. (The price of foreign currency is the exchange rate measured in sterling per unit of foreign currency, which is the inverse of the way the exchange rate is measured elsewhere in this book.) It was assumed that supply of, and demand for, each of these three assets was always brought into line by movements in their prices. Thus for each of these three assets, the price was obtained by adding up all the supplies, equating this total to the sum of the demands, and re-arranging.

A similar procedure had been used for the Treasury model exchange rate equation used in the mid-1970s and described in Section 7.2 above, but the LBS model incorporated several important developments. Three asset prices, not just one, were now being modelled simultaneously, and many other asset demands were also included explicitly. More important than this, the LBS model was used under the assumption of rational expectations. The resulting LBS exchange rate equation had properties that were approximated by the uncovered interest parity equation used in the Liverpool model (and in the model of Chapter 4).

The uncovered interest parity condition was assumed to hold only approximately in the LBS model, implying that investors were willing to receive a slightly lower total expected return on one currency than on another. This was because they had eventually to make a payment in the first currency and did not wish to take the risk of an adverse exchange rate movement. This type of behaviour is said to be *risk-averse*. For similar reasons, the total expected return on gilts and equities in the LBS model was generally not equal to the return that could be obtained on riskless short-term deposits.

In this version of the LBS model, the real demand for cash was determined as for other assets, so that it declined when the returns rose on other financial assets. This was an LM curve (although the impact of output on demand for cash was indirect). The various expenditure equations, for consumption, exports and other components of demand, could be combined to give an IS curve, in exactly the way described in Chapter 4. The earnings and prices equations, as in the late 1970s version of the LBS model discussed in Section 7.2, tended to move domestic costs and prices back towards a given long run relationship with foreign prices measured in sterling.

Taking all these features together, the LBS model had a similar structure although far larger and more disaggregated, to the small model presented in Chapter 4, and also had many similarities to the Liverpool model. As demonstrated in Section 8.3, such models under the assumption of rational expectations suggest that the exchange rate will jump sharply in response to an announcement of a future reduction in monetary growth, thus providing a possible explanation for the exchange rate movements after 1979.

7.6 Further reading

This chapter has shown how macro-econometric models are always in the process of development, with minor changes being introduced almost all the time and major changes occurring on occasion. Developments that are likely to occur in the mid-1980s include detailed modelling of supply factors in goods and labour markets for the LBS model; a fully revised disaggregated financial sector in the Treasury model, with some similarities to that in the LBS model; and more widespread use of rational expectations for regular forecasting.

More generally, there will probably be a tendency to make explicit the assumption about market structure (i.e., whether there is perfect or imperfect competition, instantaneous or long run market clearing). There will also probably be attempts to reduce the vulnerability of the models to the Lucas critique (which argues that most models alter when government policies change; see Chapter 8).

There are various sources that will give information about these developments. Articles by the forecasting groups in their own journals are often the most up to date readily available source. These publications include the *National Institute Economic Review*, the *LBS Economic Outlook* and *Financial Outlook*, the *Liverpool University Economic Outlook* and the *City University Business School Economic Review*; see the list given in Table 1.1. The Treasury *Economic Progress Report* occasionally contains information about recent modelling developments and all these institutions publish working paper series.

A comprehensive and also reasonably up to date source of information is given by the manuals listing the equations of each of the models. These are published by all the groups, either when significant changes have occurred or at regular intervals. In the past these have been difficult to follow, for even when a description of the underlying theory is included, the properties of the model as a whole are usually understood most easily with the use of simulations. Simulations may be included in future editions of some model manuals.

Meanwhile, a series of books planned by the ESRC macro-econometric modelling bureau at Warwick (see Chapter 1) will provide full sets of simulations on all the models mentioned here, with full description, using versions of the models that will be about two years out of date at the time of publication. The first of these is Wallis (1985). Another source of information is the journal *Economic Modelling*, which is publishing a series of descriptive articles on macro-econometric models, although it is uncertain how frequently these will be updated. Recent examples of such articles are the descriptions of the Liverpool University model in Minford *et al.* (1984) and of the LBS model in Budd *et al.* (1984).

8

Policy analysis

The importance of macro-econometric models for policy analysis is considerable, and the process of trying out different policies on these models also gives insight into how they work and can reveal problems that would otherwise go undetected. In this chapter, the techniques used in policy analysis are discussed and illustrated. The first section describes policy simulations, and this is followed by an examination of the effect of policy changes under the assumption of rational expectations. The next section considers the use of optimal control for policy analysis; this is in principle the most systematic way of choosing policies but in practice is difficult to implement. The chapter concludes by considering the plausibility of policies, and the danger that the models themselves may change when policies are altered.

The subjects covered by this chapter tend to be more technical than those dealt with by previous chapters. Although the discussion is intended to be as simple as possible, it is in places inevitably more difficult than in the earlier parts of the book.

8.1 Policy simulations

The basic tool for evaluating policies with macro-econometric models is the use of *simulations*. The economist prepares a forecast, which will be referred to as the *base forecast*, then alters one or several of the exogenous policy variables, and recalculates the forecast. The new projection is called a simulation, or policy simulation. Comparison of the base forecast with the simulation shows how the economy would be affected by the policy change, according to the model. As an illustration, this section discusses a policy simulation made using the macro-econometric model of Chapter 4, and two simulations carried out on the Treasury model are also considered.

Table 8.1 reproduces the forecast of Section 5.4. This was made using exogenous exchange rate expectations and is used as the base forecast in this section. Table 8.2 shows a simulation in which government spending (exogenous policy variable G in the model) is raised £0.5 billion per quarter at 1980 prices. The figures in Table 8.2 were calculated using the same historical data, the same constant adjustments and the same projections of exogenous variables as were used in computing the base forecast,

Table 8.1 The base forecast
(This table reproduces key variables from the forecast given in Chapter 5 – made using exogenous, not rational, expectations.)

	Real GDP at factor cost GDPE £bn. 1980 prices	Real personal disposable income RPDI (1) £bn. 1980 prices	Employment ET 000s	Average earnings WSI index 1980 = 100	Consumer prices PC index 1980 = 100	Money stock MO £bn.	Short term interest rates RLB % points	Exchange rate EER index 1980 = 100	Current balance BAL £bn.	PSBR £bn.
1984 1	52.4	40.3	23558	136	131	13.3	8.9	87.8	0.0	1.2
2	52.6	40.6	23504	139	132	13.7	8.8	87.8	−0.2	2.2
3	53.0	40.7	23462	142	134	13.7	11.1	88.3	0.0	2.1
4	53.3	40.7	23434	144	137	14.7	11.5	88.4	0.1	2.0
Year 1985	215.5	164.2	23382	154	144	15.0	11.2	88.3	−1.9	9.0
1986	218.1	168.4	23305	169	154	16.1	11.5	88.3	−4.5	8.9
1987	220.8	172.0	23152	185	164	17.2	10.9	88.2	−7.2	9.3
1988	224.4	175.6	23953	200	173	18.2	10.6	88.1	−10.7	10.6

Note: (1) Real personal disposable income RPDI is obtained from model variables by the formula YD/(PC/100).

Table 8.2 Simulation of higher public spending

(This simulation uses the same exogenous assumptions and adjustments as the base forecast in Table 8.1, except for the increase in government spending (variable G in the model of Chapter 5) of £500m. per quarter at 1980 prices, worth around £2¼ billion at 1984 prices.)

	Real GDP at factor cost GDPE £bn. 1980 prices	Real personal disposable income RPDI (1) £bn. 1980 prices	Employment ET 000s	Average earnings WSI index 1980=100	Consumer prices PC index 1980=100	Money supply M0 £bn.	Short term interest rates RLB % points	Exchange rate EER index 1980=100	Current balance BAL £bn.	PSBR £bn.
1984 1	52.9	40.7	23558	136	131	13.3	8.9	87.8	0.0	1.8
2	53.1	41.0	23514	139	132	13.7	9.9	88.1	−0.2	2.8
3	53.4	41.0	23489	142	134	13.7	12.7	88.7	−0.2	2.8
4	53.5	40.8	23478	144	138	14.7	12.9	88.8	−0.3	2.7
Year 1985	215.9	164.2	23447	155	145	15.0	12.2	88.6	−3.5	11.6
1986	218.5	168.4	23375	170	155	16.1	12.5	88.5	−6.0	11.7
1987	221.2	172.2	23214	186	166	17.2	11.8	88.4	−9.0	12.5
1988	224.8	175.8	23008	202	175	18.2	11.5	88.3	−12.8	14.1

Note: (1) Real disposable income RPDI is obtained from model variables by the formula YD/(PC/100).

except that variable G has been changed. Since money supply MO is one of the exogenous variables held at the same level in the base forecast and in the simulation, the higher government borrowing caused by increased spending must be entirely financed by higher bond (gilts) sales.

Exchange rate expectations in the simulation are assumed to be exogenous, at the same level as in the base forecast. This simplifying assumption, which is relaxed in Section 8.3, usually leads to misleading results when computing simulations (as demonstrated in that section), but exceptionally has relatively small effects in this particular simulation.

The differences between the base forecast and the simulation are shown in Table 8.3. This is a widely used way to present the results. For most of the variables, the differences are expressed as a percentage of the base forecast level. For example the rise in GDP in 1984 second quarter from £52.4 billion (1980 prices) in the base forecast to £52.9 billion in the simulation appears as $100 \times (52.9 - 52.4)/52.4$, which is about 1.0 per cent, in Table 8.3. For a few of the variables, such as interest rates, it would be confusing to use percentages and the actual difference is presented.

The impact of the policy change on GDP is to raise it by about £0.5 billion in each of the early quarters, but this effect falls away in later quarters. The model thus exhibits strong crowding out, i.e. private sector spending (net of imports) falls by almost as much as the increase in government spending. The most important reason for this is a large and rapid increase in imports in response to higher domestic demand; this is not shown explicitly in Table 8.3 but is reflected in the worsening of the current account. The adverse movement in net trade is aggravated by a fall in competitiveness, caused by the combination of higher wages (which are themselves due to increased domestic demand) with an approximately unchanged exchange rate. Another important reason for the crowding out is the rise in inflation in the first few years, which has the effect in this model of reducing consumer spending.

Against these negative factors, fixed investment and inventories (not shown in the table) rise in response to higher demand and to improved real profits. Note that profits do not appear as a model variable but we can deduce that they have risen in real terms, because the percentage rise in real personal incomes is negative, or less than the rise in GDP, throughout the simulation.

When forecasting employment, this model treats government spending in the same way as other components of GDP. This approximation will cause little inaccuracy when the government raises its spending on goods and services purchased from the private sector (this is called procurement spending; an example is road building by private contractors), but when the higher spending takes the form of direct government employment, the impact on total employment will be greater than suggested by the model equation.

To use this macro-econometric model to simulate the impact of higher

Table 8.3 Simulation of higher public spending, expressed as difference from base forecast

(This table gives the differences (1) between the base forecast shown in Table 8.1 and the simulation in Table 8.2. This can be seen easily by comparing the last five columns with those in the first five columns, although rounding errors make it less clear for the first five columns.)

	Real GDP at factor cost GDPE %	Real personal disposable income RPDI (2) %	Employment ET 000s	Average earnings WSI %	Consumer prices PC %	Money stock MO %	Short term interest rates RLB % points	Exchange rate EER %	Current balance BAL £bn.	PSBR £bn.
1984 1	0.9	0.0	0	0.0	0.0	–	0	0.0	0.0	0.6
2	1.0	0.0	10	0.0	0.1	•	1.1	0.3	0.0	0.6
3	0.7	–0.2	27	0.1	0.3	–	1.6	0.4	–0.2	0.7
4	0.3	–0.3	44	0.2	0.5	–	1.4	0.4	–0.4	0.7
Year 1985	0.2	0.0	65	0.6	0.7	–	1.0	0.3	–1.6	2.6
1986	0.2	0.0	70	0.8	0.8	–	1.0	0.2	–1.5	2.8
1987	0.2	0.1	62	0.8	0.8	–	0.9	0.2	–1.8	3.2
1988	0.2	0.1	55	0.8	0.8	–	0.9	0.2	–2.1	3.5

Notes: (1) Columns 1, 2, 4 to 6 and 8 are the percentage difference between base and simulation. The other columns are differences in the units shown.
(2) Real personal disposable income RPDI is obtained from model variables by the formula YD/(PC/100).

government spending on direct employment, it would be possible to replace the employment equation with a newly estimated one that treats government spending separately. Alternatively, it would be possible to alter not merely the exogenous variable G when preparing the simulation, but also the constant adjustment on the employment equation, by an amount which reflected our judgement of the size of the missing effect.

Simulations like the one in Tables 8.2 and 8.3 that differ from the base forecast only because of changed exogenous variables are called *clean simulations* and show the properties of the model. Simulations in which adjustments are also changed are called *dirty simulations* and show what the forecaster believes will happen when the exogenous variables are altered. Research work appearing in the academic literature almost always uses clean simulations, while dirty simulations are often used for articles in the press.

In the Treasury model and other large models, government spending on direct employment is a separate variable and is allowed for in the employment equation. However, dirty simulations are sometimes carried out on these models to allow for other inadequacies. An example is given by the simulations on the Treasury model prepared for the National Economic Development Office (NEDO) in April 1982. These simulations included extensive alterations to the constant adjustments. Unsurprisingly this gave very different results from earlier work and even though this was partly due to developments in the model itself, the alterations to a large number of adjustments cast doubt on the validity of the results.

As a result of the widespread surprise over these simulations, NEDO produced a detailed paper describing the then current version of the Treasury model, the impact of recent changes, and the effect of the adjustments on the simulations. See NEDO (1983). Table 8.4 presents some of their results. It shows a clean simulation on the 1982 version of the Treasury model of higher government spending on procurement (specifically, increased spending on capital goods purchased from the private sector). The increase is £250 million per quarter at 1975 prices, which is roughly the same size as the increase of £500 million at 1980 prices used for the simulation in Table 8.3.

The Treasury model simulation in Table 8.4 assumes that money supply sterling M3 is held at the same level as in the corresponding base forecast. This assumption is significantly different from the assumption of unaltered MO used in the simulation on the model of Chapter 4, shown in Table 8.3. The difference arises because demand for MO (which is entirely non-interest bearing) is more interest-sensitive than demand for sterling M3 (much of which earns interest). Thus when higher output and prices in these simulations tend to raise the demand for money, interest rates must rise by more to hold sterling M3 unaltered than to hold MO unchanged. This problem, which is typical of the difficulties encountered when comparing models, cannot easily be avoided because the Treasury model

Table 8.4 Treasury model clean simulation of higher public spending

(The simulation is of an increase in public investment of £1 billion per annum at 1975 prices, worth around £2¼ billion at 1984 prices. Figures are the difference between the simulation and the base run (1).)

Financial year	Real GDP at factor cost %	RPDI %	Unemployment 000s	Average earnings %	RPI %	£M3 %	Short term interest rates % points	Exchange rate %	Current balance £bn.	PSBR £bn.
1983/84	0.6	0.2	−23	0.2	0.1	–	0.5	0.2	−0.9	1.7
1984/85	0.7	0.6	−64	0.4	0.3	–	1.0	0.3	−1.8	1.6
1985/86	0.5	0.6	−48	0.8	0.6	–	1.3	0.3	−2.1	1.8
1986/87	0.3	0.5	−12	1.0	0.8	–	1.7	0.5	−2.1	2.4
1987/88	0.2	0.5	18	1.1	0.8	–	2.1	0.9	−2.5	3.1

Source: NEDO (1983).
Note: (1) Columns 1, 2, 4 to 6 and 8 are differences as a percentage. The other columns are differences in the units indicated.

in 1982 did not include MO while the model of Chapter 4 ignores sterling M3.

The results in Table 8.4 show rapid crowding out, with the rise in GDP initially equal to the increase in public spending but soon falling back. These results are similar to those in Table 8.3, although some of the causes are different. There is more downward effect on private spending through higher interest rates in the Treasury model simulation (interest rates are increased 2 per cent in the last two years of the Treasury simulation, which is about twice as large as in the simulation shown in Table 8.3). Against this the Treasury model suggests that wages rise ahead of, not behind, the rise in prices in the early part of the simulation, which provides a short run stimulus to consumer spending that does not occur in the simulation on the model of Chapter 4.

Table 8.5 shows a dirty simulation, in which the same exogenous change is made to public spending as that used in Table 8.4, but in addition trade and productivity performance are assumed to improve. This is achieved by altering the constant adjustments on appropriate equations. For example the adjustment on the export equation is altered by an amount equivalent to the direct effect of a 6 per cent rise in the level of world trade.

Comparing the dirty simulation with the equivalent clean simulation, GDP is about 0.3 or 0.4 per cent higher in each year except the first, and price inflation is reduced by up to 0.6 per cent; unemployment is slightly worse throughout because the higher output is insufficient to offset the effects of increased productivity. The problem is that the changes to the adjustments, on which these results are based, are arbitrary. This means that there is no reason why larger adjustments to trade performance and a smaller adjustment to productivity should not be made to give even more favourable results in which unemployment is reduced.

8.2 Multipliers

In the first of the simulations discussed in the previous section, a rise of £0.5 billion in government spending boosted GDP by £0.5 billion in the first two quarters, with the effect falling away to only about £0.1 billion in 1988. See Table 8.3. A convenient way to describe these results is to divide the change in GDP by the alteration in government spending which caused it. This ratio is 1.0 in the first two quarters, falling to 0.2 at the end of the simulation. These ratios are known as *multipliers*; more specifically, the value of the ratio in the quarter when the policy change occurred is called an impact multiplier, the values in later quarters are called dynamic multipliers, and the eventual value, after all the effect has worked its way through, is known as a long-run multiplier. It is possible to calculate multipliers for each of the endogenous variables in respect of each of the exogenous variables.

Dynamic and long-run multipliers can be defined in an alternative way,

Table 8.5　Treasury model dirty simulation (1) of higher public spending

(The simulation is of an increase in public investment of £1 billion per annum at 1975 prices, worth around £2¼ billion at 1984 prices. Figures are the difference between the simulation and the base run (2).)

Financial year	Real GDP at factor cost %	RPDI %	Unemployment 000s	Average earnings %	RPI %	£M3 %	Short term interest rates % points	Exchange rate %	Current balance £bn.	PSBR £bn.
1983/84	0.7	0.2	29	0.1	0.0	–	0.5	0.4	– 0.7	1.9
1984/85	1.0	0.6	2	0.3	0.0	–	1.1	0.8	– 1.6	1.7
1985/86	0.9	0.8	– 6	0.6	0.1	–	1.5	0.9	– 2.1	1.7
1986/87	0.7	0.8	25	0.9	0.3	–	1.9	1.2	– 2.1	2.1
1987/88	0.5	0.7	59	0.9	0.2	–	2.3	1.7	– 2.4	2.8

Source:　NEDO (1983).

Notes:　(1)　This was a dirty simulation, i.e. it included adjustments as follows: exports were boosted by an adjustment equal to the effect of world trade being 6 per cent higher. Productivity and import performance were improved by about 1 per cent.

(2)　Columns 1, 2, 4 to 6 and 8 are differences as a percentage. The other columns are differences in the units indicated.

using the effect on an endogenous variable of a temporary movement in an exogenous variable that lasts for only one quarter, instead of the sustained change used above. This distinction does not affect the definition of impact multipliers. We will use the definition given in the previous paragraph.

Because they measure the reaction of one variable to a small change in another variable, multipliers are approximately equal to derivatives, and exactly equal in linear models. The multipliers calculated from a linear model will always be the same whatever base forecast is used, but the values of multipliers computed from non-linear models depend on the base forecast used. All macro-econometric models used for forecasting, including that in Chapter 4, are non-linear, but it is usually the case that the multipliers are little changed by small alterations to the base forecast. This is a convenient property, for it means that the forecasters have an approximate idea of the value of the multipliers even if they do not recompute them every time the base forecast is altered. Against this, it is unrealistic for multipliers to be completely unaffected by changes in the base forecast.

Multipliers can be useful for policy-making, as a way of comparing and combining the effects of policies. For example, the simulations in Section 8.1 showed the effect of altering government spending by £0.5 billion per quarter. An alternative policy might be to change spending by £1.5 billion. It would be possible to compute another forecast, but it is easier to use the multipliers calculated above. The impact multiplier for GDP in respect of government spending is 1.0, suggesting that a £1.5 billion rise in spending raises GPD by about £1.5 billion initially; and the dynamic multiplier for five years later is 0.2, suggesting that the effect on GDP is £0.3 billion after five years. There calculations would be exact in linear models, but are only approximate for the non-linear model of Chapter 4, with the inaccuracy becoming greater when larger changes are considered.

8.3 Simulations using rational expectations

The assumption of rational expectations, it will be recalled from Chapter 5 Section 5.5, means that people are assumed not to make systematic mistakes when forming expectations. Since the model itself is in principle a description of how the economy has behaved in the past and will continue to behave, rational expectations are usually interpreted to mean that expectations are consistent with the projections made by the model itself. The computer techniques used to ensure this consistency were discussed in that chapter.

The first part of this section gives an example of a simulation made under the assumption of rational expectations, contrasting it with a simulation that uses exogenous expectations. Next there is a discussion of why rational expectations do not simply mean self-justifying circularity, in which any set of expectations is consistent with some set of forecasts from the model; instead, it is explained that under certain conditions, there is only one set of expectations that is consistent with the model's projections. The final parts of this section describe in detail the rational expectations simulation, and show how the results are altered when policy changes are known about before they occur.

Contrast between simulations using rational expectations and using exogenous expectations

The assumption of rational expectations seems logical and use of it ensures that the small macro-econometric model used in this book has the intended properties. However, it involves many repeated computations and very occasionally, for some applications, it may be acceptable to approximate the results by using a different assumption. For example, the forecast in Chapter 5 based on the assumption of exogenous expectations was not very different from that made using rational expectations, and the simulation presented earlier in this chapter would not have been greatly altered if rational expectations had been used. It must be emphasized that these were exceptional cases. In general, a model designed for use with rational expectations gives misleading results under other assumptions. We will illustrate this by describing a simulation of a cut in monetary growth, first assuming exogenous expectations and then assuming rational expectations.

Table 8.6 shows a simulation of the effect of a cut in money supply MO growth, by 1 per cent per annum, which is one quarter of a per cent each quarter. Fiscal policy variables (government spending and tax rates) are unaltered and exchange rate expectations are exogenous, at base forecast levels.

Consumer prices are initially unchanged but in the later years of the simulation they fall slightly compared to the base forecast, in response to a small increase in the exchange rate and because GDP falls. (The lower level of GDP is induced mainly by higher interest rates.) The fall in prices is much smaller than the reduction in nominal money supply, so real money supply declines throughout the simulation. This causes real interest rates to become higher and higher, which seems implausible. Another unlikely aspect of the simulation is that the exchange rate appreciation is much less than the reduction in monetary growth.

These implausible effects are caused by the assumption that expectations about the exchange rate are the same in the simulation as in the base forecast. This is clearly nonsense. It implies that for several years a depreciation of sterling is anticipated, forcing UK interest rates to be above world rates. This expectation is never fulfilled. Instead, sterling rises slightly. For example, from Table 8.6, in 1987 interest rates are 2.1 percentage points above the base forecast and the exchange rate is rising, from 0.5 per cent above base in 1987 to 0.7 per cent above in the following year. Compared to the base forecast, investors in sterling have the benefit of both a 0.2 per cent appreciation and a 2.1 percentage point favourable

Table 8.6 Simulation of cut in money supply growth presented as differences from base

(This table shows a simulation of a 1 per cent per annum reduction in money supply (MO) growth, from 1985 first quarter. The results are presented as differences (1) from the base forecast, and expectations are assumed to be at the same exogenously fixed level in both base and simulation.)

	Real GDP at factor cost GDPE %	Real personal disposable income RPDI (2) %	Employment ET 000s	Average earnings WSI %	Consumer prices PC %	Money supply MO %	Short term interest rates RLB % points	Exchange rate EER %	Current balance BAL £bn.	PSBR £bn.
1984 1	0	0	0	0	0	0	0	0	0	0
2	0	0	0	0	0	0	0	0	0	0
3	0	0	0	0	0	0	0	0	0	0
4	0	0	0	0	0	0	0	0	0	0
1985 1	0.0	0.0	0	0.0	0.0	−0.3	0.7	0.2	0.0	0.0
2	−0.1	0.0	0	0.0	0.0	−0.5	0.9	0.2	0.1	0.0
3	−0.1	0.0	−1	0.0	0.0	−0.8	1.0	0.3	0.1	0.0
4	−0.1	0.0	−4	0.0	−0.1	−1.0	1.1	0.3	0.1	0.1
Years 1986	−0.1	−0.1	−11	−0.1	−0.2	−1.6	1.5	0.4	0.5	0.3
1987	−0.1	−0.2	−23	−0.3	−0.4	−2.6	2.1	0.5	0.7	0.6
1988	−0.1	−0.2	−31	−0.6	−0.6	−3.6	2.8	0.7	0.9	0.8

Notes: (1) Columns 1, 2, 4 to 6 and 8 are the percentage difference between base and simulation. The other columns are differences in the units shown.
(2) Real personal disposable income (RPDI) is obtained from model variables by the formula YD/(PC/100).

interest rates differential, an implausible total gain of 2.3 per cent per annum.

In a rational expectations simulation, anticipations are in line with the model's predictions and so these implausible results cannot occur. Table 8.7 shows a rational expectations simulation of the same policy change, i.e. a 1 per cent per annum cut in monetary growth announced and implemented in 1985 first quarter. The case where a policy change is announced ahead of its implementation is considered later. (The base forecast used to calculate the differences shown in Table 8.7 is the rational expectations forecast of section 5.5, not the slightly different exogenous expectations forecast.) In this simulation, interest rates in 1987 are 0.7 percentage points below the base forecast level, while the exchange rate rises from 5.1 per cent above base in 1987 to 6.0 per cent above in 1988. This gives the plausible result that the cut in interest rates approximately offsets the benefit to investors from the appreciation in sterling. (The offset is not exact because of errors due to rounding and averaging across years.)

The assumption of rational expectations has not only removed the implausible combination of exchange rates and interest rates. It has also caused widespread changes to the other results. We will now examine in detail how these results come about, and consider some of the underlying theory.

The uniqueness of rational expectations results

In the model, EER depends partly on this period's foreign and domestic interest rates, and partly on anticipations about next period's value for EER. Under the assumption of rational expectations, these anticipations in turn depend on next period's interest rates, and on the expected value of EER one period further ahead; and so on for all future periods. Hence the exchange rate depends on current expectations of interest rates in all future periods. When there is a change in expectations about those interest rates, which may be due to an alteration in UK monetary policy or some other factor, then the exchange rate usually has to jump suddenly and discontinuously from last period's level to reflect the new information. This is demonstrated by the simulation of an unexpected policy change shown in Table 8.7, and by Fig. 8.1, which compares the values of EER from that simulation with those from the base forecast.

The jump in the exchange rate also causes jumps in many other variables, such as competitiveness. These are known as *jump* variables. By contrast some variables, such as the consumer prices index, depend only on lagged values of the jump variables and are unaffected in the period when new information is received, although their values in later quarters are altered. These are known as *backward-looking* variables.

In all periods, whether or not new information has been received, all variables must be at values which satisfy the equations of the model; and at which expectations for all future periods are consistent with the model's

Table 8.7 Simulation of unanticipated cut in money supply growth assuming rational expectations

(This simulation is of a 1 per cent per annum cut in the growth of MO from 1985 first quarter. Expectations are assumed to be rational, but it is assumed that the change is not known about until it actually begins. The results are presented as differences (1) from the base rational expectations forecast given in Section 5.5 of Chapter 5.)

	Real GDP at factor cost GDPE %	Real personal disposable income RPDI (2) %	Employment ET 000s	Average earnings WSI %	Consumer prices PC %	Money supply MO %	Short term interest rates RLB % points	Exchange rate EER %	Current balance BAL £bn.	PSBR £bn.	Real exchange rate COMP %
1984 1	0	0	0	0	0	0	0	0	0	0	0
2	0	0	0	0	0	0	0	0	0	0	0
3	0	0	0	0	0	0	0	0	0	0	0
4	0	0	0	0	0	0	0	0	0	0	0
1985 1	-0.2	0.0	0	0.0	0.0	-0.3	0.7	3.9	0.7	0.0	3.9
2	-0.4	0.1	-2	0.0	-0.1	-0.5	0.7	3.9	0.6	0.0	3.9
3	-0.5	0.3	-9	-0.1	-0.4	-0.8	0.2	3.8	0.5	0.0	3.8
4	-0.3	0.4	-20	-0.3	-0.7	-1.0	-0.2	3.9	0.5	0.0	3.7
Years 1986	-0.3	0.4	-47	-1.1	-1.7	-1.6	-0.3	4.3	1.6	0.0	3.2
1987	-0.2	0.4	-81	-2.6	-3.1	-2.6	-0.7	5.1	0.9	0.1	2.9
1988	0.0	0.4	-89	-4.0	-4.4	-3.6	-0.5	6.0	1.0	0.0	2.8

Notes: as Table 8.3.

forecasts. Intuitively, these conditions sound little more than the circular requirement that expectations be self-justifying, and indeed it can be shown mathematically that these two requirements are usually not suffi-cient to pinpoint a unique value for each variable. Some extra requirement is needed to prevent there being infinitely many possible values. Another

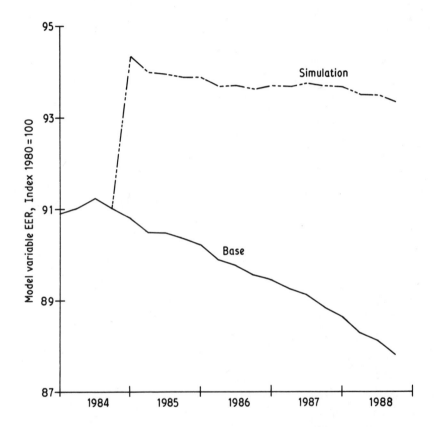

Figure 8.1a   Simulation of MO cut: effect on nominal exchange rate

way to understand intuitively this property of models under rational expectations is to note that jump variables, in the period when new information is received, jump in response to this extra information about the future, and are not tied down by events in the past.

To explain this extra requirement, we return to the notion of the steady-state. This was defined in Chapter 4 Section 4.3, for models without rational expectations, as the state in which all variables are unchanging, or

growing at constant rates. Such models are or ought to be designed so that
in the absence of irregular movements in exogenous variables, all the
endogenous variables tend towards their steady-state values whatever the
starting point. This is known as *global stability*. An example is given by
the equation for PC, in which UK consumer prices gradually regain a fixed
ratio to world prices measured in sterling.

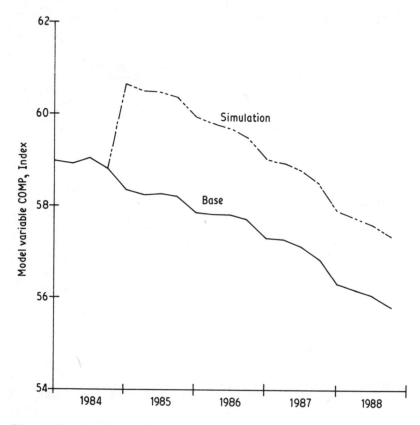

Figure 8.1b   Simulation of MO cut: effect on real exchange rate

Under the assumption of rational expectations, the steady-state of an
equation or a model is defined in the same way, except that additionally,
expectations must be fulfilled. However, in contrast to the above, useful
rational expectations models must not be globally stable. Instead for each
period, there must exist one and only one value for each jump variable
from which there is a tendency to move towards the steady-state. All other

values must lead to explosive future movements further and further from the steady-state. Although each jump variable has such a unique value, this value will not be constant from one period to another, but will instead vary as the backward-looking variables change over time, and as new information is received.

This resolves the problem, identified above, of choosing a single correct value for the exchange rate (and other variables). There is only one value for each jump variable in the current period that is consistent with future values that tend to the steady-state.

The simulation in detail

Returning to the rational expectations simulation of a 1 per cent per annum cut in MO growth shown in Table 8.7, the discontinuous movements referred to above are clearly visible. The variables EER, COMP and several others jump by a significant amount in 1985 first quarter, the period in which the policy change is announced. The unique correct value for each of these variables depends on expectations of future events, and changes when the assumption about MO in future periods is altered.

It is convenient to describe the results in Table 8.7 by comparing the steady-state of the simulation with that of the base forecast. The steady-state cannot be reached in the finite time period covered by the simulation, but the later years probably provide a reasonable guide. With money supply growth in the simulation 1 per cent per annum below the base forecast rate, the analytical model of Buiter and Miller (1981) on which this macro-econometric model is based suggests that the nominal exchange rate EER should be rising 1 per cent per annum faster in the steady-state. Table 8.7 suggests that in the later years of the simulation, this is approximately true.

The analytical model also suggests that the steady-state real exchange rate, variable COMP, will be unaffected by the change in monetary growth. This implies that steady-state consumer price inflation will be cut by about 1 per cent per annum. In line with this theory, Table 8.7 shows inflation reduced by approaching 1 per cent in the later years, with COMP gradually returning towards the base forecast level. (Strictly speaking, in the macro-econometric model used here the steady-state real exchange rate alters when inflation is changed, as described by Smith (1985), but this effect is not strong.)

The level of real economic activity in this model is heavily influenced by the real exchange rate, a high value depressing output by worsening the trade balance. With the steady-state value of the real exchange rate approximately unaffected by the simulation, steady-state output is also unlikely to be greatly altered. This is confirmed by Table 8.7, which shows that the effect on GDP is negligible by the end of the simulation. There is some adverse effect on employment in the later years but it is becoming smaller, suggesting that it may eventually return to the base forecast levels but only after a long delay.

We can now consider the early periods of the simulation. These are of more practical interest than the long run, but considerable insight into the causes of early effects is provided by considering the steady-state, as we have done. Because the changes in the early periods can be thought of as being on the route towards the steady-state, they are sometimes described as the *transitional path*.

The most prominent feature of the early periods is the large rise in the nominal exchange rate. We will analyse the causes of this. The nominal exchange rate must eventually have risen by the same amount as the fall in UK prices, in order to return the steady-state real exchange rate approximately to its base forecast level (see above). Provided that expectations are fulfilled, the form of the exchange rate equation only allows an appreciation equal to the amount of any reduction in UK interest rates. Although interest rates in the later years have fallen by about two-thirds of a percentage point (and should reach about one full point in the steady-state), allowing the exchange rate to appreciate by that amount, in the early periods interest rates fall by less than this (at the very start of the simulation they actually increase, because real money supply is cut and GDP has not yet fallen enough to offset this). Thus the values for the interest rate do not give enough scope for the exchange rate to rise. Instead, there has to be an initial jump, which does not have to be consistent with the interest rate differential in the previous period, because it is a response to an unanticipated change.

The jump in the nominal exchange rate at the start of the simulation implies a large increase in the real exchange rate, because prices and wages take some time to react. This adverse movement in competitiveness causes some immediate fall in GDP as net trade worsens, and this effect builds up as exports and imports respond to the lagged competitiveness terms in their equations. After about a year, the reduction in GDP, and the explicit exchange rate term in the prices equation, both start to have the effect of reducing UK prices and hence wages. This begins to reverse the initial rise in the real exchange rate, which in turn means that net trade and GDP start to recover. This regaining of lost output puts some upward pressure on prices, which is more than offset by the effect from the continuing appreciation of the nominal exchange rate, and so prices continue to fall and competitiveness and output continue to recover.

Anticipated policy changes

This concludes the discussion of the simulation shown in Table 8.7, in which the policy change was announced and implemented at the same time. It is interesting to contrast this with a simulation in which the policy change, of a 1 per cent per annum cut in monetary growth, is announced at the start of 1984 but not implemented until a year later. We assume that the policy announcement is fully credible; this assumption is relaxed in Section 8.5. This simulation is shown in Table 8.8, and Fig. 8.2 compares the two simulations and the base forecast.

Table 8.8   Simulation of anticipated cut in money supply growth assuming rational expectations
(This table shows a simulation of a 1 per cent annum reduction in money supply (MO) growth, which begins in 1985 first quarter and is known about during the four previous quarters. Results are presented as differences (1) from the base rational expectations forecast shown in Section 5.5 of Chapter 5.)

	Real GDP at factor cost GDPE %	Real personal disposable income RPDI (2) %	Employment ET 000s	Average earnings WSI %	Consumer prices PC %	Money supply MO %	Short term interest rates RLB % points	Exchange rate EER %	Current balance BAL £bn.	PSBR £bn.	Real exchange rate COMP %
1984 1	-0.2	0.0	0	0.0	0.0	–	0.0	3.6	0.5	0.1	3.6
2	-0.3	0.0	-2	0.0	-0.1	–	-0.2	3.6	0.4	0.1	3.6
3	-0.3	0.1	-6	-0.1	-0.3	–	-0.7	3.6	0.3	-0.1	3.6
4	-0.2	0.5	-14	-0.2	-0.6	–	-1.1	3.8	0.3	0.0	3.5
1985 1	-0.2	0.5	-22	-0.5	-0.7	-0.3	-0.6	4.0	0.3	0.0	3.5
2	-0.2	0.4	-29	-0.7	-1.1	-0.5	-0.5	4.1	0.3	0.0	3.4
3	-0.2	0.4	-35	-1.1	-1.4	-0.8	-0.5	4.2	0.2	0.0	3.1
4	-0.3	0.5	-43	-1.3	-1.7	-1.0	-0.7	4.4	0.1	0.0	3.0
Years 1986	-0.2	0.5	-61	-2.0	-2.4	-1.6	-0.8	5.0	0.7	0.1	2.9
1987	-0.0	0.4	-73	-3.1	-3.5	-2.6	-0.6	6.2	0.8	0.0	2.8
1988	0.0	0.4	-66	-4.1	-4.4	-3.6	-0.4	7.2	0.9	-0.2	2.8

Notes: as Table 8.3.

One very important point is that the exchange rate, and other jump variables, jump in the period when the policy is announced, not in the period when it is implemented. This is because, as mentioned above, it is only when new information is received that the exchange rate can move in such a way that expectations are not fulfilled. Another important point from this simulation is that the values of variables in the later years suggest

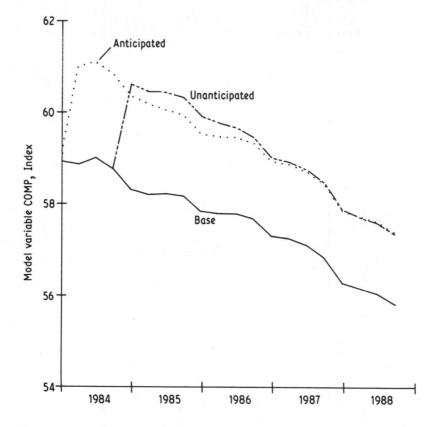

Figure 8.2 Anticipated and unanticipated cases compared – simulation of MO cut: effect on real exchange rate

that the steady-state is approximately the same as in the unanticipated case. Finally, the maximum size of the movements in many important variables is less when the change is anticipated (Table 8.8) than when it is unanticipated (Table 8.7). Gross domestic product and the real exchange rate are good examples of this. This is because the anticipation of the policy change allows the impact to be spread out over more periods, with less effect in any single one.

One final point concerns multipliers in rational expectations models. These are defined in an analagous way to those in other models, except that they allow not only for the reaction of endogenous variables to changes in current and past exogenous variables, but also for changes in expectations about future variables. As we have demonstrated, these can have a very substantial effect.

8.4 Optimal control

Optimal control methods are in principle the most systematic way to use large macro-econometric models for policy analysis. There are many practical difficulties in implementing optimal control techniques, including the very large amounts of computer capacity usually required, but even so they can provide considerable insights into the working of models.

The basic characteristic of optimal control methods as applied to macro-econometric models is that the user specifies an objective and the computer then tries out many different policies on the model until it finds the policy that does as well as possible in terms of the objective.

The user's objectives have to be specified as a *welfare function*, often also called an *objective function*, which puts a value on the utility given by combinations of economic variables. A typical welfare function might give a large value for low inflation combined with low unemployment, a small value for high inflation and high unemployment, and a value in between for low inflation plus high unemployment.

To make solution possible, only a few variables can usually be included in the welfare function. A simple example is:

$$\text{Welfare} = -5 \times (\text{Unemployment in millions})^2 - (\text{Inflation in per cent per annum})^2$$

This is known as a quadratic welfare function, because it involves the squares of variables. Properties of such functions are relatively easy to analyse. It would have a value of

$$-5 \times 9 - 25 = -70$$

for unemployment of three million and inflation of 5 per cent per annum. A fall in unemployment, or inflation, or both would raise welfare (make it less negative). For example, a quarter million cut in unemployment would give the value

$$-5 \times 7.56 - 25 = -62.8$$

which is a gain of just over seven. A fall of three-quarters of a per cent in inflation would give a similar gain. The size of these effects depends on the initial magnitudes of the variables; if unemployment was three and a half million and inflation still at 5 per cent, then a cut of only one fifth of a million would give a welfare gain of seven, while a 0.75 per cent cut in inflation would still be needed to give this gain. Thus this function has the property of declining marginal utility.

The choice of the number 5 in the above welfare function is meant to reflect the preferences of the government, or other user. Such numbers are known as *weights*. In practice choice of appropriate weights can be difficult; one approach is to experiment with different weights and use those that give the most attractive results. The overall scaling is irrelevant, so exactly the same conclusions about policy would be obtained by using, say, 10 and 2 or 20 and 4, instead of the 5 and 1 shown above. This means that the value of utility calculated above is meaningful only for comparisons. The variables that appear in the welfare function are called *target variables* or simply *targets*.

The welfare function given above only includes variables from one period. For most applications, a many-period welfare function is more appropriate. This is typically the sum of a series of single-period functions, such as that given above, usually with the later periods discounted. However, it is possible that governments are mainly or solely interested in welfare in a single election period.

Once the welfare function has been specified, the problem is to choose the policy which, given the macro-econometric model, makes the welfare function as large as possible. Choice of policy means selecting values for one or more *policy instruments*. These are the exogenous variables that have previously been referred to as policy variables and typical examples include tax rates (e.g. income tax, variable T in the model), government spending (variable G) and money supply (variable MO). They are often referred to as simply *instruments*, for brevity.

This can be regarded as a mathematical problem of maximization subject to constraints. The welfare function is to be maximized, with respect to the instruments, and subject to the constraints implied by the macro-econometric model. In simple cases, the usual mathematical procedure can be applied. This involves substituting the constraints into the welfare function, setting the first derivatives to zero and solving the resulting simultaneous equations to give values for the instruments. An equivalent mathematical procedure is to use a Lagrangian to impose the constraints.

It is rarely possible to carry out this mathematical procedure directly, because of the complexity and size of macro-econometric models. Instead a computer program is used which carries out a repetitive search until it finds the values of the instruments that make the welfare function as large as possible. This search does not involve random experiments with many different values of the instruments to see which give the highest welfare; that would take an extremely long time and there would be no guarantee that the correct result had been found. Instead a type of controlled search is carried out.

There are a variety of different search techniques used for this purpose, but almost all of them can be referred to by the generic name of *Newton* methods. These have the feature of using information about both the first derivatives of target variables with respect to the instruments, and the second derivatives.

The derivatives are often unobtainable by analytical methods and a numerical approximation must be used. For the first derivatives, the multipliers (defined in Section 8.2 of this chapter) provide a good estimate, because they are the movement in an endogenous variable caused by a small change in an exogenous policy variable, expressed as a ratio to that small change. In linear models the multipliers are exactly equal to the first derivatives. An estimate for the second derivatives is often obtained by use of a formula which relates them approximately to the first derivatives.

The search begins from some arbitrarily chosen values for the instruments. Using these, a base forecast is prepared, and the resulting projections for the targets are used to compute the value of the welfare function. They are also used to calculate the values of the derivatives of the welfare function with respect to the instruments. These are not, of course, the same as the derivatives of the targets with respect to the instruments, and will in general change, perhaps fairly significantly and perhaps from positive to negative or vice versa, as the values of the targets change. For example, writing U for unemployment, its first derivative with respect to income tax rates is dU/dT and writing $\triangle PC$ for inflation, its first derivative with respect to T is $d\triangle PC/dT$. These derivatives depend on the relationship between U and T, and between $\triangle PC$ and T, given by the equations of the model and allow for all indirect effects (the complication caused by the need to consider an objective function for many time periods is ignored). Then the first derivative with respect to T of the simple welfare function referred to earlier is:

$$-10 \times U \times dU/dT - 2 \times \triangle PC \times d\triangle PC/dT$$

This will clearly change as unemployment and inflation change, even if dU/dT and $d\triangle PC/dT$ are assumed approximately constant.

The next stage is to choose new values for the instruments and recompute the forecast. For those instruments with respect to which the welfare function has a positive derivative, the program will usually choose a higher value, and where there is a negative derivative the instrument will typically be reduced. This accords with intuition, for a positive derivative means that larger values boost welfare. However, the program will occasionally not choose in this way because of information from the second derivatives.

Since the derivatives of welfare with respect to the instruments change during the exercise, the program may (for example) reduce the value of an instrument several times and then increase it, although it is unlikely to reverse more than a fraction of the earlier reduction.

This process of choosing new values for the instruments and recomputing the forecast continues until the gain in welfare between one set of values for the instruments and the next is less than some small, user-specified limit (alternative criteria are sometimes used to indicate that the process is complete). The values taken by the instruments at this stage are those that maximize the welfare function.

This concludes the description of the application of optimal control methods to macro-econometric models. We will now consider some drawbacks and problems.

Limitations of using optimal control methods

It can be shown that the use of a Newton method, as just described, is guaranteed to locate a maximum value for the welfare function, provided that derivatives exist at all the policy values that are tried. However this is only guaranteed to be a *local maximum*, i.e. relatively small changes in the instruments from the values chosen by the program will cause a reduction in welfare, although relatively large changes may increase welfare. Users are likely to be more interested in a *global maximum*, which is the highest possible value obtainable for the welfare function and cannot be bettered by any alternative values for the instruments.

For linear models, with a quadratic welfare function, there can only be a global maximum, but there may be many local maxima in non-linear models and as emphasized in Section 8.2 of this chapter, most large macro-econometric models are non-linear. The program will provide no indication about any other maxima apart from the one it has found. To deal with this problem, the economist must rely on instinct and perhaps try several repeated attempts at the whole process, each beginning from different starting values for the instruments. When different starting values generate the same result, confidence in that result is increased.

Another problem is that the program may use an unacceptably large amount of computer time before finding the optimal solution. The time taken generally increases with the size of the model being used, the number of time periods covered, the number of instruments and the number of targets. The user may therefore have to restrict the number of targets and instruments.

Possibly more important than the above problems is another difficulty. Optimal control methods can often be applied to problems in engineering with confidence that the results will be of practical use, because the models used are generally robust representations of the real world. By contrast macro-econometric models are imperfect, over-simplified descriptions of reality. This does not always matter when they are used for forecasting, or for policy analysis without optimal control methods, because the forecaster can make judgemental adjustments to allow for known weaknesses. When a macro-econometric model is used in an optimal control exercise, the program will detect weak or missing links in the model that allow odd policy combinations to yield attractive results.

For example, in the model of Chapter 4, cutting indirect taxes (variable TREF) will tend to lower consumer price inflation. This in turn will tend to reduce wages, thus improving competitiveness, boosting output and raising employment. If TREF is one of the policy instruments and the welfare function includes inflation and unemployment as above, then the optimal control methods will attempt to reduce TREF to very low levels, perhaps even making it negative (i.e. replacing the taxes by a subsidy), because this will have a beneficial effect on both parts of the welfare function. The model will cause some limit to this, for with very high output the pressure of demand terms in the prices equation will eventually make it difficult to reduce prices further even with large cuts in TREF; interest rates will also tend to rise, restricting the growth in output.

However it is likely that TREF will be reduced to a very low, perhaps implausible, level before the program stops. This is because another important link, which in the real world restricts the governments ability to cut indirect taxes, is missing from the model. This is a relationship between the stock of government debt and interest rates. The model includes an equation for public borrowing (the PSBR), and as indirect taxes are cut, it will indicate higher borrowing and will increase the rate of growth in the outstanding stock of government debt (variable GOVTB). However, this will not have any effect on interest rates (although the government will have to make higher interest payments, because its debt is greater).

The lack of this particular link mattered relatively little for forecasting, and even during policy simulations it would be possible for the user to make some judgemental adjustment to allow for it. However when optimal control methods are used, this type of missing link is generally detected very rapidly by the program. This type of problem is widespread in macro-econometric models; when this link is included, others will probably be missing. As mentioned in Chapter 4, the economists who construct models have limited resources and have to choose to omit some aspects of the real world.

When optimal control methods detect a missing link in the model, corrective action can be taken. In this case, it would be possible either to alter the interest rate equation to include some effect from the stock of government debt, or to include GOVTB in the welfare function so that restricting its size became part of the objective. This illustrates a surprising feature of optimal control methods as applied to macro-econometric models. While their use in suggesting practical policies for governments to follow is limited, they can be an extremely useful tool for detecting inadequacies in the models and suggesting improvements.

This view is supported by the committee set up by the Wilson administration to examine the possible use of optimal control for macro-economic policy-making by UK governments. The committee's report states:

> We do not believe that the use of optimal control techniques could, or should, result in any organisational changes in the policy making process in the foreseeable future. The potential value of optimal control techniques is at the operational level.
>
> (Ball, 1978, para 40)

Box 8.1   Uncertainty about which model is correct

Suppose that there is more than one structure of model that might describe how the world works. In principle this can be dealt with very easily. Assume that there are two possible models under consideration and that there is no uncertainty about the coefficients of each model. (The technique described below can be easily generalized to finite numbers of models greater than two. It can also in principle be generalized to allow for uncertainty about coefficients.)

Suppose that our welfare function is of the type shown in the text. Then the problem is:

$$\text{Max } E(-5U^2 - \triangle PC^2) \tag{1}$$

where the E outside the bracket is the expectational operator. Assume that we know the probability p that the first model is correct. This will in practice usually be guessed. The expression (1) then becomes

$$\text{Max } p(-5U_1^2 - \triangle PC_1^2) + (1-p)(-5U_2^2 - \triangle PC_2^2) \tag{2}$$

where U_1 and U_2 are the figures for unemployment obtained from the first and second models respectively, and $\triangle PC_1$, $\triangle PC_2$ are defined analogously. Notice that (2) is the expectation of the utility and differs from the expression $-5(p U_1 + (1-p)U_2)^2 - (p \triangle PC_1 + (1-p)\triangle PC_2)^2$ that is obtained by taking the utility of the expectations.

The maximization problem (2) is in principle no different from the optimal control problems considered in the text. It has four targets, U_1, U_2, $\triangle PC_1$ and $\triangle PC_2$. It has to be maximized with respect to the same set of instruments (tax rates, bond finance, government spending etc.) as were available before – there is no increase in the number of instruments despite the doubling in the number of targets. The econometric model that provides the constraints has now roughly doubled in length. Our first view of the world forms the first half of the model, our second view forms the second half. Exogenous variables, including our instruments, are common to both halves. By contrast endogenous variables appear twice, once in each half. In particular our targets, U and $\triangle PC$, each appear twice, as U_1 and $\triangle PC_1$ in the first half and as U_2 and $\triangle PC_2$ in the second half. Set up in this way the problem can be handled by conventional software, if size constraints permit.

It is possible to estimate at least two macro-econometric models of the UK (or other) economy neither of which is rejected by the data, which yield very different policy prescriptions if analysed in isolation from one another. Techniques of the type described above offer a way of resolving this conflict.

This concludes the main discussion of optimal control methods as applied to macro-econometric models. Box 8.1 includes a brief description of how these methods can be used to allow for uncertainty about how the world works. A detailed, technical description of optimal control methods appears in Holly and Hughes-Hallett (forthcoming).

8.5 The credibility of policies and time inconsistency

In the discussion of rational expectations in Section 8.3, we assumed that the financial markets and individuals (whom we will refer to in this section as *private agents*) believe the government when it announces a change of policy. What happens when the government is not believed, or if people think it will only go some of the way down the route it has promised? Conversely, what happens if a policy is announced and believed, but the government later reneges on its commitment? In practice, both of these things happen fairly often.

It turns out that both can be taken account of, provided that the forecaster knows, or feels confident in assuming, two things: what the government is actually going to do; and what private agents think it is going to do. In practice, it can be very difficult to make assumptions about these things, particularly the second, and later in this section we show that economic theory can give us some limited information about the links between them. Meanwhile, we assume that they are both known.

The government's plans, and the beliefs of private agents about those plans, can be summarized as two sets of projections for the exogenous policy variables in the model. The forecaster computes expectations by using the second set to generate a simulation of what the private sector believes will happen, and then combines these expectations with the first set of exogenous variables to compute the actual forecast. This can be difficult to implement in complex cases, but is often relatively easy.

Table 8.9 and Fig. 8.3 show three policy simulations designed to illustrate this process. In all three, the government is assumed to announce early in 1984 that it will cut monetary growth by 1 per cent per annum with effect from a year later. In the first simulation, private agents believe this and the government implements the policy as promised (this simulation was also shown in detail in Table 8.8 above). In the second simulation, private agents do not believe the government until the policy is actually implemented, when they are assumed suddenly to accept that the policy will continue. In the third simulation, private agents initially believe the announcement, but the government fails to implement the policy, and when this occurs private agents realize their mistake and suddenly accept that the policy change will never occur. Other simulations could be carried out that assumed less abrupt changes in private agents' beliefs, and would give the same broad results.

These assumptions about private agents' beliefs, and about whether or not the policy is actually implemented, are summarized in the 'truth table' below. (A fourth simulation could involve two No's, i.e. private agents do not believe the policy, and it is never implemented; this would be uninteresting because the simulation would be no different at all from the base forecast.)

	Simulation 1	Simulation 2	Simulation 3
Is the policy announcement believed during 1984?	Yes	No	Yes
Is the policy actually implemented?	Yes	Yes	No

In the first simulation, the exchange rate and some other variables jump at the beginning of 1984 when the policy change is first announced and believed. In the second simulation, there is no change in any variable until the policy is implemented and believed in, early in 1985; because there is no period of anticipation over which the effect can be spread out, the jump is larger than in the first simulation for the real exchange rate and many other variables, although after some years these variables slowly approach the values that they took in the first simulation.

The most interesting feature of the third simulation is that although no policy change actually takes place, there are still significant effects on the economy from the false anticipation. Moreover, these effects continue even after private agents have realized their earlier mistake.

Ideally, we would like an indication from economic theory of the way in which a government's actions affect its credibility. An appealing notion is to argue that when a government reneges on earlier commitments, its credibility will thereafter be greatly reduced. This area is currently the subject of considerable research. Meanwhile, we can make some comments on the converse problem: the way in which a government's credibility, assumed to be given, affects the availability of policy choices to the government.

We can identify the best policy available to the government on each of two extreme assumptions about its credibility. By policy in this section we mean the values taken by all exogenous policy variables for the current and all future periods. At one extreme, we assume that the government has complete credibility with private agents, and can choose the very best policy, i.e. the one which maximizes its objective function which includes discounted values of targets in future periods. In general, such a policy may be *time inconsistent*, which means that in future periods, if it were to re-compute its then optimal policy using the same objective function, it would choose a different policy. It must be emphasized that this occurs even though the objective function is unchanged and no unexpected events occur (in general, changes in the objective function and unexpected events always cause a change of policy even from a policy that is not time inconsistent). By our assumption of credibility, private agents will believe that the government is going to stick to its pre-announced policy, even though they know in advance that there will be future periods when the government is tempted to change to what will then be a better policy.

At the other extreme, we assume that private agents are totally lacking any belief in the government's ability to keep to pre-announced policies. A government in this position has to follow a *time consistent* policy, that is to say one in which at no point in the future can the government ever do better by suddenly switching to a new policy. (Of course, unexpected events or a change in objective function could still make it desirable for the government to change policies, but in the absence of these things it will not want to change.) In general, the value of the objective function given by a time consistent policy is below that obtainable from a time inconsistent one. It is therefore in the government's interest to have credibility with

Table 8.9 Three policy simulations with different assumptions about credibility
(This table shows the effect of an announcement, made in early 1984, that monetary growth will be cut by 1 per cent per annum from early 1985. The results are differences (1) from the base run.)

	Simulation 1			Simulation 2			Simulation 3		
Is the policy announcement believed during 1984?	YES			NO			YES		
Is the policy actually implemented?	YES			YES			NO		
	Effective exchange rate EER %	Real exchange rate COMP %	Employment ET 000s	Effective exchange rate EER %	Real exchange rate COMP %	Employment ET 000s	Effective exchange rate EER %	Real exchange rate COMP %	Employment ET 000s
1984 1	3.6	3.6	0	0	0	0	3.6	3.6	0
2	3.6	3.6	−2	0	0	0	3.6	3.6	−2
3	3.6	3.6	−6	0	0	0	3.6	3.6	−6
4	3.8	3.5	−14	0	0	0	3.8	3.5	−14
1985 1	4.0	3.5	−22	3.9	3.9	0	0.1	−0.4	−22
2	4.1	3.4	−29	3.9	3.9	−2	0.2	−0.5	−27
3	4.2	3.1	−35	3.8	3.8	−9	0.4	−0.7	−26
4	4.4	3.0	−43	3.9	3.7	−20	0.5	−0.7	−23
Years 1986	5.0	2.9	−61	4.3	3.2	−47	0.7	−0.4	−14
1987	6.2	2.8	−73	5.1	2.9	−81	1.1	−0.1	+8
1988	7.2	2.8	−66	6.0	2.8	−89	1.2	0.3	+23

Note: (1) Figures for EER and COMP are percentage differences from base, while those for ET are the absolute difference in thousands.

private agents, or failing that, to find some way of locking itself now into future policies.

This type of analysis is relatively new. See Buiter (1984) for a technical description and further references. As yet no attempt has been made to

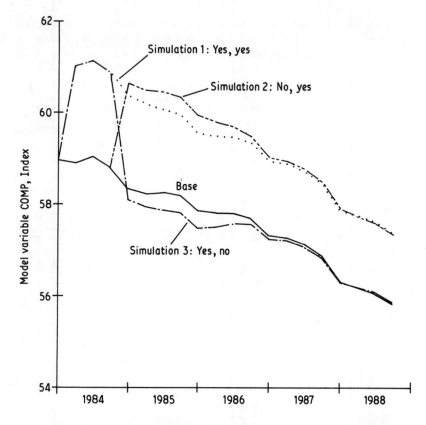

Figure 8.3   The influence of belief about policy announcements – simulation of MO cut: effect on real exchange rate

compare time consistent and time inconsistent policies on a large macroeconometric model and such an operation would probably involve very substantial amounts of computer time.

8.6 The Lucas critique

A severe problem in using macro-econometric models for policy analysis is that the parameters in the models may alter when government policies are altered. The classic discussion of this subject is by Lucas (1976). This problem is known as the *Lucas critique* and in principle is avoided by ensuring that the model depends only on the most fundamental aspects of the economy, which are the tastes of individuals and the available technology (or the factors determining the ability of the economy to generate technological change).

In practice this is difficult or impossible to achieve and instead a partial avoidance of the problem is obtained by making explicit allowance for people's expectations of government policy and other events. When these expectations are assumed to be rational, as in Section 8.3 above, then the model captures one of the most important ways in which people react to government policy.

An example of the effect of ignoring the Lucas critique is given by the simulation of reduced monetary growth with fixed expectations, shown in Table 8.6. Because this takes as a constant one of the main routes through which government policy operates, it produces implausible results, and the simulation of the same policy change under rational expectations gives a more likely description of what would happen. However, the small macro-econometric model used in these simulations remains subject to the Lucas critique; the use of rational expectations merely reduces the problem. In general, this is a problem that cannot be avoided completely. The forecaster, as in many other aspects of forecasting, has to judge how severe the problem is likely to be for any particular application, and take action, if necessary, for example by using rational expectations.

APPENDIX 1

Full listing of the equations from the forecasting model of Chapter 4

Notes

(1) All logs are natural logarithms (to base e); 'exp' indicates that e is to be raised to the power of the expression that follows.

(2) When a 'W' appears in the first column, a working variable is being defined. No historical data are required for working variables. They are merely a means of simplifying the presentation of the equations.

(3) Items such as 'DV79Q1' are dummy variables, intended to capture the effect of exceptional events such as dock strikes. During estimation, they took the value 1 in the period indicated (1979 first quarter for DV79Q1) and zero in all other periods; they are set to zero for forecasting.

(4) Definitions and sources for all variables (apart from working and dummy variables) are given in Appendix 4.

(5) Standard errors are shown in brackets under estimated coefficients.

(6) The long run versions of the equations are shown in Box 4.10.

(7) Stability tests were applied to most of the equations, and the numbers given in brackets for these tests indicate how many post-sample periods were used. The statistics shown are asymptotically distributed as χ^2 with degrees of freedom equal to the number shown in brackets. Critical values at the 5 per cent (one-tailed) level are 18.31 with 10 degrees of freedom and 15.51 with 8 degrees of freedom.

(8) An LM test against autocorrelation of up to fifth order was also applied. This is shown as LM (5). This is asymptotically distributed as χ^2 with five degrees of freedom. The critical value for this at the 5 per cent (one-tailed) level is 11.07.

Prices

First define trend production as a working variable:

$$\text{W} \quad \text{PROD} = 1.0057^{(\text{TIME}_t - 32)}$$

$$
\begin{aligned}
\text{PC}_t = \exp \Big[&\log(\text{PC}_{t-1}) \\
&+ \underset{(0.083)}{0.636} \log(\text{PC}_{t-1}/\text{PC}_{t-2}) + \underset{(0.017)}{0.0600} \log(\text{TREF}_t) \\
&- \underset{(0.019)}{0.0750} \log(\text{TREF}_{t-1}) + \underset{(0.0115)}{0.0199} \log(\text{TREF}_{t-4}) \\
&- \underset{(0.014)}{0.0275} \log(\text{PC}_{t-1}/(\text{WWPI}_{t-1}/\text{EER}_{t-1})) \\
&+ \underset{(0.0561)}{0.1144} \log(\text{GDPE}_{t-1}/\text{PROD}) - \underset{(0.623)}{1.080} \Big]
\end{aligned}
$$

Estimation period from 1964Q1 to 1980Q4
$\bar{R}^2 = 0.748$
Standard error = 0.75 per cent
Durbin-Watson = 2.22
Stability test (10) 10.36
LM(5) 4.39

Interest rates

$$
\begin{aligned}
\text{RLB}_t = \underset{(0.00109)}{(1/0.00346)} \Big[&- \log(\text{MO}_t/\text{PC}_{t-1}) \\
&+ \underset{(0.088)}{0.719} \log(\text{MO}_{t-1}/\text{PC}_{t-2}) \\
&+ \underset{(0.139)}{0.442} \log(\text{GDPE}_{t-1} - \text{O}_{t-1}) - \underset{(0.00062)}{0.00160} (\text{TIME}_t - 32) \\
&- \underset{(0.0072)}{0.0909}\text{Q1} - \underset{(0.0055)}{0.0520}\text{Q2} - \underset{(0.0055)}{0.0698}\text{Q3} - \underset{(1.12)}{3.26} \Big]
\end{aligned}
$$

Estimation period from 1964Q1 to 1980Q4
$\bar{R}^2 = 0.912$
Standard error = 1.57 per cent
Durbin-Watson = 1.69
Two-stage least squares instruments T, G/GDP, XWM, RSW, lagged RLB.
Stability test (10) 14.43
LM(5) 6.32

Note: This equation was estimated with log MO as the dependent variable, and has been re-arranged to give the equation for RLB shown here. All the statistics shown refer to the equation as it was estimated.

Exchange rate

Assumes uncovered interest parity:

$$EER_t = XEER_t (1 + (RLB_t - RSW_t)/400)$$

where XEER is today's expectation of EER next period.

The exchange rate equation above relies on the assumption that the market is dominated by speculators who will take the highest total return (interest plus any expected capital gain or loss) regardless of whether this involves holding sterling or foreign currency. This behaviour is termed 'risk neutral' and implies that speculative funds, and hence the exchange rate, will shift until the total return is the same for both sterling and foreign currency. The above equation simply states that the two total returns are equal.

Wages

$$
\begin{aligned}
WSI_t = \exp \Big[& \log(WSI_{t-1}) + \log(WSI_{t-1}/WSI_{t-2}) \\
& + \underset{(0.098)}{0.221} \, (\log(WSI_{t-2}/WSI_{t-3}) - \log(WSI_{t-3}/WSI_{t-4})) \\
& - \underset{(0.127)}{0.752} \, (\log(WSI_{t-1}/(1.0057PC_{t-1})) - \log(WSI_{t-2}/PC_{t-2})) \\
& - \underset{(0.200)}{0.222} \, (\log(PC_{t-1}/PC_{t-2}) - \log(PC_{t-2}/PC_{t-3})) \Big]
\end{aligned}
$$

Estimation period from 1964Q1 to 1980Q4
$\bar{R}^2 = 0.381$
Standard error = 1.51 per cent
Durbin-Watson = 2.18
Stability test (10) 3.56
LM(5) 8.79

Competitiveness

$$COMP_t = WSI_t/(PROD \times WWPI_t/EER_t)$$

Export demand

$$
\begin{aligned}
X_t = \exp \Big[& 0.510 \log(X_{t-1}) + 0.131 \log(X_{t-2}) \\
& (0.067) \qquad\qquad (0.056) \\
& + 0.207 \log(XWM_t) - 0.171 \log(COMP_t) \\
& (0.042) \qquad\qquad\quad (0.034) \\
& - 0.0867 \, DV67Q4 - 0.0559 \, DV70Q3 \\
& (0.0148) \qquad\quad\; (0.0142) \\
& - 0.111 \, DV72Q3 - 0.120 \, DV79Q1 \\
& (0.015) \qquad\quad (0.015) \\
& + 3.19 \\
& (0.49) \Big]
\end{aligned}
$$

Estimation period from 1966Q2 to 1981Q4
$\overline{R}^2 = 0.992$
Standard error = 2.00 per cent
Durbin-Watson = 1.62
Stability test (6) 24.4
LM(5) 6.16

Export prices

$$
\begin{aligned}
PX_t = \exp \Big[& 0.762 \log(PX_{t-1}) + 0.0965 \log(WSI_{t-1}/PROD) \\
& (0.033) \qquad\qquad (0.0299) \\
& + 0.152 \log(WWPI_{t-1}/EER_{t-1}) + 0.705 \\
& (0.025) \qquad\qquad\qquad\qquad (0.114) \Big]
\end{aligned}
$$

Estimation period from 1963Q2 to 1980Q4
$\overline{R}^2 = 0.999$
Standard error = 1.21 per cent
Durbin-Watson = 1.64
Stability test (10) 21.07
LM(5) 6.69

Fixed investment

The stock of private sector fixed investment:

$$
\begin{aligned}
KI_t = KI_{t-1} + ICHS_t \\
+ GDPE_{t-1}\exp \Big[& 0.608 \log((KI_{t-1} - KI_{t-2} - ICHS_{t-1})/GDPE_{t-2}) \\
& (0.129) \\
& - 2.12 \log(KI_{t-1}/GDPE_{t-1}) \\
& (0.84) \\
& - 2.31 \log(GDPE_{t-1}/GDPE_{t-2}) \\
& (1.00) \\
& - 1.05 \log \left(\frac{WSI_{t-1} \times ET_{t-1}}{PC_{t-1} \times 1.0057^{TIME_t}} \right) + 13.1 \\
& (0.48) \qquad\qquad\qquad\qquad\qquad\quad (5.3) \Big]
\end{aligned}
$$

Estimation period from 1970Q1 to 1980Q4
$\overline{R}^2 = 0.560$
Standard error = 10.7 per cent
Durbin-Watson = 1.99
Stability test (8) 17.03
LM(5) 2.15

To calculate GDP, the flow of gross fixed private investment is needed, so this is computed as a working variable, which equals the change in the stock, plus the amount of fixed investment that offsets depreciation:

$$
W \qquad IFP = KI_t - KI_{t-1} + 4610 \times 1.0086^{TIME_t - 100}
$$

Inventories

First, a working variable for the expected real interest rate is defined:

$$
\begin{aligned}
\text{W} \quad \text{RREAL} = {} & 0.503\ \text{RLB}_{t-1} \\
& (0.177) \\
& - 0.086 \times 400(\text{EER}_{t-1}/\text{EER}_{t-1} - 1) \\
& (0.054) \\
& - 0.155 \times 400 \left(\frac{\text{WWPI}_{t-1} \times \text{EER}_{t-2}}{\text{WWPI}_{t-2} \times \text{EER}_{t-1}} - 1 \right) \\
& (0.042) \\
& - 0.400 \times 400\ (\text{WSI}_{t-1}/\text{WSI}_{t-2} - 1) + 1.20 \\
& (0.071) \hspace{5.5cm} (1.47)
\end{aligned}
$$

Estimation period from 1963Q3 to 1983Q1
$\overline{R}^2 = 0.339$
Standard error = 4.28
Durbin-Watson = 1.69

The equation for the stock of inventories is as follows (note that it is the change in this stock that contributes to GDP):

$$
\begin{aligned}
\text{KII}_t = \exp \Big[& \log(\text{KII}_{t-1})\ - 0.000351\ \text{RREAL} \\
& \hspace{2cm} (0.000234) \\
& + 0.486\ \log(\text{KII}_{t-1}/\text{KII}_{t-2}) \\
& (0.089) \\
& - 0.154\ \log(\text{KII}_{t-1}/\text{GDPE}_{t-1}) \\
& (0.028) \\
& - 0.0148\ \text{DV74Q1}\ + 0.0507 \Big] \\
& (0.0043) \hspace{1.8cm} (0.0088)
\end{aligned}
$$

Estimation period from 1963Q3 to 1980Q4
$\overline{R}^2 = 0.607$
Standard error = 0.60 per cent of change
Durbin-Watson = 2.03
Stability test (10) 24.15
LM(5) 6.09

Employment (whole economy)

$$ET_t = \exp \left[\log(ET_{t-1}) \right.$$

$$+ 0.544 \log(ET_{t-1}/ET_{t-2})$$
$$(0.104)$$
$$- 0.0479 \log(ET_{t-1} \times PROD/GDPE_{t-1})$$
$$(0.0166)$$
$$- 0.00742 \log(TREF_{t-1}/PC_{t-1})$$
$$(0.00328)$$
$$- 0.0242 \log(WSI_{t-1}/(PROD \times PC_{t-1}))$$
$$(0.0128)$$
$$\left. - 0.0259 \right]$$
$$(0.0094)$$

Estimation period from 1963Q3 to 1980Q4
$\overline{R}^2$ squared $= 0.466$
Standard error $= 0.27$ per cent
Durbin-Watson $= 2.16$
Stability test (10) 7.82
LM(5) 4.48

Personal disposable income at current prices (variable YD)

For this variable, it is necessary to define several working variables, for receipts of grants, debt interest, rent and income from companies:

Working variable for receipts of current grants from government

$$W \quad GRANTS = \frac{PC_t}{100} \left[- 0.631\ ET_t + 6762\ WSI_t/PC_t \right.$$
$$(0.137) \qquad (3150)$$
$$- 42.5\ ((WSI_{t-1}/PC_{t-1})/(WSI_{t-5}/PC_{t-5}) - 1)100$$
$$(19.2)$$
$$\left. - 15.0\ (PC_{t-1}/PC_{t-5} - 1)100 + 15875 \right]$$
$$(11.9) \qquad\qquad\qquad (6241)$$

Estimation period from 1979Q1 to 1983Q2
$\overline{R}^2 = 0.971$
Standard error $= 108$
Durbin-Watson $= 1.51$
LM(5) 10.63

Working variable for personal sector net receipts of debt interest from government

W   NETINT = $0.000673\,RLB_{t-1} \times GOVTB_{t-1}$
           (0.000105)
           $+ 16.36PC_{t-1}$
           (2.26)

Estimation period from 1969Q4 to 1980Q4
$\bar{R}^2 = 0.710$
Standard error = 1.39
Durbin-Watson = 2.21
Stability test (8) 13.97
LM(5) 8.71
(Divided through by PC_{t-1} during estimation)

Working variable for company tax and dividend payments

W $YCA = GDPE_{t-4} \times PC_{t-4}/100 - 1.347WSI_{t-4} \times ET_{t-4}/100$

Working variable for personal receipts of rent

W $JRENT = 0.046\,GDPE_{t-1} \times PC_{t-1}/100$

Personal disposable income at current prices

$YD_t = \{$ income from private and government employment
       $\{ ET_t \times 1.347 \times WSI_t(1 - T_t) \times (1 + 0.07)/100$
       $\{$ plus net interest and dividend receipts
       $\{ + NETINT\,(1 - 0.1\,T_t) \times 0.65 + 0.1\,YCA$
       $\{$ less tax on interest receipts
       $\{ - (RLB_{t-1}/400)\,(GDPE_{t-1} \times PC_{t-1}/100)$
       $\{$ less net interest payments to banks and companies
       $\{ - (RLB_{t-1}/400) \times 1.2 \times (GDPE_{t-1} \times PC_{t-1} \times 0.2/100)$
       $\{$ plus grants and rent
       $\{ + GRANTS + JRENT$

Consumer spending

$$
\begin{aligned}
C_t = \exp \Big[& \log(C_{t-1}) + 0.0057 \\
& - \underset{(0.099)}{0.239}\,(\log(C_{t-1}/C_{t-2}) - 0.0057) \\
& - \underset{(0.0350)}{0.0806}\,\log\!\left(\frac{C_{t-1}}{YD_{t-1}/(PC_{t-1}/100)} \right) \\
& - \underset{(0.163)}{0.419}\,(\log(PC_{t-1}/PC_{t-2}) + 0.0057) \\
& + \underset{(0.081)}{0.110}\;\left(\log\left(\frac{YD_{t-1}/PC_{t-1}}{YD_{t-2}/PC_{t-2}} \right) - 0.0057\right) \\
& - \underset{(0.00125)}{0.00280}\,(RLB_{t-1} - RLB_{t-2}) \Big]
\end{aligned}
$$

Estimation period from 1956Q4 to 1980Q4
$\overline{R}^2 = 0.157$
Standard error = 1.18 per cent
Durbin-Watson = 2.11
Stability test (10) 5.35
LM(5) 5.16

Note: An inflation term that allows for deviations between income from
employment and total personal disposable income was used during
estimation, but for simplicity a simpler form is given in the
equations as shown here and in Chapter 4: the parameter estimates
are virtually unaltered by this.

Imports (non oil)

$$
\begin{aligned}
M_t = \exp \Big[& \underset{(0.106)}{0.572}\,\log(M_{t-1}) + \underset{(0.362)}{0.858}\,\log(C_t/C_{t-1}) \\
& + \underset{(0.67)}{1.40}\,\log\!\left(\frac{KII_t/KII_{t-1}}{KII_{t-1}/KII_{t-2}} \right) + \underset{(0.33)}{1.39}\,\log(GDPE_{t-2}) \\
& + \underset{(0.130)}{0.234}\,\log(WGNP_{t-1}/XWM_{t-1}) \\
& - \underset{(0.099)}{0.138}\,\log(WWPI_{t-6}/EER_{t-6}) \\
& + \underset{(0.132)}{0.181}\,\log\!\left(\frac{WSI_{t-6}}{1.0057^{TIME_t-38}} \right) - \underset{(3.3)}{11.7} \Big]
\end{aligned}
$$

Estimation period from 1965Q2 to 1980Q4
$\overline{R}^2 = 0.975$
Standard error = 4.11 per cent
Durbin-Watson = 2.33
Stability test (10) 7.03
LM(5) 10.15

Balance of payments

Current account balance

$$\mathrm{BAL}_t = \begin{cases} \text{exports net of imports} \\ \mathrm{PX}_t \times \mathrm{X}_t/100 - \mathrm{M}_t \times \mathrm{WWPI}_t/(\mathrm{EER}_t \times 1.05) \\ + \mathrm{O}_t \times \mathrm{POILWC}_t/\mathrm{EER}_t \end{cases}$$
$$\begin{cases} \text{plus net interest and dividends paid to the UK by} \\ \text{foreigners} \\ + \mathrm{OJ}_{t-1} \times 0.8\,\mathrm{RSW}_{t-1}/400 \end{cases}$$

Capital account

Because foreign exchange markets are assumed to be cleared by specula-tors indifferent between sterling and foreign currency assets (see above), there will automatically be capital account transactions equal and opposite to the current account, less any government intervention (such intervention has no effect on the exchange rate in this model because of the speculators, but is relevant for determining money stock):

$$\mathrm{OJ}_t = \mathrm{OJ}_{t-1} + \mathrm{BAL}_t - \mathrm{DRESV}_t$$

The expenditure measure of GDP

First, define a working variable for the adjustment to factor cost at 1980 prices (i.e. taxes on expenditure less subsidies)

W $F = 0.158\,C_t + 0.07\,\mathrm{IFP} + 0.43\,X_t + 0.077\,G_t$

The expenditure measure of GDP equals the sum of expenditure compo-nents at market prices, less F:

$$\mathrm{GDPE}_t = C_t + \mathrm{IFP} + \mathrm{KII}_t - \mathrm{KII}_{t-1} + G_t + X_t - M_t + O_t - F$$

The public sector borrowing requirement (PSBR)

For this variable, working variables for company sector payments of tax and for government receipts of rent are defined. The working variables for grants and debt interest payments, defined earlier, are also used:

Company tax (net of grants to companies)

W $\mathrm{CTAX} = 0.056\,\mathrm{YCA} + 0.80\,\mathrm{O}_{t-4} \times \mathrm{POILWC}_{t-4}/\mathrm{EER}_{t-4}$

Government receipts of rent

W $\mathrm{GRENT} = 0.018\,\mathrm{GDPE}_{t-1} \times \mathrm{PC}_{t-1}/100$

Public sector borrowing requirement

PSBR_t = $\Big\{$ spending on goods and services
$PC_t \times G_t/100$

$\Big\{$ less taxes on incomes of persons (including
employee's NIC, employers' NIC and NIS)
$- (T_t + 0.09) \times ET_t \times 1.347 \times WSI_t/100$
$- (RLB_{t-1}/400) \times T_t \times (GDPE_{t-1} \times PC_{t-1}/100)$

$\Big\{$ less tax receipts from company incomes
$- CTAX$

$\Big\{$ less expenditure tax receipts
$- F \times TREF_t/100$

$\Big\{$ less receipts of rent
$- GRENT$

$\Big\{$ less profits of public corporations and government
$- 0.037\, GDPE_{t-1} \times PC_{t-1}/100$

$\Big\{$ plus grants
$+ GRANTS$

$\Big\{$ plus debt interest payments on gilts and other debt
$+ (1 - T_t \times 0.72 \times 0.1) \times NETINT$

Financing the PSBR

The PSBR has to be financed either through the issue of high powered money (the stock of which is variable MO), which consists of notes and coin and bankers' balances at the Bank of England; or through changes in foreign currency reserves (the flow of which is variable DRESV); or through other debt (mainly long-term bonds, i.e. gilts but also including National Savings and short-term bill transactions). By identity, a working variable for the flow of this other debt can be defined:

W $DGG = PSBR_t - (MO_t - MO_{t-1}) + DRESV_t.$

Assuming that revaluations can be ignored, the stock of this debt is given by:

$$GOVTB_t = GOVTB_{t-1} + DGG.$$

APPENDIX 2

Full results from the first forecast presented in Chapter 5, made using exogenously imposed expectations

Table A.2.1. Expenditure on gross domestic product

	GDPE	C	G	KI	KII	X	M	O
	GDP (exp. measure)	Consumer spending	Public spending	Fixed capital stock	Stock of inventories	Non-oil exports	Non-oil imports	Net oil trade
	Annual values							
1979	201385	138004	60800	379970	70933	56808	51960	− 1492
1980	196394	137324	60600	388770	70210	56776	50776	− 496
1981	194448	137559	58612	394559	66395	54188	50648	2140
1982	199008	139552	59036	399831	65630	54284	52916	3432
1983	205079	144673	61376	405873	65396	54048	56044	4444
1984	211304	149479	62372	414637	65408	58668	61908	4100
1985	215546	152298	63344	425435	66388	61648	67084	4500
1986	218054	155569	64204	436516	67771	63316	70588	4800
1987	220807	159557	64916	447186	68736	64884	73244	4800
1988	224395	163669	65740	457441	69687	66740	76436	4952
	Quarterly values							
1983 1	51591	35473	15536	403405	65459	13528	13854	1215
2	50627	36055	15167	404830	65411	13329	13891	1030
3	50941	36395	15308	406614	65363	13289	14001	1200
4	51920	36750	15366	408643	65350	13900	14300	1000
1984 1	52355	37076	15498	410872	65294	14246	14777	1000
2	52619	37303	15577	413294	65312	14575	15387	1000
3	53009	37546	15615	415860	65418	14819	15735	1000
4	53320	37555	15683	418520	65609	15027	16010	1100
1985 1	53505	37742	15729	421257	65873	15211	16390	1100
2	53761	37901	15815	424041	66193	15362	16636	1100
3	53997	38222	15861	426832	66555	15485	16924	1100
4	54283	38433	15937	429610	66931	15591	17134	1200
1986 1	54380	38589	15974	432385	67308	15693	17343	1200
2	54414	38675	16040	435162	67650	15787	17546	1200
3	54546	39048	16067	437908	67941	15872	17800	1200
4	54714	39258	16124	440606	68184	15962	17899	1200
1987 1	54904	39535	16151	443266	68403	16066	18056	1200
2	55100	39717	16218	445899	68623	16168	18195	1200
3	55305	40045	16245	448502	68847	16269	18414	1200
4	55498	40259	16302	451078	69069	16380	18580	1200
1988 1	55700	40533	16330	453642	69297	16508	18798	1200
2	55948	40706	16400	456181	69540	16627	18967	1250
3	56256	41110	16470	458709	69809	16743	19240	1250
4	56491	41320	16540	461233	70102	16864	19431	1250

Note: All figures are in £million at 1980 prices.

Table A.2.2.   Expenditure on gross domestic product (percentage changes)

	GDPE	C	G	KI	KII	X	M
	GDP (exp. measure)	Consumer spending	Public spending	Fixed capital stock	Stock of invent-ories	Non-oil exports	Non-oil imports
Annual percentage changes							
1979	1.7	5.0	0.8	2.6	3.6	0.5	12.2
1980	− 2.5	− 0.5	− 0.3	2.3	− 1.0	− 0.1	− 2.3
1981	− 1.0	0.2	− 3.3	1.5	− 5.4	− 4.6	− 0.3
1982	2.3	1.4	0.7	1.3	− 1.2	0.2	4.5
1983	3.1	3.7	4.0	1.5	− 0.4	− 0.4	5.9
1984	3.0	3.3	1.6	2.2	0.0	8.5	10.5
1985	2.0	1.9	1.6	2.6	1.5	5.1	8.4
1986	1.2	2.1	1.4	2.6	2.1	2.7	5.2
1987	1.3	2.6	1.1	2.4	1.4	2.5	3.8
1988	1.6	2.6	1.3	2.3	1.4	2.9	4.4
Quarterly percentage changes							
1983 1	4.8	3.6	5.8	1.4	− 0.7	− 2.1	4.7
2	2.3	4.2	3.8	1.4	− 1.1	− 3.9	2.6
3	3.0	3.8	3.9	1.5	− 0.3	2.2	7.8
4	2.1	3.1	2.4	1.7	0.7	2.3	8.7
1984 1	1.5	4.5	− 0.2	1.9	− 0.3	5.3	6.7
2	3.9	3.5	2.7	2.1	− 0.2	9.3	10.8
3	4.1	3.2	2.0	2.3	0.1	11.5	12.4
4	2.7	2.2	2.1	2.4	0.4	8.1	12.0
1985 1	2.2	1.8	1.5	2.5	0.9	6.8	10.9
2	2.2	1.6	1.5	2.6	1.3	5.4	8.1
3	1.9	1.8	1.6	2.6	1.7	4.5	7.6
4	1.8	2.3	1.6	2.6	2.0	3.8	7.0
1986 1	1.6	2.2	1.6	2.6	2.2	3.2	5.8
2	1.2	2.0	1.4	2.6	2.2	2.8	5.5
3	1.0	2.2	1.3	2.6	2.1	2.5	5.2
4	0.8	2.1	1.2	2.6	1.9	2.4	4.5
1987 1	1.0	2.5	1.1	2.5	1.6	2.4	4.1
2	1.3	2.7	1.1	2.5	1.4	2.4	3.7
3	1.4	2.6	1.1	2.4	1.3	2.5	3.4
4	1.4	2.6	1.1	2.4	1.3	2.6	3.8
1988 1	1.5	2.5	1.1	2.3	1.3	2.7	4.1
2	1.5	2.5	1.1	2.3	1.3	2.8	4.2
3	1.7	2.7	1.4	2.3	1.4	2.9	4.5
4	1.8	2.6	1.5	2.3	1.5	3.0	4.6

Table A.2.3. Other key indicators

	PC	YD	RLB	EER	WSI	ET
	Consumer price index	Personal disposable income	Short-term interest rates	Exchange rate index	Average earnings (whole economy)	Employment
	1980 = 100	£m.current prices	%p.a.	1980 = 100	1980 = 100	000s
Annual values						
1979	86	135928	13.7	91	83	25367
1980	100	160727	16.3	100	99	25121
1981	111	174328	13.3	99	111	24276
1982	120	188274	11.9	94	121	23870
1983	127	201037	9.8	87	131	23679
1984	134	216698	10.1	88	140	23489
1985	144	236437	11.2	88	154	23383
1986	154	259424	11.5	88	169	23305
1987	164	282078	10.9	88	185	23152
1988	173	303808	10.6	88	200	22953
Quarterly values						
1983 1	125	49035	10.8	84	129	23699
2	126	49574	10.0	88	130	23717
3	127	50645	9.5	88	132	23681
4	129	51783	9.0	87	134	23619
1984 1	131	52760	8.9	88	136	23558
2	132	53600	8.8	88	139	23504
3	134	54611	11.1	88	142	23462
4	137	55726	11.5	88	144	23434
1985 1	140	57013	11.7	88	148	23410
2	142	58399	11.0	88	152	23388
3	145	59813	10.9	88	155	23373
4	148	61212	11.2	88	159	23359
1986 1	151	62662	12.2	89	163	23343
2	153	64132	11.4	88	167	23320
3	155	65609	11.5	88	171	23294
4	158	67021	10.8	88	175	23263
1987 1	161	68471	11.0	88	179	23222
2	163	69878	10.7	88	183	23175
3	165	71223	11.1	88	187	23129
4	168	72506	10.7	88	190	23082
1988 1	170	73896	11.1	88	194	23030
2	172	75282	10.2	88	198	22976
3	174	76660	10.6	88	202	22925
4	177	77970	10.4	88	205	22879

Table A.2.4.   Other key indicators (percentage changes)

	PC	YD	EER	WSI	ET
	Consumer price index	Personal disposable income	Exchange rate index	Average earnings (whole economy)	Employment
	Annual percentage changes				
1979	13.4	20.0	7.2	15.2	1.3
1980	16.5	18.2	10.1	20.3	– 1.0
1981	11.1	8.5	– 1.2	11.7	– 3.4
1982	8.3	8.0	– 4.7	9.3	– 1.7
1983	5.3	6.8	– 8.0	8.1	– 0.8
1984	5.5	7.8	1.6	6.9	– 0.8
1985	7.4	9.1	0.3	9.4	– 0.5
1986	7.4	9.7	0.1	10.2	– 0.3
1987	6.4	8.7	– 0.1	9.2	– 0.7
1988	5.6	7.7	– 0.1	8.2	– 0.9
	Quarterly percentage changes				
1983 1	6.3	6.4	– 11.6	8.9	– 1.4
2	5.0	5.9	– 6.6	7.8	– 0.9
3	5.0	7.4	– 7.2	8.2	– 0.6
4	5.0	7.4	– 6.6	7.5	– 0.4
1984 1	4.8	7.6	4.6	5.8	– 0.6
2	5.3	8.1	0.0	6.8	– 0.9
3	5.5	7.8	– 0.1	7.0	– 0.9
4	6.4	7.6	2.0	7.9	– 0.8
1985 1	7.0	8.1	0.7	8.5	– 0.6
2	7.4	9.0	0.5	9.3	– 0.5
3	7.6	9.5	0.0	9.8	– 0.4
4	7.7	9.8	– 0.1	10.1	– 0.3
1986 1	7.7	9.9	0.1	10.2	– 0.3
2	7.6	9.8	0.1	10.3	– 0.3
3	7.4	9.7	0.1	10.1	– 0.3
4	7.1	9.5	– 0.1	10.0	– 0.4
1987 1	6.8	9.3	– 0.3	9.7	– 0.5
2	6.5	9.0	– 0.2	9.4	– 0.6
3	6.2	8.6	– 0.1	9.1	– 0.7
4	6.0	8.2	0.0	8.8	– 0.8
1988 1	5.8	7.9	0.0	8.5	– 0.8
2	5.7	7.7	– 0.1	8.3	– 0.9
3	5.5	7.6	– 0.1	8.1	– 0.9
4	5.5	7.5	– 0.1	8.0	– 0.9

Table A.2.5.   World variables

	RSW	XWM	WWPI	WGNP	POILWC
	World short-term interest rates	*World exports of manufactures*	*World wholesale prices*	*World GNP*	*World oil prices*
	Annual values				
1979	8.7	95	87	99	57
1980	11.9	100	100	100	100
1981	12.7	103	110	102	124
1982	11.4	100	118	101	132
1983	8.6	99	124	104	122
1984	9.0	104	132	108	121
1985	9.0	109	141	110	121
1986	9.0	114	151	112	121
1987	9.0	118	162	115	121
1988	9.0	123	173	117	121
	Quarterly values				
1983 1	9.1	100	122	102	128
2	8.2	100	123	103	119
3	8.7	98	125	104	121
4	8.5	100	127	106	121
1984 1	9.0	102	130	106	121
2	9.0	104	131	107	121
3	9.0	105	133	108	121
4	9.0	106	135	109	121
1985 1	9.0	108	138	109	121
2	9.0	109	140	110	121
3	9.0	110	142	110	121
4	9.0	111	145	111	121
1986 1	9.0	112	148	112	121
2	9.0	113	150	112	121
3	9.0	114	152	113	121
4	9.0	115	155	113	121
1987 1	9.0	116	158	114	121
2	9.0	118	160	114	121
3	9.0	119	163	115	121
4	9.0	120	166	116	121
1988 1	9.0	122	169	116	121
2	9.0	123	172	117	121
3	9.0	124	174	118	121
4	9.0	126	177	118	121

Note: World interest rates are in % per annum. Other series are indices, 1980 = 100.

Table A.2.6.   World variables (percentage changes)

	XWM	WWPI	WGNP	POILWC
	World exports of manufactures	World wholesale prices	World GNP	World oil prices
Annual percentage changes				
1979	5.1	10.6	3.5	42.2
1980	5.4	14.6	1.1	74.3
1981	3.5	10.3	1.8	23.9
1982	− 3.7	6.8	− 0.5	6.8
1983	− 0.3	5.5	2.4	− 7.7
1984	4.8	6.5	3.8	− 0.9
1985	4.9	6.7	2.3	0.0
1986	3.9	7.0	2.0	0.0
1987	4.2	7.0	2.1	0.0
1988	4.4	6.9	2.3	0.0
Quarterly percentage changes				
1983 1	− 2.9	5.2	0.6	0.8
2	0.7	5.2	1.5	− 7.9
3	− 1.3	5.4	3.1	− 10.9
4	2.4	6.3	4.2	− 12.3
1984 1	2.0	6.7	4.6	− 5.3
2	4.0	6.7	4.2	2.1
3	6.7	6.5	3.4	0.0
4	6.6	6.1	3.0	0.0
1985 1	5.9	6.5	2.7	0.0
2	5.0	6.7	2.3	0.0
3	4.6	6.8	2.2	0.0
4	4.2	6.9	2.1	0.0
1986 1	4.0	7.0	2.0	0.0
2	3.9	7.0	2.0	0.0
3	3.9	7.0	2.0	0.0
4	4.0	6.9	2.0	0.0
1987 1	4.1	7.0	2.1	0.0
2	4.2	7.0	2.1	0.0
3	4.3	7.0	2.2	0.0
4	4.4	7.1	2.2	0.0
1988 1	4.4	7.1	2.2	0.0
2	4.3	7.0	2.2	0.0
3	4.3	6.8	2.3	0.0
4	4.4	6.7	2.4	0.0

Table A.2.7. UK financial variables

		MO	PSBR	GOVTB	BAL	OJ	XEER	COMP
		Money supply MO	Public sector borrowing	Gov't non-money debt	Current account balance	Net overseas assets	Expected exchange rate	Real exchange rate
		Annual values						
1979		9852	12638	62336	− 653	10242	94	59
1980		10630	12173	73962	3235	14069	102	67
1981		11201	10730	87608	6547	19918	96	65
1982		11512	5448	93093	5378	11874	91	62
1983		12710	10292	102973	998	8255	87	57
1984		13845	7525	109081	− 22	8363	88	57
1985		14956	8969	116688	− 1857	7379	88	57
1986		16087	8937	124473	− 4502	3937	88	58
1987		17155	9275	132450	− 7164	− 2263	88	58
1988		18184	10596	141483	− 10662	− 11562	88	57
		Quarterly values						
1983	1	12098	4374	100013	781	7936	88	56
	2	12554	2152	102165	− 171	8053	88	58
	3	12587	2616	104787	603	8623	87	58
	4	13599	1150	104925	− 215	8408	87	56
1984	1	13275	1182	106431	63	8470	88	57
	2	13683	2225	108249	− 151	8319	88	57
	3	13677	2087	110341	− 45	8275	88	57
	4	14746	2032	111304	111	8386	88	57
1985	1	14330	1962	113682	− 255	8131	88	57
	2	14723	2509	115798	− 396	7736	88	57
	3	14790	2502	118233	− 616	7120	88	57
	4	15981	1995	119038	− 591	6529	88	58
1986	1	15493	1889	121415	− 832	5697	88	58
	2	15877	2518	123548	− 1039	4659	88	58
	3	15872	2527	126081	− 1294	3365	88	58
	4	17107	2002	126848	− 1338	2027	88	58
1987	1	16583	1868	129240	− 1593	433	88	58
	2	16953	2545	131415	− 1675	− 1242	88	58
	3	16905	2630	134093	− 1867	− 3109	88	58
	4	18178	2233	135052	− 2029	− 5137	88	57
1988	1	17577	2123	137777	− 2418	− 7555	88	57
	2	17970	2887	140271	− 2502	− 10057	88	57
	3	17921	3006	143326	− 2781	− 12838	88	57
	4	19268	2580	144558	− 2962	− 15800	88	57

Note: The first five variables are in £million at current prices. The two exchange rate series are indices.

Table A.2.8.   UK financial variables (percentage changes)

	MO	PSBR	GOVTB	XEER	COMP
	Money supply MO	Public sector borrowing	Gov't non-money debt	Expected exchange rate	Real exchange rate
	Annual percentage changes				
1979	12.2	51.6	21.9	11.3	9.1
1980	7.9	– 3.7	18.7	9.3	13.0
1981	5.4	– 11.9	18.5	– 6.1	– 2.2
1982	2.8	– 49.2	6.3	– 4.8	– 4.6
1983	10.4	88.9	10.6	– 4.5	– 7.9
1984	8.9	– 26.9	5.9	0.6	– 0.3
1985	8.0	19.2	7.0	0.0	0.5
1986	7.6	– 0.4	6.7	0.0	0.7
1987	6.6	3.8	6.4	0.0	– 0.3
1988	6.0	14.2	6.8	0.0	– 1.1
	Quarterly percentage changes				
1983 1	9.4	1108.3	10.4	– 6.6	– 10.6
2	11.6	35.8	10.9	– 7.2	– 6.5
3	10.5	37.4	11.4	– 6.6	– 6.9
4	10.1	– 28.0	9.7	3.1	– 7.7
1984 1	9.7	– 73.0	6.4	0.1	1.5
2	9.0	3.4	6.0	– 0.6	– 2.2
3	8.7	– 20.2	5.3	1.4	– 1.9
4	8.4	76.6	6.1	1.5	1.4
1985 1	7.9	66.1	6.8	0.0	0.2
2	7.6	12.7	7.0	0.0	0.7
3	8.1	19.9	7.2	0.0	0.4
4	8.4	– 1.8	6.9	0.0	0.6
1986 1	8.1	– 3.7	6.8	0.0	0.9
2	7.8	0.4	6.7	0.0	0.8
3	7.3	1.0	6.6	0.0	0.8
4	7.0	0.4	6.6	0.0	0.4
1987 1	7.0	– 1.1	6.4	0.0	0.0
2	6.8	1.1	6.4	0.0	– 0.2
3	6.5	4.0	6.4	0.0	– 0.4
4	6.3	11.5	6.5	0.0	– 0.7
1988 1	6.0	13.7	6.6	0.0	– 1.0
2	6.0	13.4	6.7	0.0	– 1.2
3	6.0	14.3	6.9	0.0	– 1.2
4	6.0	15.6	7.0	0.0	– 1.1

Table A.2.9. Other variables

		PX	T	TREF	DRESV	TIME	ICHS
		Non-oil export prices	Average income tax rate	Average indirect tax rate	Change in reserves etc.	Time trend 1955 Q1 equals 1	Council house sales
		1980 = 100	ratio	1980 = 100	£m. current prices	–	£m. 1980 prices
		Annual values					
1979		89	0.20	80	1576	98.5	563
1980		100	0.20	100	940	102.5	976
1981		107	0.22	121	– 1128	106.5	1139
1982		114	0.22	135	– 1056	110.5	2261
1983		126	0.22	136	– 431	114.5	1773
1984		141	0.22	143	0	118.5	1480
1985		152	0.22	154	0	122.5	1160
1986		164	0.22	165	0	126.5	1000
1987		176	0.22	176	0	130.5	1000
1988		189	0.22	186	0	134.5	940
		Quarterly values					
1983	1	120	0.22	137	– 176	113	495
	2	123	0.22	134	– 288	114	430
	3	127	0.22	134	33	115	428
	4	132	0.22	141	0	116	420
1984	1	136	0.22	144	0	117	400
	2	139	0.22	140	0	118	380
	3	142	0.22	141	0	119	360
	4	145	0.22	149	0	120	340
1985	1	148	0.22	153	0	121	320
	2	151	0.22	150	0	122	300
	3	153	0.22	152	0	123	280
	4	156	0.22	160	0	124	260
1986	1	159	0.22	165	0	125	250
	2	162	0.22	161	0	126	250
	3	165	0.22	163	0	127	250
	4	168	0.22	172	0	128	250
1987	1	171	0.22	177	0	129	250
	2	174	0.22	172	0	130	250
	3	178	0.22	174	0	131	250
	4	181	0.22	183	0	132	250
1988	1	184	0.22	187	0	133	250
	2	187	0.22	182	0	134	230
	3	191	0.22	184	0	135	230
	4	194	0.22	193	0	136	230

Table A.2.10. Other variables (percentage changes)

	PX	T	TREF	ICHS
	Non-oil export prices	Average income tax rate	Average indirect tax rate	Council house sales
	Annual percentage changes			
1979	11.2	− 6.3	26.3	20.3
1980	12.1	0.7	24.3	73.3
1981	7.3	9.5	20.8	16.7
1982	6.2	2.9	11.6	98.5
1983	10.1	− 0.1	1.1	− 21.6
1984	12.0	0.0	5.2	− 16.5
1985	8.2	0.0	7.1	− 21.6
1986	7.7	0.0	7.6	− 13.8
1987	7.6	0.0	6.7	0.0
1988	7.3	0.0	5.7	− 6.0
	Quarterly percentage changes			
1983 1	7.7	0.0	− 1.3	− 17.2
2	8.2	− 0.1	1.3	− 23.0
3	10.9	− 0.1	− 0.4	− 23.9
4	13.6	− 0.1	5.0	− 22.6
1984 1	12.8	− 0.1	5.0	− 19.2
2	13.4	0.0	4.8	− 11.6
3	11.6	0.0	5.3	− 15.9
4	10.3	0.0	5.5	− 19.0
1985 1	8.9	0.0	6.4	− 20.0
2	8.3	0.0	7.0	− 21.1
3	7.9	0.0	7.4	− 22.2
4	7.8	0.0	7.6	− 23.5
1986 1	7.7	0.0	7.7	− 21.9
2	7.7	0.0	7.7	− 16.7
3	7.7	0.0	7.6	− 10.7
4	7.6	0.0	7.4	− 3.8
1987 1	7.6	0.0	7.1	0.0
2	7.6	0.0	6.8	0.0
3	7.6	0.0	6.5	0.0
4	7.5	0.0	6.2	0.0
1988 1	7.4	0.0	6.0	0.0
2	7.3	0.0	5.8	− 8.0
3	7.2	0.0	5.7	− 8.0
4	7.1	0.0	5.5	− 8.0

APPENDIX 3

Full results from the second forecast presented in Chapter 5, made on the assumption of rational expectations

Table A.3.1. Expenditure on gross domestic product

	GDPE	C	G	KI	KII	X	M	O
	GDP (exp. measure)	Consumer spending	Public spending	Fixed capital stock	Stock of inventories	Non-oil exports	Non-oil imports	Net oil trade
Annual values								
1979	201385	138004	60800	379970	70933	56808	51960	– 1492
1980	196394	137324	60600	388770	70210	56776	50776	– 496
1981	194448	137559	58612	394559	66395	54188	50648	2140
1982	199008	139552	59036	399831	65630	54284	52916	3432
1983	205079	144673	61376	405873	65396	54048	56044	4444
1984	210831	149625	62372	414619	65352	58108	61812	4100
1985	215503	153056	63344	425295	66312	61052	67156	4500
1986	218224	156583	64204	436316	67791	63064	71104	4800
1987	221319	160374	64916	447052	68912	64940	73752	4800
1988	224960	164141	65740	457472	69967	67056	76800	.4952
Quarterly values								
1983 1	51591	35473	15536	403405	65459	13528	13854	1215
2	50627	36055	15167	404830	65411	13329	13891	1030
3	50941	36395	15308	406614	65363	13289	14001	1200
4	51920	36750	15366	408643	65350	13900	14300	1000
1984 1	52273	37076	15498	410872	65294	14160	14777	1000
2	52462	37303	15577	413292	65275	14439	15375	1000
3	52857	37583	15615	415842	65339	14654	15706	1000
4	53238	37663	15683	418470	65499	14854	15956	1100
1985 1	53500	37901	15729	421164	65756	15042	16320	1100
2	53807	38089	15815	423908	66096	15204	16580	1100
3	53982	38424	15861	426672	66495	15341	16982	1100
4	54214	38642	15937	429435	66899	15466	17275	1200
1986 1	54332	38826	15974	432198	67291	15596	17501	1200
2	54432	38935	16040	434963	67650	15713	17680	1200
3	54629	39313	16067	437701	67969	15823	17913	1200
4	54831	39509	16124	440403	68253	15932	18011	1200
1987 1	55025	39767	16151	443081	68519	16055	18183	1200
2	55219	39929	16218	445743	68784	16173	18332	1200
3	55435	40241	16245	448383	69045	16292	18542	1200
4	55640	40437	16302	450999	69299	16419	18694	1200
1988 1	55850	40689	16330	453606	69552	16565	18900	1200
2	56093	40838	16400	456189	69817	16697	19062	1250
3	56393	41215	16470	458763	70100	16828	19328	1250
4	56623	41399	16540	461331	70399	16964	19509	1250

Note: All figures are in £million at 1980 prices.

Table A.3.2. Expenditure on gross domestic product (percentage changes)

	GDPE	C	G	KI	KII	X	M
	GDP (exp. measure)	Consumer spending	Public spending	Fixed capital stock	Stock of inventories	Non-oil exports	Non-oil imports
	Annual percentage changes						
1979	1.7	5.0	0.8	2.6	3.6	0.5	12.2
1980	− 2.5	− 0.5	− 0.3	2.3	− 1.0	− 0.1	− 2.3
1981	− 1.0	0.2	− 3.3	1.5	− 5.4	− 4.6	− 0.3
1982	2.3	1.4	0.7	1.3	− 1.2	0.2	4.5
1983	3.1	3.7	4.0	1.5	− 0.4	− 0.4	5.9
1984	2.8	3.4	1.6	2.2	− 0.1	7.5	10.3
1985	2.2	2.3	1.6	2.6	1.5	5.1	8.6
1986	1.3	2.3	1.4	2.6	2.2	3.3	5.9
1987	1.4	2.4	1.1	2.5	1.7	3.0	3.7
1988	1.6	2.3	1.3	2.3	1.5	3.3	4.1
	Quarterly percentage changes						
1983 1	4.8	3.6	5.8	1.4	− 0.7	− 2.1	4.7
2	2.3	4.2	3.8	1.4	− 1.1	− 3.9	2.6
3	3.0	3.8	3.9	1.5	− 0.3	2.2	7.8
4	2.1	3.1	2.4	1.7	0.7	2.3	8.7
1984 1	1.3	4.5	− 0.2	1.9	− 0.3	4.7	6.7
2	3.6	3.5	2.7	2.1	− 0.2	8.3	10.7
3	3.8	3.3	2.0	2.3	0.0	10.3	12.2
4	2.5	2.5	2.1	2.4	0.2	6.9	11.6
1985 1	2.3	2.2	1.5	2.5	0.7	6.2	10.4
2	2.6	2.1	1.5	2.6	1.3	5.3	7.8
3	2.1	2.2	1.6	2.6	1.8	4.7	8.1
4	1.8	2.6	1.6	2.6	2.1	4.1	8.3
1986 1	1.6	2.4	1.6	2.6	2.3	3.7	7.2
2	1.2	2.2	1.4	2.6	2.4	3.4	6.6
3	1.2	2.3	1.3	2.6	2.2	3.1	5.5
4	1.1	2.2	1.2	2.6	2.0	3.0	4.3
1987 1	1.3	2.4	1.1	2.5	1.8	2.9	3.9
2	1.4	2.6	1.1	2.5	1.7	2.9	3.7
3	1.5	2.4	1.1	2.4	1.6	3.0	3.5
4	1.5	2.3	1.1	2.4	1.5	3.1	3.8
1988 1	1.5	2.3	1.1	2.4	1.5	3.2	3.9
2	1.6	2.3	1.1	2.3	1.5	3.2	4.0
3	1.7	2.4	1.4	2.3	1.5	3.3	4.2
4	1.8	2.4	1.5	2.3	1.6	3.3	4.4

Table A.3.3. Other key indicators

	PC	YD	RLB	EER	WSI	ET
	Consumer price index	Personal dispos- able income	Short- term interest rates	Exchange rate index	Average earnings (whole economy)	Employ- ment
	1980 = 100	£m. current prices	%p.a.	1980 = 100	1980 = 100	000s
	Annual values					
1979	86	135928	13.7	91	83	25367
1980	100	160727	16.3	100	99	25121
1981	111	174328	13.3	99	111	24276
1982	120	188274	11.9	94	121	23870
1983	127	201037	9.8	87	131	23679
1984	133	216522	9.6	91	140	23484
1985	142	234492	9.9	91	152	23354
1986	152	255685	9.9	90	166	23269
1987	161	277536	9.8	89	182	23134
1988	171	299792	10.0	88	197	22966
	Quarterly values					
1983 1	125	49035	10.8	84	129	23699
2	126	49574	10.0	88	130	23717
3	127	50645	9.5	88	132	23681
4	129	51783	9.0	87	134	23619
1984 1	131	52760	8.9	91	136	23558
2	132	53594	8.6	91	139	23502
3	134	54565	10.4	91	141	23456
4	136	55603	10.4	91	144	23419
1985 1	139	56759	10.5	91	147	23388
2	141	57979	9.7	90	151	23361
3	143	59241	9.7	90	154	23342
4	146	60513	9.8	90	157	23326
1986 1	148	61866	10.6	90	161	23307
2	151	63247	9.7	90	165	23282
3	153	64624	9.9	90	168	23257
4	155	65948	9.5	90	172	23229
1987 1	158	67342	9.8	89	176	23194
2	160	68728	9.6	89	180	23153
3	162	70079	10.1	89	184	23114
4	165	71386	9.8	89	187	23075
1988 1	168	72808	10.3	89	191	23032
2	170	74239	9.6	88	195	22986
3	172	75678	10.0	88	199	22943
4	175	77066	10.0	88	203	22905

Table A.3.4. Other key indicators (percentage changes)

	PC	YD	EER	WSI	ET
	Consumer price index	Personal Disposable income	Exchange rate index	Average earnings (whole economy)	Employment
	Annual percentage changes				
1979	13.4	20.0	7.2	15.2	1.3
1980	16.5	18.2	10.1	20.3	– 1.0
1981	11.1	8.5	– 1.2	11.7	– 3.4
1982	8.3	8.0	– 4.7	9.3	– 1.7
1983	5.3	6.8	– 8.0	8.1	– 0.8
1984	5.2	7.7	5.1	6.8	– 0.8
1985	6.5	8.3	– 0.6	8.6	– 0.6
1986	6.9	9.0	– 0.7	9.4	– 0.4
1987	6.4	8.5	– 0.8	9.0	– 0.6
1988	6.0	8.0	– 1.1	8.5	– 0.7
	Quarterly percentage changes				
1983 1	6.3	6.4	– 11.6	8.9	– 1.4
2	5.0	5.9	– 6.6	7.8	– 0.9
3	5.0	7.4	– 7.2	8.2	– 0.6
4	5.0	7.4	– 6.6	7.5	– 0.4
1984 1	4.8	7.6	8.4	5.8	– 0.6
2	5.1	8.1	3.8	6.8	– 0.9
3	5.2	7.7	3.3	6.9	– 1.0
4	5.8	7.4	5.1	7.6	– 0.8
1985 1	6.1	7.6	– 0.1	8.0	– 0.7
2	6.4	8.2	– 0.6	8.5	– 0.6
3	6.6	8.6	– 0.8	8.8	– 0.5
4	6.8	8.8	– 0.7	9.1	– 0.4
1986 1	6.9	9.0	– 0.6	9.2	– 0.3
2	7.0	9.1	– 0.7	9.4	– 0.3
3	6.9	9.1	– 0.8	9.4	– 0.4
4	6.8	9.0	– 0.9	9.4	– 0.4
1987 1	6.6	8.9	– 0.9	9.3	– 0.5
2	6.4	8.7	– 0.7	9.1	– 0.6
3	6.3	8.4	– 0.7	9.0	– 0.6
4	6.2	8.2	– 0.8	8.8	– 0.7
1988 1	6.1	8.1	– 0.9	8.6	– 0.7
2	6.0	8.0	– 1.1	8.5	– 0.7
3	6.0	8.0	– 1.1	8.5	– 0.7
4	6.0	8.0	– 1.2	8.4	– 0.7

Table A.3.5. World variables

	RSW	XWM	WWPI	WGNP	POILWC
	World short-term interest rates	World exports of manufactures	World wholesale prices	World GNP	World oil prices
	Annual values				
1979	8.7	95	87	99	57
1980	11.9	100	100	100	100
1981	12.7	103	110	102	124
1982	11.4	100	118	101	132
1983	8.6	99	124	104	122
1984	9.0	104	132	108	121
1985	9.0	109	141	110	121
1986	9.0	114	151	112	121
1987	9.0	118	162	115	121
1988	9.0	123	173	117	121
	Quarterly values				
1983 1	9.1	100	122	102	128
2	8.2	100	123	103	119
3	8.7	98	125	104	121
4	8.5	100	127	106	121
1984 1	9.0	102	130	106	121
2	9.0	104	131	107	121
3	9.0	105	133	108	121
4	9.0	106	135	109	121
1985 1	9.0	108	138	109	121
2	9.0	109	140	110	121
3	9.0	110	142	110	121
4	9.0	111	145	111	121
1986 1	9.0	112	148	112	121
2	9.0	113	150	112	121
3	9.0	114	152	113	121
4	9.0	115	155	113	121
1987 1	9.0	116	158	114	121
2	9.0	118	160	114	121
3	9.0	119	163	115	121
4	9.0	120	166	116	121
1988 1	9.0	122	169	116	121
2	9.0	123	172	117	121
3	9.0	124	174	118	121
4	9.0	126	177	118	121

Note: World interest rates are in % per annum. Other series are indices, 1980 = 100.

Table A.3.6.   World variables (percentage changes)

	XWM	WWPI	WGNP	POILWC
	World exports of manufactures	World wholesale prices	World GNP	World oil prices
	Annual percentage changes		·	
1979	5.1	10.6	3.5	42.2
1980	5.4	14.6	1.1	74.3
1981	3.5	10.3	1.8	23.9
1982	– 3.7	6.8	– 0.5	6.8
1983	– 0.3	5.5	2.4	– 7.7
1984	4.8	6.5	3.8	– 0.9
1985	4.9	6.7	2.3	0.0
1986	3.9	7.0	2.0	0.0
1987	4.2	7.0	2.1	0.0
1988	4.4	6.9	2.3	0.0
	Quarterly percentage changes			
1983 1	– 2.9	5.2	0.6	0.8
2	0.7	5.2	1.5	– 7.9
3	– 1.3	5.4	3.1	– 10.9
4	2.4	6.3	4.2	– 12.3
1984 1	2.0	6.7	4.6	– 5.3
2	4.0	6.7	4.2	2.1
3	6.7	6.5	3.4	0.0
4	6.6	6.1	3.0	0.0
1985 1	5.9	6.5	2.7	0.0
2	5.0	6.7	2.3	0.0
3	4.6	6.8	2.2	0.0
4	4.2	6.9	2.1	0.0
1986 1	4.0	7.0	2.0	0.0
2	3.9	7.0	2.0	0.0
3	3.9	7.0	2.0	0.0
4	4.0	6.9	2.0	0.0
1987 1	4.1	7.0	2.1	0.0
2	4.2	7.0	2.1	0.0
3	4.3	7.0	2.2	0.0
4	4.4	7.1	2.2	0.0
1988 1	4.4	7.1	2.2	0.0
2	4.3	7.0	2.2	0.0
3	4.3	6.8	2.3	0.0
4	4.4	6.7	2.4	0.0

The production and use of economic forecasts

Table A.3.7. UK financial variables

		MO	PSBR	GOVTB	BAL	OJ	XEER	COMP
		Money supply MO	Public sector borrowing	Gov't non-money debt	Current account balance	Net overseas assets	Expected exchange rate	Real exchange rate
		Annual values						
1979		9852	12638	62336	− 653	10242	94	59
1980		10630	12173	73962	3235	14069	102	67
1981		11201	10730	87608	6547	19918	96	65
1982		11512	5448	93093	5378	11874	91	62
1983		12710	10292	102973	998	8255	87	57
1984		13845	7397	109039	1542	9484	91	59
1985		14956	8721	116391	− 1825	9127	90	58
1986		16087	8679	123946	− 5644	4793	90	58
1987		17155	8918	131606	− 8534	− 2638	89	57
1988		18184	10102	140190	− 12355	− 13514	88	56
		Quarterly values						
1983	1	12098	4374	100013	781	7936	88	56
	2	12554	2152	102165	− 171	8053	88	58
	3	12587	2616	104787	603	8623	87	58
	4	13599	1150	104925	− 215	8408	87	56
1984	1	13275	1187	106437	616	9024	91	59
	2	13683	2218	108246	320	9344	91	59
	3	13677	2048	110299	276	9620	91	59
	4	14746	1945	111176	329	9949	91	59
1985	1	14330	1890	113481	− 85	9865	90	58
	2	14723	2436	115523	− 276	9589	90	58
	3	14790	2441	117897	− 661	8928	90	58
	4	15981	1955	118661	− 803	8125	90	58
1986	1	15493	1844	120994	− 1152	6972	90	58
	2	15877	2451	123059	− 1331	5641	90	58
	3	15872	2452	125517	− 1565	4076	90	58
	4	17107	1933	126214	− 1596	2480	89	58
1987	1	16583	1796	128534	− 1896	584	89	57
	2	16953	2460	130625	− 2008	− 1424	89	57
	3	16905	2532	133205	− 2235	− 3658	89	57
	4	18178	2129	134061	− 2396	− 6054	89	57
1988	1	17577	2012	136674	− 2823	− 8877	88	56
	2	17970	2762	139044	− 2902	− 11779	88	56
	3	17921	2875	141968	− 3212	− 14991	88	56
	4	19268	2452	143073	− 3418	− 18409	88	56

Note: The first five variables are in £million at current prices. The two exchange rate series are indices.

Table A.3.8.   UK financial variables (percentage changes)

	MO	PSBR	GOVTB	XEER	COMP
	Money supply MO	Public sector borrowing	Gov't non-money debt	Expected exchange rate	Real exchange rate
	Annual percentage changes				
1979	12.2	51.6	21.9	11.3	9.1
1980	7.9	− 3.7	18.7	9.3	13.0
1981	5.4	− 11.9	18.5	− 6.1	− 2.2
1982	2.8	− 49.2	6.3	− 4.8	− 4.6
1983	10.4	88.9	10.6	− 4.5	− 7.9
1984	8.9	− 28.1	5.9	4.2	3.0
1985	8.0	17.9	6.7	− 0.7	− 1.1
1986	7.6	− 0.5	6.5	− 0.8	− 0.8
1987	6.6	2.7	6.2	− 0.7	− 1.1
1988	6.0	13.3	6.5	− 1.1	− 1.8
	Quarterly percentage changes				
1983 1	9.4	1108.3	10.4	− 6.6	− 10.6
2	11.6	35.8	10.9	− 7.2	− 6.5
3	10.5	37.4	11.4	− 6.6	− 6.9
4	10.1	− 28.0	9.7	3.1	− 7.7
1984 1	9.7	− 72.9	6.4	3.7	5.1
2	9.0	3.1	6.0	3.1	1.5
3	8.7	− 21.7	5.3	5.0	1.3
4	8.4	69.1	6.0	4.8	4.2
1985 1	7.9	59.2	6.6	− 0.5	− 1.1
2	7.6	9.8	6.7	− 0.9	− 1.1
3	8.1	19.2	6.9	− 0.7	− 1.3
4	8.4	0.5	6.7	− 0.6	− 1.0
1986 1	8.1	− 2.4	6.6	− 0.7	− 0.8
2	7.8	0.6	6.5	− 0.7	− 0.7
3	7.3	0.5	6.5	− 0.9	− 0.8
4	7.0	− 1.1	6.4	− 0.8	− 0.9
1987 1	7.0	− 2.6	6.2	− 0.6	− 0.9
2	6.8	0.4	6.1	− 0.7	− 1.0
3	6.5	3.3	6.1	− 0.8	− 1.2
4	6.3	10.2	6.2	− 0.9	− 1.5
1988 1	6.0	12.0	6.3	− 1.0	− 1.8
2	6.0	12.3	6.4	− 1.1	− 1.9
3	6.0	13.5	6.6	− 1.1	− 1.9
4	6.0	15.2	6.7	− 1.2	− 1.8

Table A.3.9. Other variables

	PX	T	TREF	DRESV	TIME	ICHS
	Non-oil export prices	Average income tax rate	Average indirect tax rate	Change in reserves etc.	Time trend 1955 Q1 equals 1	Council house sales
	1980 = 100	ratio	1980 = 100	£m. current prices	–	£m. 1980 prices
	Annual values					
1979	89	0.20	80	1576	98.5	563
1980	100	0.20	100	940	102.5	976
1981	107	0.22	121	– 1128	106.5	1139
1982	114	0.22	135	– 1056	110.5	2261
1983	126	0.22	136	– 431	114.5	1773
1984	140	0.22	143	0	118.5	1480
1985	150	0.22	152	0	122.5	1160
1986	161	0.22	163	0	126.5	1000
1987	173	0.22	173	0	130.5	1000
1988	186	0.22	184	0	134.5	940
	Quarterly values					
1983 1	120	0.22	137	– 176	113	495
2	123	0.22	134	– 288	114	430
3	127	0.22	134	33	115	428
4	132	0.22	141	0	116	420
1984 1	136	0.22	144	0	117	400
2	138	0.22	140	0	118	380
3	141	0.22	141	0	119	360
4	143	0.22	148	0	120	340
1985 1	146	0.22	152	0	121	320
2	148	0.22	149	0	122	300
3	151	0.22	150	0	123	280
4	154	0.22	158	0	124	260
1986 1	156	0.22	162	0	125	250
2	159	0.22	159	0	126	250
3	162	0.22	160	0	127	250
4	165	0.22	169	0	128	250
1987 1	168	0.22	173	0	129	250
2	172	0.22	169	0	130	250
3	175	0.22	171	0	131	250
4	178	0.22	180	0	132	250
1988 1	181	0.22	184	0	133	250
2	185	0.22	180	0	134	230
3	188	0.22	181	0	135	230
4	192	0.22	193	0	136	230

Table A.3.10.   Other variables (percentage changes)

	PX	T	TREF	ICHS
	Non-oil export prices	Average income tax rate	Average indirect tax rate	Council house sales
	Annual percentage changes			
1979	11.2	– 6.3	26.3	20.3
1980	12.1	0.7	24.3	73.3
1981	7.3	9.5	20.8	16.7
1982	6.2	2.9	11.6	98.5
1983	10.1	– 0.1	1.1	– 21.6
1984	11.2	0.0	5.0	– 16.5
1985	7.2	0.0	6.2	– 21.6
1986	7.5	0.0	6.9	– 13.8
1987	7.7	0.0	6.5	0.0
1988	7.7	0.0	6.1	– 6.0
	Quarterly percentage changes			
1983 1	7.7	0.0	– 1.3	– 17.2
2	8.2	– 0.1	1.3	– 23.0
3	10.9	– 0.1	– 0.4	– 23.9
4	13.6	– 0.1	5.0	– 22.6
1984 1	12.8	– 0.1	5.0	– 19.2
2	12.8	0.0	4.8	– 11.6
3	10.5	0.0	5.1	– 15.9
4	8.9	0.0	5.2	– 19.0
1985 1	7.4	0.0	5.8	– 20.0
2	7.2	0.0	6.1	– 21.1
3	7.2	0.0	6.4	– 22.2
4	7.3	0.0	6.6	– 23.5
1986 1	7.3	0.0	6.8	– 21.9
2	7.4	0.0	6.9	– 16.7
3	7.5	0.0	7.0	– 10.7
4	7.6	0.0	6.9	– 3.8
1987 1	7.7	0.0	6.8	0.0
2	7.7	0.0	6.6	0.0
3	7.7	0.0	6.4	0.0
4	7.7	0.0	6.3	0.0
1988 1	7.7	0.0	6.2	0.0
2	7.7	0.0	6.1	– 8.0
3	7.7	0.0	6.0	– 8.0
4	7.7	0.0	6.0	– 8.0

APPENDIX 4

Variables sources and definitions

Abbreviations and notes:

All data are seasonally adjusted except for MO, RSW, RLB, and DRESV.

ET means CSO *Economic Trends*.
MDStat means CSO *Monthly Digest of Statistics*.
OECD MEI means *Main Economic Indicators* published by OECD.
FS means CSO *Financial Statistics*.
BB means CSO *National Income and Expenditure*, often called the blue book.

All these publications appear monthly (except for the blue book which is annual) and are available through HMSO.

The ET national accounts appendix appears quarterly in January, April, July and October.

£m. 80 means £million at constant 1980 prices
80 = 100 means an index based at 100 in 1980
£m. means £million at current prices

Note 1:   See Table 1.1 in MDStat or Table 1 in the ET national accounts annex.

Name	Units	Definition	Source
G	£m. 80	General government final consumption plus total public sector fixed investment	ET national accounts annex (Table 1 for government consumption, Table 14 for investment). Or MDStat Table 1.1 (for government consumption) plus Table 1.7 (for public investment).
GDPE	£m. 80	Gross domestic product, expenditure estimate	See note 1.
C	£m. 80	Consumers' expenditure	See note 1.
X	£m. 80	Non-oil exports	Total exports are obtained from the tables given in note 1. Oil exports are taken as exports of fuels, MDStat Table 15.8. Figures in that table are monthly index numbers. Work out the quarterly average and multiply by 16.07 to convert to a figure at 1980 prices. Non-oil exports equal total exports minus oil exports.
M	£m. 80	Non-oil imports	Total imports are obtained from the tables in note 1. Oil imports are taken as imports of fuels, MDStat Table 15.8. Figures in that table are monthly index numbers. Work out the quarterly average and multiply by 17.19 to convert to a figure at 1980 prices. Non-oil imports equal total imports minus oil imports.
O	£m. 80	Oil exports net of oil imports	Subtract the oil import figure obtained when calculating M from the oil

Name	*Units*	*Definition*	*Source*
			export figure derived when computing X.
KII	£m. 80	Stock of inventories	A recent end-year figure at current prices appears in a footnote to BB Table 12.4. To obtain an end-1980 figure subtract the annual increases in book value (the last line of Table 12.4) for each year back to, but not including, 1980. Update using the stockbuilding figures in the tables shown in note 1.
KI	£m. 80	Stock of fixed capital of the private sector	End-1980 figures appear in BB Table 11.7 (for private sector add personal, IC companies and financial companies). Update to latest available end-year using net capital formation figures at 1980 prices in BB Table 11.4. Update quarterly from then adding private sector gross fixed capital formation from MDStat Table 1.7, less an allowance for depreciation each quarter of $4610 \times 1.0086^{time}$ where time = 1 in 1980 first quarter, time = 7 in 1981 third quarter, etc.
PC	80 = 100	Consumer prices index	Take consumer spending at current prices from the tables in note 1 and divide it by consumer spending at constant prices from the same source. Multiply the result by 100.

Name	Units	Definition	Source
YD	£m.	Personal disposable income	MDStat Table 1.4 or ET quarterly national accounts appendix, Table 4.
RLB	% p.a.	UK banks' base rates	FS Table 13.10, or daily in the press.
EER	80 = 100	Sterling's effective (trade-weighted) exchange rate	FS Table 13.3 (code AJHT), or daily in the press (divided by 0.961).
ET	000s	Employed labour force	ET Table 36
WSI	80 = 100	Index of average wages and salaries	Divide total wages and salaries (MDStat Table 1.4 or ET national accounts annex Table 4) by ET. Divide the result by 0.01169.
RSW	% p.a.	World short-term interest rates	Use 3-month US Treasury bill rate from FS Table 13.3 (code AJIB).
WWPI	80 = 100	World wholesale price index	Use OECD producer prices, from table headed 'Producer prices' in Part 1 of OECD MEI. Alternatively, *National Institute Economic Review* statistical appendix Table 19.
XWM	80 = 100	Index of world exports of manufactures	*National Institute Economic Review* statistical appendix Table 23.
POILWC	80 = 100	Index of oil prices in 'world' currency	Take $ per barrel price (from NIER statistical appendix Table 26 or daily press). Divide this by 0.3189 (the price in 1980 was $31.89) and then divide by the dollar effective exchange rate (from NIER statistical appendix Table

Name	Units	Definition	Source
			18 or daily press). Finally multiply by 100.
WGNP	80 = 100	Index of world GNP	From tables at back of LBS *Economic Outlook*, Table 13.
MO	£m.	Money supply MO, not seasonally adjusted	Update figures given in this book by subtracting the notes and coin issue in FS Table 1.6 (column 6, code AAGE). This ignores changes in bankers' balances, which are small.
PSBR	£m.	Public sector borrowing requirement	ET Table 56 (use seasonally adjusted figure) or MDStat Table 17.2 or FS Table 2.3 (code ABFB).
DRESV	£m.	Change in reserves etc.	FS Table 1.6, columns 16 plus 17 plus 18 (codes AAGN plus AAGO plus AAGP).
GOVTB	£m.	Stock of non-money government debt (ignoring revaluations)	Update figures given in this book by adding the PSBR, subtracting changes in MO, and adding variable DRESV.
BAL	£m.	Current account balance	ET Table 48 or MDStat Table 16.3 (use seasonally adjusted figures).
OJ	£m.	Private sector net overseas financial assets (ignoring revaluations)	Update the figures given in this book by adding BAL and subtracting DRESV.
XEER	Index	Expectations for the exchange rate one period ahead	Use the actual value taken by the exchange rate EER one period on.
COMP	Index	Index of competitiveness (higher means less competitive), i.e. the real exchange rate	Divide average wages and salaries WSI by the trend level of productivity. This level is 1.0057^{time} where time = 1 in 1980 first

Name	Units	Definition	Source
			quarter, time = 7 in 1981 third quarter etc. Then multiply by EER and divide by WWPI.
PX	80 = 100	Non-oil export price index	Obtain current price non-oil exports by subtracting fuel exports (MDStat Table 15.1) from total exports (MDStat Table 1.1). Divide the result by variable X (non-oil exports at 1980 prices) and multiply by 100.
T	Ratio	Average income tax rate	Divide income tax payments (MDStat Table 1.4 or ET national accounts annex Table 4) by total wages and salaries (from the same tables).
TREF	80 = 100	Average indirect tax rate	Subtract subsidies from taxes on expenditure (both at current prices from MDStat Table 1.1 or ET national accounts annex Table 1) and divide by the adjustment to factor cost (1980 prices, same tables). Then multiply by 100.
TIME	–	Time trend	Equals 1 in 1955 first quarter, 7 in 1956 third quarter, 100 in 1980 first quarter etc.
ICHS	£m. 80	Sales of council houses	From Table 4 in the tables at the back of LBS *Economic Outlook*, or from *Building and Construction Statistics* (Department of Environment).

APPENDIX 5

Blank tables to be used for preparing your own forecast

Table A.5.1. Exogenous variables

	G	O	RSW	XWM	WWPI	WGNP	POILWC
	Public spending	Net oil trade	World short interest rate	World exports of manufactures	World wholesale prices	World GNP	World oil prices
	£m.80	£m.80	% p.a.	80 = 100	80 = 100	80 = 100	80 = 100
198							
198							
198							
198							
198							
198							
198							
198							
198							
198 1							
2							
3							
4							
198 1							
2							
3							
4							
198 1							
2							
3							
4							
198 1							
2							
3							
4							

Note: All the tables in Appendix 5 may be photocopied without permission from the publishers.

Table A.5.1. *continued*

	MO	XEER	T	DRESV	TIME	ICHS
	Money supply MO	Expected exchange rate	Average income tax rate	Change in reserves etc.	Time trend (1955 Q1 equals 1)	Council house sales
	£m.	index	ratio	£m.	–	£m. 80
198						
198						
198						
198						
198						
198						
198						
198						
198						
198 1						
2						
3						
4						
198 1						
2						
3						
4						
198 1						
2						
3						
4						
198 1						
2						
3						
4						

Table A.5.2. Expenditure on gross domestic product and key indicators

		GDPE	C	G	KI	KII	X	M
		GDP (exp. measure)	Consumer spending	Public spending	Fixed capital stock	Stock of inventories	Non-oil exports	Non-oil imports
		£m. 80	£m. 80	£m. 80	£m. 80	£m. 80	£m. 80	£m. 80
198								
198								
198								
198								
198								
198								
198								
198								
198								
198	1							
	2							
	3							
	4							
198	1							
	2							
	3							
	4							
198	1							
	2							
	3							
	4							
198	1							
	2							
	3							
	4							

Table A.5.2. *continued*

	O	PC	YD	RLB	EER	WSI	ET
	Net oil trade	Consumer price index	Personal disposable income	Short-term interest rates	Exchange rate index	Average earnings (whole economy)	Employment
	£m. 80	80 = 100	£m.	% p.a.	80 = 100	80 = 100	000s
198							
198							
198							
198							
198							
198							
198							
198							
198							
198 1							
2							
3							
4							
198 1							
2							
3							
4							
198 1							
2							
3							
4							
198 1							
2							
3							
4							

Table A.5.3. UK financial and other variables

	MO	PSBR	GOVTB	BAL	OJ	XEER	COMP
	Money supply MO	Public sector borrowing	Gov't non-money debt	Current account balance	Net overseas assets	Expected exchange rate	Real exchange rate
	£m.	£m.	£m.	£m.	£m.	80 = 100	80 = 100
198							
198							
198							
198							
198							
198							
198							
198							
198							
198 1							
2							
3							
4							
198 1							
2							
3							
4							
198 1							
2							
3							
4							
198 1							
2							
3							
4							

Table A.5.3.   *continued*

	PX	T	TREF	DRESV	TIME	ICHS
	Non-oil export prices	Average income tax rate	Average indirect tax rate	Change in reserves etc.	Time trend (1955 Q1 equals 1)	Council house sales
	80 = 100	ratio	80 = 100	£m.	–	£m. 80
198						
198						
198						
198						
198						
198						
198						
198						
198						
198 1						
2						
3						
4						
198 1						
2						
3						
4						
198 1						
2						
3						
4						
198 1						
2						
3						
4						

References

Artis, M.J. (1982), 'Why do forecasts differ?', paper presented to the panel of academic consultants, no. 17, Bank of England, London.

Balance, D.C. and Burton, C.P.H. (1983), 'Answering practices in the CBI industrial trends survey', in *Twenty Five Years of Ups and Downs*, Confederation of British Industry, London.

Ball, R.J. (1978), *Report of Committee on Policy Optimisation*, Cmnd 7148, HMSO, London.

Ball, R.J., Burns, T. and Laury, J.S.E. (1977), 'The role of exchange rate changes in balance of payments adjustment: the UK case', *Economic Journal*, vol. 87, 1–29.

Barker, T. (ed.) (1976), *Economic Structure and Policy*, Cambridge Studies in Applied Econometrics 2, Chapman & Hall, London.

Begg, D.K.H. (1982), *The Rational Expectations Revolution in Macroeconomics: Theories and Evidence*, Philip Allan, Oxford.

Begg, D.K.H., Fischer, S. and Dornbush, R. (1984), *Economics*, British edition, McGraw-Hill, London.

Brittan, A. (ed.) (1983), *Employment, Output and Inflation: The National Institute Model of the UK Economy*, Heinemann, London.

Brooks, S., and Henry, B. (1983), 'Re-estimation of the National Institute model', *National Institute Economic Review*, no. 103, February, 62–70.

Budd, A., Dicks, G., Holly, S., Keating, G. and Robinson, W. (1984), 'The London Business School econometric model', *Economic Modelling*, vol. 1, no. 4, December, 355–420.

Buiter, W.H. (1984), 'Policy evaluation and design for continuous time linear rational expectations models: some recent developments', London School of Economics DEMEIC econometrics programme, discussion paper A 42.

Buiter, W.H. and Miller M. (1981), 'Monetary policy and international competitiveness: the problems of adjustment', in Eltis, W.A. and Sinclair, P.J.N. (eds), *The Money Supply and the Exchange Rate*, Oxford University Press.

Corker, R.J. (1983), 'Forecasting uncertainty: how accurate can we be?', *LBS Economic Outlook*, vol. 7, no. 5, 33–41.

CSO (1983), *Economic Trends*, no. 360, October, 77–8, HMSO, London.

Department of Energy (1983), *Development of the Oil and Gas Resources of the United Kingdom 1983*, HMSO, London.

FCEC (1981), 'Capital spending and the UK economy', mimeo, Federation of Civil Engineering Contractors, London.

Fisher, P., Holly, S. and Hughes-Hallett, A. (1985), 'Efficient solution techniques for dynamic nonlinear rational expectations models', London Business School Centre for Economic Forecasting discussion paper, no. 145.

Harvey, A. (1981), *Econometric Analysis of Time Series*, Philip Allan, Oxford.

Heathfield, D. (1984), 'The Southampton economic model', *Economic Modelling*, vol. 1, no. 1, January, 108–25.

Hibbert, J. (1981), 'Revisions to estimates of economic growth', *Economic Trends*, no. 331, May, 82–7, HMSO, London.

Holly, S. and Hughes-Hallett, A. (forthcoming), *Optimal Control, Expectations and Uncertainty*, Cambridge University Press.

Holly, S. and Zarrop, M.B. (1983), 'On optimality and time consistency when expectations are rational', *European Economic Review*, vol. 21, February, 23–40.

Johnston, J. (1972), *Econometric Methods*, McGraw-Hill, New York.

Keating, G. (1983), 'The effect of answering practices on the relationship between CBI survey data and official data', *Applied Economics*, vol. 15, no. 2, April, 213–24.

Klein, L.R. and Goldberger, A.S. (1955), *An Econometric Model of the United States 1929–1952*, North-Holland Publishing Company, Amsterdam.

Klein, P.A. and Moore, G.H. (1981), 'Industrial surveys in the UK – parts I and II', *Applied Economics*, vol. 13, 167 and 465.

Laury, J.S.E., Lewis, S.R. and Ormerod, P.A. (1978), 'Properties of macro-economic models of the UK: a comparative study', *National Institute Economic Review*, no. 83, February, 52–72.

Lucas Jr, R.E. (1976), 'Econometric policy evaluation: a critique', in Brunner, K. and Meltzer, A. (eds), *The Phillips Curve and Labour Markets*, supplement to the *Journal of Monetary Economics*.

Maddala, G.S. (1977), *Econometrics*, McGraw-Hill, Tokyo.

Maurice, R. (1968), 'National accounts statistics: sources and methods', *Studies in Official Statistics*, no. 13, HMSO, London.

Minford, P., Marwaha, S., Matthews, K. and Sprague, A. (1984), 'The Liverpool macroeconomic model of the United Kingdom', *Economic Modelling*, vol. 1, no. 1, January, 24–62.

NEDO (1983), 'Report on the Treasury simulations presented to Council in April 1982, and the role of demand in the economy', memoranda by the Director General, mimeo, National Economic Development Council, London.

Nickell, S.J. and Andrews, M. (1983), 'Unions, real wages and employment in Britain 1951–79', *Oxford Economic Papers*, vol. 35 supplement; reprinted in Greenhalgh, C.A., Layard, P.R.G and Oswald, A.J. (eds) (1983), *The Causes of Unemployment*, Oxford University Press.

Ormerod, P.A. (1979), *Economic Modelling*, Heinemann, London.

Savage, D. (1975), 'Interpreting the investment intentions data', *National Institute Economic Review*, no. 73, 41–6.

Smith, P.N. (1985), 'Current account movements, wealth effects and the deter-mination of the exchange rate', London Business School Centre for Economic Forecasting discussion paper, no. 147.

Stewart, J. (1976), *Understanding Econometrics*, Hutchinson, London.

Surrey, M.J.C. (1971), *The Analysis and Forecasting of the British Economy*, Cambridge University Press.

SSRC (1981), 'Report on macro-economic research in the UK,' Social Science Research Council, London.

Theil, H. (1966), *Applied Economic Forecasting*, North-Holland Publishing Company, Amsterdam.

Theil, H. (1971), *Principles of Econometrics*, North-Holland Publishing Company, Amsterdam.

Treasury (1984), also earlier years, *Financial Statement and Budget Report 1984–85*, HMSO, London.

Wallis, K.F. (1979), *Topics in Applied Econometrics*, second edition, Basil Blackwell, Oxford.

Wallis, K.F. (ed.) (1985), *Models of the UK Economy: A Review by the ESRC Macroeconomic Modelling Bureau*, Oxford University Press.

Index

Note: entries in italics are defined on the page number shown in italics.